UNTIMELY TRACTS

By the same author

ART AND IMAGINATION
THE AESTHETICS OF ARCHITECTURE
THE MEANING OF CONSERVATISM
A SHORT HISTORY OF MODERN PHILOSOPHY
KANT
FORTNIGHT'S ANGER
THE POLITICS OF CULTURE
A DICTIONARY OF POLITICAL THOUGHT
THE AESTHETIC UNDERSTANDING
THINKERS OF THE NEW LEFT
SEXUAL DESIRE
SPINOZA

Untimely Tracts

Roger Scruton
Professor of Aesthetics
Birkbeck College, London

M
MACMILLAN
PRESS

First published 1987

Published by
THE MACMILLAN PRESS LTD
Houndmills, Basingstoke, Hampshire RG21 2XS
and London
Companies and representatives
throughout the world

Printed in Hong Kong

British Library Cataloguing in Publication Data
Scruton, Roger
Untimely tracts.
I. Title
082 AC8
ISBN 0–333–43862–0
ISBN 0–333–43863–9 Pbk

Contents

Preface

The following articles, written for *The Times* over a period of four years, consist of reflections, outbursts and exhortations on subjects which, with two exceptions, I chose myself. (The two exceptions are the short essays on Sisson and Hayek, commissioned by the editor.) The purpose of a newspaper column is neither to argue from first principles nor to engage in debate, but to present, as briefly as possible, a distinct point of view. For a variety of reasons, the outlook expressed in these articles is unfashionable and could be made tolerable to its critics only by a long and mild-mannered argument, of a kind that has no place in a daily newspaper. I do not deny the need for such an argument; but, in reprinting these untimely thoughts, I reaffirm the conviction that gave rise to them – namely, that opinions which are out of fashion may nonetheless be true.

I am extremely grateful to the late editor of *The Times*, Charles Douglas-Home, for tolerating, and to the then features editor, Peter Stothard, for first commissioning, utterances which have been so widely disapproved. I am also grateful to the many readers who sent messages of encouragement and for whose sake I have prepared this volume for the press. The articles are reprinted by kind permission of Times Newspapers Limited.

R.S.
London

The Virtue of Irrelevance

The power of education is mysterious. It exerts itself through complicity and influence, rather than through coercion or control. Such power is more durable and more popular than force. Hence political movements tend to posture as the friends of education, whether or not their real purpose is to destroy or limit it.

The defenders of privilege argue for quality, and therefore standards; the defenders of equality argue for quantity, and therefore the destruction of standards. In their hearts, however, they are each suspicious of education, which, by making privilege accessible, both challenges those at the top and perpetuates the distinction between top and bottom. Each side aims secret blows at education. Some try to prevent it from spreading, while others try to destroy it altogether by spreading it too thin.

Recently, however, a more effective strategy has been discovered. This is to make all education 'relevant'. Traditionally a large part of learning was devoted to subjects which are wilfully 'irrelevant' – like Latin, Greek, ancient history, higher mathematics, philosophy and literary criticism. The syllabus recommended by ancient thinkers consisted almost entirely of such subjects. And the ancient instinct was wise. The more irrelevant a subject, the more lasting is the benefit that it confers. Irrelevant subjects bring understanding of the human condition, by forcing the student to stand back from it. They also enhance the appetite for life, by providing material for thought and conversation.

This is the secret which civilisation has guarded: that power and influence come through the acquisition of useless knowledge. The answer is, therefore, to destroy the effect of education by making it relevant. Replace pure by applied mathematics, logic by computer programming, architecture by engineering, history by sociology: the result will be a new generation of well-informed philistines, whose charmlessness will undo every advantage which their learning might otherwise have conferred.

Not surprisingly, the main objects of this attack have been the humanities. A person who knows only engineering or microbiology finds himself hampered by his knowledge, which casts little light on his experience and leads to no new communication with his fellow humans. A person with a classical or literary education, however, inhabits a transformed world and sees meaning where others see facts. He is equipped not just to change the world, but to interpret it. Hence he will interpret it in his own favour and become master of his condition. The major task is to destroy the majestic irrelevance which confers this power.

Considerable ingenuity has been spent in inventing 'relevant' humanities. The problem has been to conserve the outward prestige of education, as an embodiment of the reasonable approach to life's problems, while persuading the uneducated that there is a learning addressed to interests which they already have. The answer has been found to lie in the word 'studies'. When added to a relevant-sounding prefix (such as 'media' or 'communications', 'black' or 'gay') this word adjoins even to the most half-baked enthusiasm an air of superior knowledge. Not only are you right, it says, to be interested in the problems of the media, of blacks, of homosexuals: there is also a way of converting enthusiasm into expertise.

Consider the subject which has done more than any other to discredit humane education in American universities: 'women's studies'. How did this subject come into being? When nineteenth-century philanthropists confronted the industrial revolution, 'more education' was their cry – and when Arnold, Ruskin, Shaftesbury and Gladstone repeated it, more education there was. Similarly, you might think, when twentieth-century philogynists campaign for 'women's studies' they are merely repeating the age-old folly of the English in seeking educational remedies for problems that are beyond intellectual control. In fact, however, the appeal of 'women's studies' is precisely in its power to undo the effects of education.

Not only is it relevant, addressing itself to social and political problems which the uneducated student will instantly recognise; it also cuts across established disciplines, adopting and discarding methods according to imperatives that have no academic rationale. It therefore ploughs like a tank through the enemy's lines, and carries a swarm of believing students behind it. Of course, no educated person is likely to take it seriously. For it is impossible to isolate the work of women from a tradition created largely by men; it is impossible to understand the social reality of womanhood without studying manhood; it is impossible to hold the jar of civilisation to the light and expect the masculine and the feminine to separate like oil and water.

But that is precisely the point. The value of such a subject is precisely that it destroys education. It keeps the student's mind so narrowly focused on his random and transient political convictions that, when he ceases to be obsessed with them, he will lack the education through which to discover what to put in their place.

4 January 1983

Against Architecture

The recent architectural competition for the National Gallery extension aroused little public enthusiasm. When Mr Heseltine decided to accept none of the designs, one hoped that it was from a decision to defend the national interest against modern architecture – which is (after Argentina and the peace movement) the country's most prominent enemy. Not so, however. It seems that Mr Heseltine's advisers had simply failed to agree.

Nevertheless, the outcome was encouraging. One of the competitors – the firm of Ahrens, Burton and Korallek – was appointed as architect of the new extension. At the same time the firm's existing design for the building was rejected, along with any future design that the gallery trustees should be disinclined to accept. This wholly reasonable solution leads one to hope that the space next to Wilkins's facade will remain empty until the final extinction of modern architecture.

Already, it seems, one of the competitors – the American firm of Skidmore, Owings and Merill – had justified its design on the ground of 'neo-classical' inspiration, claiming Schinkel as a spiritual ancestor. If the architects of Chicago's Hancock Center feel compelled to pay lip service to the classical tradition, then, who knows, perhaps they may one day begin to study that tradition sufficiently to discover that Schinkel is not really part of it. Perhaps we may look forward to a general recovery from the campaign of diseducation initiated by the pedagogues and demagogues of the Modern Movement.

Of course there is a long way to go. It is necessary to undo a vast web of innocent and not so innocent confusions. It is also necessary to resist architecture in every available way, perhaps even to organise women and children to link hands around major building sites and lie down unresisting in front of bulldozers. We must convince architects of the need to recuperate some of the knowledge which they wilfully threw away. We must begin by destroying the illusion that architects are necessary. Architecture, like clothing, is a vernacular art. It provides predictable answers to predictable problems. Architects have conned us into an exaggerated view of their significance. Sometimes they produce wonderful things. But for the most part they are as dispensable as dress designers, and far more dangerous.

An old-fashioned builder armed with a pattern book, and forbidden to use materials that he does not understand, might make an agreeable botched job of the gallery extension, and the public, in its sovereign indifference to everything that is merely normal, would not complain. But of course, if you suggest such a thing, a hundred architects rise up to rebuke you, with arguments which have had considerable success in persuading people in power to find employment for them. They will tell you that buildings have specific functions and must be carefully designed so as to fulfil those functions. Only an architect, they will say, has the skills required to design an art gallery, a theatre or a concert hall.

The argument is nonsense. Buildings no more have specific functions than do clothes. All successful buildings are, like Covent Garden or the lofts of Lower Manhattan, infinitely adaptable, precisely because they address themselves not to specific functions but to the general and vacillating requirements of human existence. First among these requirements – as the example of clothing displays – is an appearance of order, agreeableness and normality. Architects must understand appearances, not functions. Until they do so they are no better qualified than anyone else.

They will then tell you that only an expert can really understand appearances. You need someone to employ the modern materials in the most sensitive way, so as to explore their 'aesthetic possibilities'. That too is nonsense. There is no such thing as an aesthetic expert. Besides, what was wrong with the old materials? And where is the proof that architects have understood the new materials – understood them, that is, in the way that generations of builders understood brick and stone?

Finally architects will tell you that they are mending their ways. They are becoming 'classicists' and they have adopted a respect for order, pattern and vertical emphasis. Don't believe them. Their obession with experiment causes them to leave out most that is essential to classicism and to incorporate most that is not.

The modern architect takes the term 'classical' to refer to a system of proportions, composed with mathematical guidance and unencumbered by detail or moulding. For the lover of the classical tradition, the term has the opposite sense. It denotes flexibility, multiplicity, ornament and moulding. It concerns not the whole, but the part, and the whole as derived from its parts. Without detail – which the old materials encourage and the new materials deny – no system of proportion is even perceivable.

Another Falklands war may see Mr Heseltine, now Defence Secretary, returning to his former position. By then he may be glad to turn from the battle against Argentina, with its short-term successes, to the battle against modern architecture, with its short-term defeats. For in this area, at least, there is hope for a final victory.

18 January 1983

The Politics of Language

If you want to control the world, first control language: such has been the unspoken maxim of revolutionary politics in our century. Looking through the *Short Guide to Political Terms* recently issued by the Novosti Press Agency in Moscow, one is struck by the outrage that communism has committed against language: all terms, especially those which might have been useful to an opponent, are torn loose from their intellectual roots and appropriated to the cause of dogma.

'Liberalism' becomes 'a political and ideological trend which unites supporters of the bourgeois-parliamentary system and freedom for capitalist enterprise . . .'; 'democracy' is genuine only if it is 'socialist democracy' (which, through the 'dictatorship of the proletariat', provides the sole guarantee of true human rights); 'anarchism' is a 'social and political creed which rejects the necessity of state authority (including working people's power)': 'imperialism' is 'monopolistic capitalism'; and 'Trotskyism' is a 'petty bourgeois opportunist movement hostile to Marxism-Leninism'. The 'collectivisation of agriculture' – perhaps the greatest crime against the peasantry that has ever been committed – is nothing more terrible than a 'uniting' of 'small individual peasant households' into 'large co-operative collective farms'.

The liturgy is astonishing in its shameless mythopoeia and in its benighted addiction to theories whose remoteness from the modern world make them now almost incomprehensible. Nevertheless, it has a certain power. There is a remarkable energy of hatred accumulated in this pamphlet – hatred of opposition, hatred of discovery and therefore hatred of truth. Its purpose is to forestall refutation by securing an unshakable bridgehead in language. Communism denies opposition not only the right to live, but also the right to die protesting. It has tried to ensure that the words of politics can be used only to express dogmas of its own – not because it believes those dogmas to be true, but because it wants lies to take the place of truth.

It seeks, indeed, to displace truth from politics. Gradually all rival creeds are to be appropriated and devoured; no words will express them, since no words will be available that have not been enslaved by falsehood. 'Genocide' describes the internal policies of South Africa; 'democracy' those of the Soviet Union; 'fascism' those of Chile. 'Terrorism' can be committed only by 'reactionary forces' (otherwise violence is a legitimate part of the 'struggle of the masses of the people for their national and social emancipation'); 'anti-semitism' is a tool whereby 'the exploiting classes undermine the class solidarity of working people'; while the 'cold war' is a 'policy' adopted by 'reactionary circles' in 'imperialist countries'. The Warsaw Treaty is a treaty of 'friendship, co-operation and mutual assistance', whereas Nato is a 'seat of aggression and reaction endangering peace and all mankind'.

A subsidiary purpose of this rhetoric is to divide mankind into friend and enemy, and so to engulf the world in suspicion. The 'class enemy' who stalks through language performs for the communist the same function as the Jew performed for the Nazi. He is omnipresent, yet also invisible. His stealthy progress justifies every violence, and in the end there is no defence against him short of the final solution – in this case the abolition of the language in which his spirit lives.

Meanwhile, however, we must fortify ourselves with invective. It is no matter that we thereby deprive ourselves of every subtlety, every ability to understand the world, every ability to perceive it as it now exists. The therapeutic function of speech replaces its descriptive meaning. This fact should be born in mind by those who are tempted to believe that when communists speak of 'peace', 'détente' and 'co-existence', they mean what they say.

On the contrary, as the definitions show, these terms do not really mean anything at all. They are to be understood not for their meaning, but for their magic. They are the needles with which the wicked effigy is pricked and the poison with which its thoughts are made unutterable.

1 February 1983

Who will Guard our Guardians?

Reading the GLC's plan to appoint a group of advisers to 'dismantle racism', each to be paid £11 500 to £13 500 a year, I recalled a passage in my old, and probably inauthentic, edition of Plato's *Republic*:

> 'If I have followed your argument, Socrates, the people are gravely in error. For they believe men to be of many kinds, and are prone to doubt that relations with another kind are as easy as relations with their own.
>
> Yes, I answered, and it is clear that in this respect too our poets and

orators are blameworthy. For they have placed in the hearts of the people the image of the nation *(ethnos)*, and caused them to reverence the nation in the place of man's universal form, of which the nation is only a semblance. The poet, who makes a semblance of this semblance, thereby doubly deceives the people. No wonder that the people have so little sympathy for mankind in general, and so much sympathy for those whom they believe to be related by blood and custom to themselves.

No wonder.

But now, I continued, must not our guardians do everything in their power to overcome this prejudice?

Indeed they must.

And will it be enough to banish the poets and orators, as we have already recommended?

I think not, Socrates, for we must also banish the images which they have made.

Then we must educate the people to larger sympathies?

Undoubtedly.

And who is to undertake this education? The people themselves, or the guardians?

The guardians, to be sure. But I confess that I am at a loss to see how they may fulfil this task. For the people have no pleasure in learning things which turn them from their ancient sympathies.

You say true, my dear Glaucon. But just now, as you spoke, a fair youth passed yonder in a Corinthian tunic. It reminded me that men of many cities are gathered here in Athens, some to do trade, some in flight from foes and creditors, some as artisans and slaves. In our ideal state too we must gather people from many parts. Let our athletes eat Syracusan dinners and lie with Lesbian courtesans. Let our youth grow with the image of variety and receive customs from every culture, so that no custom gains pre-eminence and nothing is impressed on the heart of our youth more deeply than the idea of the underlying unity of man.

Most certainly, he said, if our idea of the State is ever carried into practice. But I fear that the people may thwart our intentions. For the customs of strangers arouse their indignation. Moreover, they are apt to believe that the good things received by strangers are taken from themselves, who, by ancient inheritance, are the rightful possessors.

You speak truly, Glaucon, I said, but in our State there will be no strangers. There will be laws restricting association, lest people gather into kinds. More, there will be laws to abolish the idea of kinds. We shall remove the word *genos* from the language, and speak instead of communities and ethnic groups. And in order that our reforms do not concern words only, we shall appoint officers to move among the people, correcting their mistaken sympathies and directing their hearts and minds towards the Universal Man.

You speak well, he answered.

But do you not envisage a new problem?

Pray tell me your meaning, Socrates.

I mean, to what class will these officers belong? Will they be of the people, or will they be guardians?

They must be of the people, I think, lest suspicion fall on them, and they be chased from the habitations of the poor.

Let me remind you again of the argument, my dear Glaucon. In the human soul there is a better and a worse principle. When, owing to evil education or association, the better principle, which is also the smaller, is overwhelmed by the greater mass of the worse, there arises once again that brutishness which divides men into friend and foe. Only in the perfect State, in which the guardians preside over the fickle instincts of the multitude, can we ensure that man will be master of his baser desires. It follows that the officers appointed to supervise the people must belong to the Guardian class.

True, he said, I had forgotten. But how can we persuade these guardians to descend again into the general underground abode, and acquire the habit of seeing in the dark?

These guardians, I replied, will be men of the people, raised from the darkness and permitted to return to it only in pursuit of duty. They will not live in poverty. Nor will they inhabit, except by day, those parts of the *polis* the experience of which might lead them to share the prejudices of the poor. Let them mix, in their private lives, with other guardians, in circumstances congenial to their enlightened mission. Let them not fear the loss of house, food or employment. Let them retain an elevated contempt for the sympathies of working people, so that they will be disposed to lend their aid to the victims of popular prejudice.

What you suggest is indeed wise, he said. But how can we compel those who live in darkness to join the Guardian class?

At this point Adeimantus, who had been listening in silence, suddenly interrupted us. If you want my opinion, Socrates, he said, 500 drachmas, rising, would do the trick. And do you also add a fringe benefit or two, lest your guardians be tempted to spend the money on necessities.'

8 February 1983

Male Domination

What's wrong with rape? The question must naturally arise when women complain of the ease with which this crime has been committed and excused. Is rape like theft, a matter of taking without consent that which belongs to another? But then, what is taken? And what kind of 'belonging' is this, which ruins the life of the person who loses it and never enriches the thief?

Masculine thinking is dominated by the idea of contract. It sees legitimate society as an exchange of rights and promises and most crime as an attempt to cheat one's way to the common goal. For such an attitude, the extremes of evil are incomprehensible, because indescribable. If it seems surprising to men that rape should carry a maximum penalty equal to that for murder, then this is because they have been misled into thinking that the sin of taking the short cut to another's private property differs only in degree from the sin of taking the short cut to her private parts.

But it is precisely because sex is a private matter that the feminine mind is better able to comprehend it. A moment's reflection should persuade us of the woman's view, which is that the rapist, unlike the thief, does not so much deprive as annihilate his victim. He is indifferent to the other's consent, since he is indifferent to the other's existence. His rage is the rage of lust, which is fired by the sight of the human body but dismayed by the presence of the human soul. His victim is therefore forced to suffer an act which expressly severs her from her body, and which causes her to see her own body as alien. The rapist plunders not property, but life itself. For it is only on the premise of an identity between soul and body that human life is livable.

Feminists are surely right, therefore, when they see in the crime of rape vital proof of the male desire to negate the female. Rape is the extreme form of a pervasive masculine ambition, which is to replace sexual desire by the pursuit of the sexual commodity. Sexual desire is a longing to be united with another person, and tenderness (which is a frenzy of mutual consent) is the essence of its bond.

Desire has nothing to do with the urge to relieve oneself upon the body of another. To women this urge is loathsome in every way, and not the least because it allows the values of the market to pollute those of the hearth. Men, however, are wary of true desire, since tenderness imbues the sexual act with responsibilities. By vividly symbolising the presence of another human soul, it hampers freedom and diminishes power. This is the true reason why men seek to debase women. The transformation of woman into a commodity raises excitement and diminishes desire. Hence it fulfils the long-term masculine ambition, which is to make women undesirable, and so to open the way to discarding them.

This ambition has achieved remarkable successes in recent years. It has used a variety of stratagems, of which three deserve mention. First, it has put about the myth that sexuality is a merely 'animal' function and the sexual act a kind of compulsive discharge, of no intrinsic moral significance: no matter how or with whom you do it, you are never really to blame. This myth has been inculcated by pseudo-scientific documents, such as the Kinsey report, and also by campaigns for sex education in schools. The initial aim has always been to replace important moral ideas such as modesty and shame (ideas without which sexual desire is inconceivable) with a tidy notion of 'sexual hygiene' which, by abolishing mystery, abolishes desire.

The second masculine stratagem is that of indecency, of which rape is merely the most fully realised and most violent form. In a persuasive analysis of pornography (the Politics of Sex, *Salisbury Review* No. 2) Robert Grant points to the damage inflicted upon human sexuality by the market in indecent publications. Pornography, he writes, effectively authorises lust, by freeing it from moral scruple. It insulates the 'consumer' from the situation depicted. Because he participates in nothing, his excitement is freed from the obstructions of tenderness and his interest in another body need never be deflected by the awareness of another soul. Pornography is therefore the perfect preparation for a sexual ambition which aims to sever soul and body, so as to possess the second without paying the price exacted by the first.

But both of these stratagems are fraught with dangers. They are too conscious, too evident, too vulnerable to popular reaction. In a world where women may ascend to positions of influence, they risk, in the long run, a strong impediment from the law: it is presumably only a normal preoccupation with inessentials that has caused our leaders to neglect this particular duty. Hence the third and most powerful stratagem, which is to infiltrate the camp of the enemy, so as to make women speak against their own interests in their own voice.

This brilliant tactic, which bears all the marks of masculine perfidy, calls itself 'feminism', rather in the way that communist enslavement calls itself 'peace'. It propagates the extraordinary myth that the division of sexual roles, the institution of the family, the ideals of modesty and chastity are all male inventions, designed to confine women to a situation which thwarts their true development. In truth, of course, these are precisely the bonds from which men have always sought to free themselves.

By propagating feminist ideology, therefore, men hope to rid the sexual impulse of its debilitating commitment. No longer subject to the pangs of sexual desire, they may then begin to regulate their relations with women by the laws of the marketplace, and so allow no claims of allegiance to extinguish the claims of power.

15 February 1983

The French Conquest of Bayreuth

Ever since the German defeat in 1945, the French have had their eyes on Bayreuth. To capture the marketplace of German culture, to inject irony and self-doubt at the very source from which the idea of Germany had seemed to emanate – this was surely the victor's duty and prize. The first idea was to bring Wagner home, bound and struggling like Alberich, to snatch from him the ring which had caused the slavery of millions, to send him back humiliated and transfigured by the laughter of the gods. Thus would an old dream of *gloire* be realised. But the French, like the Russians, are master strategists. They soon understood that lasting victory requires conquest: Wagner must be bound and held in his own citadel. For some years they bided their time, saturating the enemy with disinformation and propaganda in the form of semiotics, structuralism and neo-Marxism. Meanwhile unilateralists like Wieland Wagner prepared the way, exhorting their countrymen to lie down before the threat beyond the Rhine, wrapped in a mystical cocoon of peace-loving surrender. When Bayreuth had been cleared of every Germanism, reduced to a bare stage without national identity, the conquest came at once, and with minimum losses.

Wagnerians everywhere shuddered at the news. It was cruel to imagine *The Ring* subjected to Boulez. No more lingering rubato; no more throbbing or heart-rending; only a precise texture of faultless orchestral sound. It was more cruel to imagine the travesty of costume and scenery: Wotan in a dressing gown, Siegfried and Gunter in dinner jackets, the Rhine Maidens swimming beneath a hydro-electric dam. And when the whole was justified in the Marxising language of the Parisian left bank, it seemed clear that the worst had happened, that Wagner had been thoroughly debunked, that irony (as happens when the French use it against the Germans) had turned into sarcasm.

Defeated, we switched on our televisions. And within minutes most of us were captivated. The gimmicks of dress and décor, the moralising and self-contradictory symbolism of the sets, the un-nuanced reading of the score – all these were as nothing beside the tremendous drive and energy of the drama, which stood out in all its riveting completeness. Patrice Chéreau had decided to humanise Wagner, to emphasise character and motive rather than metaphysics. The clumsy *gauchisme* of the sets crumbles before the use that he makes of them and persists only as a minor irritation against which the action has occasionally to struggle. The conductor, too, seized by an evident human sympathy, carries the orchestra along with the drama, and the singers respond with gestures and expressions that give the final lie to the view that Wagner's theatre is declamatory and static.

One is struck most of all by the truth of the drama – its truth to life and character – and by the extraordinary skill with which Wagner contrives and negotiates his climaxes. The great turning points of the cycle – the theft of the ring, the unsheathing of the sword, the death of Siegfried – are both exciting in themselves and also fraught with meaning. This meaning comes not from stage sets or costumes or portentous commentary, but from the action itself. The words and music compel the gestures, which compel the plot, so that a producer who humanises Wagner also reveals a meaning that no *décorateur* can spoil. And this meaning is the real meaning of *The Ring*. To summarise it in a doctrine is to deny its life.

Of course, followers of Schopenhauer, of Hegel, of Marx and Nietzsche, even Christians and Buddhists have found confirmation for their ideas in this stupendous drama. Any artist who succeeds in showing – as Wagner shows – the complex interplay of love, force and justice, and who manages to run the gamut of human relations from the most intimately erotic to the most abstrusely political in a work whose action is generated by entirely human motives, will lend himself to every kind of political and religious interpretation. Philosophies designed to interpret life will also interpret art that is true to life. But Chéreau shows that the drama is sufficiently strong to wrest itself free from the flimsy bondage imposed by the ideological décor.

Of course there are problems: one can never quite put the contradictions out of mind. A battle between a bourgeois householder and his bohemian rival ought not, one feels, to require sword and spear. Most irritating of all is the woodbird which, in obedience to an extremely superficial reading both of Marx and of Wagner, sings out its revelations from a cage, so spoiling one of the most relaxed and poetic of Wagner's images. But in Chéreau's hands, *The Ring* gains more than it loses: the result is a more or less total defeat for French irony and a triumph for German art.

22 February 1983

The Supreme Punishment

Ours is an age of abundant and vociferous moral insecurity. The public voice is one of guilt and self-castigation, which praises the acts of enemies and denounces the efforts of friends. The morbid literature of the 'peace' movement is but one example of a widespread spirit of abnegation, which calls on us to lay down our responsibilities at the critical moment and to take refuge in dreams of universal goodness or in a kind of self-indulgent puzzlement at the fact of human sin. This guilt, which muddles our perceptions, blinds us to the guilt of others, and so rids us of the consciousness of crime. When everyone is to blame, no one is to blame: *tout mal comprendre, c'est tout pardonner.*

An example of this process is provided by the case of Klaus Barbie, who was brought with a great show of triumph from Bolivia in order to be elaborately protected from the fate which he deserves. The only punishment which could register a consciousness of his crimes is precisely the punishment which our rulers (who speak with the public voice of abnegation) forbid. Barbie is to be kept as a living memorial to a guilt that we cannot expiate and to a past that we lack the will to redeem. His case, which vividly displays our reluctance to punish, shows also the need to punish and the moral absurdity of a system of punishment without the penalty of death.

Moral insecurity establishes an empire of pusillanimity and reacts with a strange outrage to any threat to its dominion. Indeed, it has only one moral conviction, which is that people with moral convictions are enemies of mankind. Thus anyone who advocates capital punishment is quickly denounced as either a mad sophist or a luster after blood. The most obvious moral truth in the world, that a cold-blooded murderer of hundreds deserves death and is unjustly served by any lesser punishment, has to be dressed up in countless disguises if it is to gain a hearing. If I now try to put the argument in a nutshell, therefore, it is only with complete confidence that the public voice will remain unaffected by what I say.

Punishment exists in order to express and confirm the consciousness of crime. It is an essential instrument of civilisation: without it a rule of law would be inconceivable, and outrage would inevitably turn to revenge. A world free from legal punishment is a world of mortal combat, in which every quarrel generates hatred and every smallest injury is the occasion for a greater. In order to forestall revenge, punishment must share the object of revenge, which is retribution. When a criminal comes before the law, he comes before an agent of justice, whose purpose is to make him suffer for his crime. Morally speaking, that is the important fact. To think of punishment either as a deterrent or as a cure is to misunderstand it; it is to commit the error of the utilitarian, who looks always to consequences and misses the meaning of the act itself.

Law is the objective order in which private conflicts are extinguished or resolved. It displaces the subjective order of vengeance not because it denies the feelings of vengeance, but on the contrary because it embodies them in impersonal and authoritative form. By making retribution into the right and responsibility of government, it effectively removes the motive from revenge and stills the anxious conscience of the victim. So long as the normal conscience regards cold-blooded murder with abhorrence, abhorrence must find its objective expression in law. The law must capture the sense that murder is different in kind from lesser crimes and that it calls forth, from its very nature, a solemn and awful punishment. Many things have changed with the advent of modern government. But in this particular the normal conscience can never be changed: it is therefore misrepresented by the public voice which purports to speak for it. One of the ironies of parliamentary democracy is that this issue, which as a matter of 'conscience' is the subject of a free vote, is decided always by the moral minority whose 'conscience' is least secure.

But when it is suggested – in the wake of some terrorist outrage – that we should learn again to treat evil with the solemnity that it merits, the moral minority assails us with the image of its irreproachable purity. It reminds us of the duty of forgiveness, while concealing the fact that it is the victim, not the judge, who must forgive. It persecutes us with slogans, fashioned from the newspeak which obliterates important distinctions.

Thus capital punishment becomes 'judicial murder'. How can you do this, we are asked, and who are you to cast the stone? The answer is simple. It is not the judge who condemns the criminal, but the criminal himself. It was he who chose to murder, and therefore he who chose to die. The idea of 'judicial murder' shows the same perversion of judgment as the beliefs of unilateralism. Those who think that in arming ourselves to deter aggression we show an intention to kill overlook the important fact, which is that the one who attacks is alone responsible for the ensuing destruction. Similarly, it is the murderer alone who is responsible for his punishment. Only if the punishment is a form of just retribution, however, can it persuade the murderer of the gravity of his crime; only then, so to speak, does it do him justice.

1 March 1983

On the Conservation of Labour

The basic premise of conservatism is that worthwhile institutions are hard to build and easy to destroy, and that a life without institutions is seriously impoverished. Institutions are created not by plans or theories, but by the co-ordinated action of several generations, by a kind of pooling of human intentions in a stream which flows free of individual ambition, providing aims and values of its own.

The Labour Party has been responsible for many unfortunate transformations; it has shown itself too permeable to ideas and insufficiently conscious of the complexity of the human condition. Nevertheless, it has succeeded in giving form and expression to emerging political forces, and a parliamentary identity to the British working class. It has developed an institutional structure which, for all its faults – and no human institution is without faults – has been genuinely responsive to the experience of those whom it claims to represent. Its achievement is the more remarkable in that it was accomplished without serious damage to parliamentary government, to national sovereignty or to our system of law.

The Labour Party has placed a succession of articulate men and women in the historically defined offices of government. At the same time it has ensured that they behave in office as the spokesmen of a class that has neither time, nor energy, nor aptitude for the arduous business of political influence. Its achievement should be compared with that of the Communist Party, which has shown itself unable in every particular to represent the interests of its supposed constituents: the mythologised 'proletariat'. Wherever the Communist Party has come to power, the working class has found itself insulted, abused and enslaved by an elite which claims exclusive insight into its interests.

By contrast, the Labour Party has been a genuine instrument of representation. It has not needed the preposterous theories and practices of Leninism; it has based its policies, instead, upon a ground of genuine human sentiment. This historical achievement has been the result of a dialectical process – although not one recorded in the Marxist liturgy. The labour movement derived its political identity from the conservative opposition. By deflecting it from its revolutionary purpose we forced the movement into the mould of parliamentary government. We opposed it as a force, so as to recognise it as an institution. The movement aimed at parliamentary representation, accepted the trappings of monarchy and constitutional government and showed itself willing to accord more respect to offices than to the ideas of their incumbents. Faced with our opposition, the Labour Party acquired the institutional character which has enabled it to endure.

While few can look without misgiving on its post-war policies in education or its present muddle over defence, we shall all be poorer for its demise. Of course its collapse is by no means a foregone conclusion. But one thing is certain: that the catastrophe at Bermondsey was, as the Marxists say, no accident. It came about because the party has lost that complex understanding of parliamentary representation which our opposition had forced on it. It has allowed itself to be taken over by people whose contempt for the procedures of representation is as great as the venom with which they affirm their loyalty to the working class.

Conservatism is neither economic dogma nor social theory. It is an attitude, founded in respect for the actual and suspicion of the merely ideal. Inevitably it must regret the passing of a great institution; but it is, in the end, the small things that matter. While the country may recover from the disappearance of the Labour Party, it is uncertain that it will be able so easily to dispense with the institutions which have provided the leading elements of its national culture. I shall conclude these thoughts, therefore, in two weeks' time – next week being the centenary of Karl Marx's death – with some remarks on a college where I was briefly privileged to be a Fellow.

8 March 1983

The Class Straggle

There is no truth whatsoever in the rumour that, if we do not write about Marx this week, there will be 'consequences' for our families. This malicious story, put about by deviationists, opportunists and the running dogs of capitalism, is a vile slander of our free institutions and an insult to the working class. We workers are more than willing to come forward at every opportunity to celebrate the genius of Marx, without whom we would be the exploited victims of imperialist lies and propaganda. Our free press allows full expression to working class opinion, and those who suggest that honest labourers such as Bernard Levin, John Vincent and Gerald Kaufman could be 'influenced' from above are enemies of the people and would deserve the full force of the people's anger, if their lies and innuendoes were not so laughably transparent.

It gives me particular pleasure to be able to remind you today of one of Marx's greatest achievements: the discovery of the class straggle. I believe that this discovery decisively influenced the history of the labour movement and pushed forward by centuries the inevitable progress of mankind. Marx observed that all previous ideas of social class rested on a single assumption: that each person belongs to only one class, proletarian, bourgeois or aristocrat. It needed the penetrating gaze of a Marx to see through this obscurantist nonsense.

Take me, for instance. In so far as I am exploited, that is to say employed, by the editor of *The Times*, I am a member of the toiling proletariat, exchanging my labour power for some small fraction of the value that I produce. At the same time I own a flat, an office, a typewriter: I have private property in the means of production and am thereby a bourgeois, who exploits the labour of secretaries, research assistants and other members of the working class. Moreover I am busily accumulating property and privileges, so as to hand them to my children, who will be heirs to my hard-won leisure. Hence I am an aristocrat, whose power resides in hereditary entitlements. When I observe my origins I am compelled to a similar conclusion. By birth, tradition, culture and connexions I derive from workers in cotton mills, country squires, barbers, shopkeepers, junkers and *szlachta*, tax inspectors and railway engineers. I belong to all classes, and to none.

It is from such observations that Marx derived his great idea. Classes are no more than bundles of straggling individuals, who totter from place to place in the scheme of things but who can be identified with no particular social position. Thus was born the theory of the class straggle, which tells us: 'Don't worry, you're all in it together'. With this simple but compelling idea, Marx removed from the minds of ordinary people the illusion that they live among enemies. This was his major contribution to peace. Previously we had been misled into thinking that the classes are at war and that there could be no final peace or justice until the proletariat had risen up and destroyed the bourgeois 'oppressor'. The idea of class straggle cast the final blow against this pernicious propaganda. It abolished the language of hatred and replaced it with that of conciliation. Each of us is proletarian and bourgeois at once; hence there need be no war, no violence, no hatred, just so long as we remain in harmony with ourselves.

To me this idea came as a revelation. For the first time I could feel confident in the future of mankind. Peace, security, goodwill among men: these were no longer empty phrases, but predictions of a state which it lies within our power to achieve. Of course there will be a long period of gestation before Marx's idea bears fruit. And meanwhile we must arm ourselves against the forces of reaction, who have a vested interest in destroying every idea that brings social harmony. But we are aware of their sinister methods. They will form themselves into exclusive societies, into elites and parties, dedicated to the pursuit of power. They will try to divide the people by setting up Jacobin clubs that rule our lives and also exclude our membership.

But we can take heart in our fight against these opportunists and man haters. The spirit of the class straggle will slowly remove the emotions on which they feed. As men come to appreciate their common destiny, the contempt for exclusive clubs, for elites and parties, will steadily grow. The new attitude will be one of amused and tolerant affection towards human weakness, in which exclusive social privileges will lose their former appeal. It was an attitude with which Marx himself was already familiar. In what was perhaps his most brilliant film – *A Night at the Opera* – he summed it up in the following immortal words: 'Why should I want to belong to a club that would have *me* as a member?'

15 March 1983

The Fate of Peterhouse

Now that lip service has been paid to the world's most over-rated thinker, I return to realities. My generation has a taste for realities. After all, we were heirs to the fantasies of our parents, and to their ridiculous notion that everything could be destroyed and made anew out of the abstract matter of equality. When we come across some real institution still standing among the ruins they left behind them, it is natural that we should feel a certain tenderness for it. It is the proof that we have not been entirely disinherited, the proof that history has not (despite the Marxists) come to an end.

The small and durable institutions matter more than the large and transient. By concealing what they offer, they also keep it safe. But because durable institutions contain more wisdom than human heads, they are the victims of envy. This is particularly true of places of education, which have therefore been strenuously attacked. Schools, universities and colleges have had to accommodate themselves to the vulgar insistence that places of education should adopt the manners, the expectations and the values of the uneducated. One by one they have capitulated. Their studies must now be 'relevant'; their policies over admission and examination must conform to the shibboleths of social policy; their 'advantages' must be offered 'fairly' and 'equally' to everyone, regardless of real distinctions, regardless even of sex. That last demand may seem the least important; in certain cases, however, it is the most important. Such a case is Peterhouse, which has finally decided to admit women, for no better reason than that times have changed. It is, of course, the character of times to change; it is also the virtue of institutions to resist them.

Peterhouse is the oldest Cambridge college and also the smallest, with some 300 undergraduates and 30 Fellows. If you knew nothing about institutions you would therefore expect it to be insignificant – or distinguished, if at all, only occasionally, by the chance election of some exceptional man. In fact it has been distinguished throughout recent times in almost every branch of learning. Kelvin and Clerk Maxwell were undergraduates, as were Whittle, the inventor of the jet engine, and Cockerell, the inventor of the hovercraft. Three of its present Fellows hold Novel prizes for their scientific research. The college has also generated a distinct school of historians, known to many – including readers of *The Times* – for their willing suspension of belief in the face of fashionable absurdities. If the writings of the present Dean have caused such a stir among churchmen, it is partly because the spirit of Peterhouse is expressed in them.

It is difficult to define this spirit: to say that it is sceptical and undeceived is to describe only its most superficial characteristics. It is in fact an acute, and poetic, scrupulousness, a sense of the preciousness of real achievement. If the Peterhouse style seems scornful and satirical, this merely reflects a respect for realities and an impatience with fraud. The same spirit which animates Peterhouse history has found expression in the writings of another Fellow, an architectural historian, whose robust refusal to swallow nonsense has enabled practitioners of his subject freely to express what they had always secretly known: that the modern movement in architecture represents not new knowledge, but a wilful loss of knowledge on a scale unprecedented in the history of art.

That is but one example of a vital and continuing process – the active defence of culture and achievement, in a world that is hostile to both. Institutions like Peterhouse, which provide the widest moral and intellectual companionship to their members, are able to support those engaged in this defence, who would otherwise, out of sheer loneliness, give up the struggle.

I have described some part of the academic achievement of Peterhouse. This achievement is a genuine one. It is not artificially engendered, as in the American Institute or the modern football team, by offering outrageous stipends to foreign stars. It has been generated by the internal vitality of the institution. But I do not believe it to be the most important element in the college's success. It is a bonus, made possible by a corporate life in which traditions of learning and humane companionship have been kept alive and passed on to many who have no interest in academic distinction.

Collegiate life is an end in itself, and only when so treated can it also be a means to the kind of education provided by Peterhouse. The move to admit women is founded on a double confusion. It stems from the theory that the college is really a machine: not an end in itself, but simply a means for generating academic achievement, whose use, like that of the photocopier, ought to be made available to all. The move also expresses the extraordinary modern idea that no voluntary association should be permitted from which one or other sex is excluded. According to this idea, the most wholesome association is that between the sexes and the primary institution that of the modern *domus* – the temporary, nomadic, two-person family. This narrowing of human possibilities condemns all forms of association which defy the tyranny of sexual impulse and all institutions which refuse the cellular structure of the sexual bond.

Collegiate life is not, and cannot be, an aggregate of domestic lives. It has a wholeness, a quotidian inwardness and a responsibility of its own. That is the true basis of Peterhouse's achievement, and it may not survive a change which will install the exclusiveness of sexual partnership at the heart of the collegiate order.

22 March 1983

Death and Destiny

The purpose of medicine is to restore the patient to normality, in so far as it lies within our power. 'Normality' is a contested notion and one that generates many of the doubts and dilemmas which face the doctor. But there is another idea which lies concealed within medical practice, and which causes an equal confusion: the idea of destiny. Many things, including death, are imposed upon us not by human choice, but by human destiny. It is only on the assumption of this destiny that a doctor can limit his obligations, and until his obligations are limited they cannot be fulfilled.

It is our destiny to die. Medicine may postpone or alleviate the process, but it cannot abolish it. Nor would it be right to try. People have sometimes hoped for permanence in this world, but a modicum of imagination suggests that earthly permanence is incompatible with our happiness. Our most valuable emotions – love, loyalty and friendship – are predicated upon the fact of death. Take away mortality, and you take away the perspective from which we view one another and the shared fragility from which our affections spring. The immortal organism does not escape tragedy; but in his joyless pleasures he can be neither pitied nor consoled, and his tragedy lies outside the reach of human compassion. If his survival could be guaranteed by an elixir, then he might endure – in the loveless manner of a Makropoulos. But it is certain that no doctor would feel obliged to assist him.

Nor should any doctor feel that he has some obligation to fight against the human condition or to postpone death beyond the point where nature ceases to resist it. The only obligation lies with the patient: to accept his destiny, and cheerfully to console his friends. Modern medicine creates a powerful fantasy: the fantasy that death may be indefinitely postponed. Patients therefore tend to shift the obligation on to the doctor: instead of preparing themselves for death, they cry out for life, and the doctor is driven to devise ever more complex ways of satisfying them, all the time aware of the futility and irrationality of their demand.

The heart transplant is a vivid and gruesome reminder of this. How easy it proves to persuade a doctor that the shrine of the dead body should be violated, for the sake of a few months of uncertain persistence in the living. The public applauds the activity, offering all its support and interest, as though promised a final victory over death. I am sure that I am not alone in sensing a certain blasphemy in this public interest – a renunciation of the duty peaceably to accept our destiny, in favour of an irrational hope which it is neither possible nor desirable to fulfil.

Surely we have come up against the natural boundary drawn by our condition, and there is something futile and impious in the attempt to pass beyond it. And is there not something morally questionable in devoting scarce medical resources on such a scale to an activity which is both uncertain in its benefits and founded in a meddlesome refusal of our lot?

Attitudes to death go hand in hand with attitudes to sex. And it is in the sphere of sex that some of the greatest of medical confusions have arisen. I refer in particular to the 'sex change' – again, an operation which has exhilarated the public, with its implication that sexuality is an elaborate accident which can be tailored to the individual need.

A person's sexuality is no longer regarded as part of his essence. It has become an accident, which he might change as he changes his clothes. The possibility of thinking in such a way shows a deep change in perception. The obligation to accept one's sex has dwindled, in the same way as the obligation to accept one's death. Consequently people call upon doctors to help them, demanding painful, expensive and dangerous operations, whose moral effects cannot really be envisaged in advance and whose premise is a kind of delusion which, however it might arouse our compassion, ought not to inspire our connivance. No doubt the time is not far distant when sex-change operations will be obtainable on the National Health, granted on the advice of 'experts' able to discern the 'real' gender-identity of the soul sheathed within each human envelope. And no doubt many arguments will be put forward for the 'compassionate' nature of this move.

But as with every attempt to undermine our power to accept our destiny, the consequences are felt not by the patient only, but by the whole community. We are forced to revise our perceptions of sexuality, in a direction which in fact deprives us of our most necessary emotions. Thus, by increasing our control over the human body, there comes a point where we lose familarity with the human soul.

29 March 1983

Who is a Fascist?

Mr Benn is not the only one to use the word 'fascist' as a term of abuse for those who are unconvinced by the theory of practice of socialism. Almost everyone on the right (to use another indiscriminate label) is liable to be faced by the following argument. You believe a, b and c. At least some fascists believed a, b and c. Ergo you are a fascist. Since fascism is evil, you too are evil. In Mrs Thatcher's case a, b and c are the ethic of work, the values of the family and national sovereignty. (*Travail, famille, patrie,* in the words of Vichy France.) They might have been love, life and happiness for all that the argument shows.

Such is the logic of Mr Benn. And it is a logic which has enormous appeal for those who have swallowed the myth that fascism is the enemy of modern civilisation, and socialism (including communism) its friend. It is proof of the good manners of the right that it seldom replies in kind; but there comes a point where good manners have to be set aside.

Fascism was a system of government introduced into Italy by Mussolini. It has something in common with the falangism introduced by Franco into Spain; it also led to an alliance with Hitler. As a result, the term 'fascism' has come to denote three very different systems of government and is used as a term of abuse largely by those who regard it as a name for the mass hysteria which facilitated Hitler's crimes.

Hitler's regime in fact called itself 'national socialism'. It had very little in common with the regimes of Mussolini and Franco, other than the fact of massive popular support. This popular support has provoked the Communist Party – an elite organisation generally incapable of persuading the mass of people spontaneously to follow it – into pouring vitriolic abuse on fascism in all its forms. But this should not blind us to the fact that the actual aims of Soviet communism have coincided very closely with those of Hitler: control from above; a command structure throughout the economy, and throughout civil life; absorption of all institutions into those of the state; destruction by whatever means, however unscrupulous, of all opposition; the control of thought, feeling, hope, fear and ambition through propaganda.

The difference between the two is fairly summarised in their names: one calls itself national socialism, the other international. Hence the first has been a little more selective in its choice of enemy. It is vitally necessary for this kind of regime to create a myth of the 'enemy'. For national socialism the enemy consisted in those within the state who did not belong to – and who 'therefore' secretly worked to destroy – the nation. For international socialism the enemy was a world-wide conspiracy, whose power base was the 'bourgeois' class: that is, everyone from capitalist to kulak. In each case the enemy enjoyed the same fate.

It is, I believe, extremely confusing to apply the term 'fascism' equally to national socialism and to the Mediterranean ideas of authoritative government espoused by Mussolini and Franco. Of course there are common features, and common dangers. But these should not be allowed to obscure the very real differences.

The essential feature of Mussolini's fascism was the corporation. The entire economic activity of the state was to be organised into corporations, subordinate to the state and answerable to it. These corporations would be composed of syndicates, representing the interests of workers, employers and professionals. Through the complex process of representation, all grievances would be removed and conflicts resolved within the corporation. Hence, if the syndicates – such as the trade unions and the associations of managers – performed their function, no other form of representation would be necessary. Government could be carried on by a small elite of dedicated professionals. Unlike national socialism, fascism did not set out to destroy autonomous institutions, but attempted to reconcile its belief in a command economy with a measure of free association at every level of society.

All very naive, of course, but remarkably similar to the political philosophy of Mr Benn, and very different from anything that has been advocated or pursued by Mrs Thatcher. Unlike Mr Benn and the fascists, Mrs Thatcher has perceived that trade unions are not normally representative of the interests of their members, that representation cannot, in general, occur outside strong parliamentary institutions resistant to rapid constitutional change, and that the law exists precisely to curtail the power of corporations, so that the individual grievance may be heard and the individual life find its purpose.

Fascism in Italy was doomed by the alliance with national socialism. In

Spain a similar system of government escaped destruction and provided one of the more flexible forms of authoritarian control. Although imposed by military force, it was able to evolve to the point where parliamentary democracy could be initiated, along with the constitutional monarchy that provides such valuable support to it. We should take comfort from the example. It shows that, if Mr Benn's philosophy ever does gain wide acceptance, we might yet recover from its imposition.

Bennite fascism therefore holds out a promise that neither national nor international socialism has been able to fulfil. If we have to choose between these three evils, then no doubt we should vote for Mr Benn. Far better, however, to remain with Mrs Thatcher.

5 April 1983

The Myth of Authenticity

During the 1960s adolescents were taught to be 'authentic'. Authenticity was sold in many forms, from oriental religion to urban terrorism; but there was a common emphasis on salvation through astonishing behaviour. To be authentic was to release your 'inner' freedom; it was to exist nakedly in a world of stuffed shirts. What a release! And, in retrospect, how priggish.

The contempt for ordinary decencies which comes over adolescents when they must leave the security of the home is a kind of fear: fear of responsibility, of work, of the sacrifices required to ensure the survival of the species. In the face of such commitments, there is comfort in a philosophy which requires us to be committed to nothing. Except that it seems like a cheat. Or at least it seemed like a cheat until Sartre showed that really 'commitment' and 'authenticity' are one and the same. Commitment, he told us, means commitment to the self, to its freedom, to its existential choice. True morality, therefore, does not condemn the 'authenticity' of the outsider. On the contrary, authenticity is the necessary and sufficient condition for a state of moral grace.

Once this rhetorical trick had been discovered, it became possible to make a handsome living by purveying it. The new existentialist guru – exemplified in the personality of R. D. Laing – could advance to positions of influence comparable to those occupied by the great preachers of the seventeenth century. He could become a psychotherapist, an entertainer, a spiritual leader. He could avail himself of the media in order to spread his gospel, and the more fervently he emphasised its youthful quality, the less attention did his audience pay to the empty nihilism of its meaning.

Authentic behaviour, however, because it is purposefully designed to offend, soon offends the agent. He can feel no great satisfaction in being original about nothing, and therefore begins to feel towards himself the kind of suspicion that he feels towards the rival authenticities of others. Authenticity gives way to cynicism, to a refusal to believe, either in the old values of society or in the new values of the self.

This whole process of moral diseducation depends upon an error of judgment. A person is imagined to have a 'real' self, hidden behind the masks of social intercourse. By tearing away the masks, it is supposed, you reveal the inner man. But what if there is nothing behind those masks? If they are all there is, any attempt wholly to discard them is an attempt to rid oneself of one's own existence. It is not surprising, therefore, if the legacy of authenticity is nothingness.

As the young were being exhorted to 'commitment', another 'authenticity' was being marketed, in the name of scholarship, discipline and reverence for the past. The principal entrepreneurs were not forward-looking gurus but impersonal corporations, such as Deutsche Grammophon, whose in many ways magnificent 'archive' series began to introduce the world to the idea of 'authentic' musical performance. Soon musicians everywhere were searching for the 'correct' instruments upon which to imitate the manners of another age. Violins lost their vibrato; flutes were replaced by recorders, pianos by fortepianos and harpsichords, cellos by viols, horns by their valveless ancestors.

Much dead sentiment was pruned away. But much live feeling was lost along with it. Authenticity came over Bach and Purcell like the kiss of death. For only the most accomplished musician can translate himself into the manners of another age without leaving behind him his full artistic sensibility. Each addition to the repertoire of musical performance changes the character of what has gone before. We do not hear the harpsichord as Bach heard it. We hear it as 'other than the piano'. And the piano – which created modern music – dominates our understanding of the keyboard. Keyboard pieces which sound ill on the piano can establish only an imperfect claim to our attention.

Were Bach still with us he would, I am sure, insist on inauthentic performance. He would know that music exists in the ear of the listener, and that the post-Romantic ear is the product of a complex musical history. Creative inauthenticity enables Bach, Brahms and Mahler to belong together, so restoring the vital continuity without which the past is an empty husk.

The two cults of authenticity seem like opposites. But they are in one sense the same. Each requires us to believe in a reality behind appearances – a real self, or a real Bach – which exists behind our spontaneous social performances. And each fails to see that true freedom requires us to surrender ourselves to social conditions, to give up the illusion that, by struggling against them, we are purer and holier than our times.

12 April 1983

Our Allies in the Warsaw Pact

A *Times* leader on 30 March pointed out that the 'Brezhnev doctrine' was invoked to justify the invasion of Czechoslovakia in 1968. That is true. According to this doctrine, the leader argued, 'communist governments must be expected to help each other militarily in times of crisis'. That, however, is false. The Brezhnev doctrine is indifferent to all crises except those which threaten Soviet power; it offers no help, but only hindrance, and its 'military assistance' takes the form of armed invasion.

What the doctrine actually says is that the 'socialist states' have 'limited sovereignty'. For in all matters which might be perceived by the Kremlin as a threat to Soviet control, the 'socialist' states are subject to military coercion. Limited sovereignty means, in effect, the absence of sovereignty. In most matters which affect social and political identity, the economic order, the legal and institutional superstructure, foreign policy and military preparedness of the 'socialist' states, no decisions can be taken by the indigenous governments. A paralysis invades the body politic, which is jerked into a semblance of life only when strings are pulled in Moscow. Limited sovereignty means not sovereignty, but subjection.

Obvious perhaps. But strangely ignored by many who discuss the military balance and the political division in Europe. We must bear in mind that the Warsaw Pact, unlike Nato, is not an alliance. An alliance is a voluntary association of sovereign states for the purpose of defence. It can be ended unilaterally by any state which sees reason to withdraw from it. It no more involves the loss of sovereignty than a contract (which is the paradigm of free association) involves the loss of freedom by those party to it. An alliance, like a contract, is an *expression* of freedom, and nations which lose the freedom to form or relinquish alliances lose the most important freedom that they have.

The Warsaw Pact is not a voluntary association between sovereign states for defence purposes. It is not voluntary; its members are not sovereign; and it has never defended, but only – as in the case of Czechoslovakia – attacked its constituents. The East European states are no more free to withdraw from the pact than they were free originally not to join. Their military and political stance is unilaterally dictated by the controlling power, which compels obedience precisely through the military structure which the 'pact' establishes.

The armies of the subject states are in a sense slave armies, and their governments puppet governments. That was why the Brezhnev doctrine was so appropriately invoked to justify the invasion of Czechoslovakia. An alliance whose entire military history has consisted in imposing itself by force upon its constituents is not an alliance, but an instrument of coercion.

The consequences for us should not go unnoticed. The Warsaw Pact is maintained at a level of military preparedness which far surpasses anything attained by the armies of Nato. It is well equipped, massively extended and brought under a single, and single-minded, command. There is no need for compromise or consultation; on the contrary, the whole military machine can be set in motion by a single order. No such systematic preparedness is, or could be, exhibited by Nato. Had it existed we should never have defied the United States so far as to fight over the Falklands.

The nature of the Warsaw Pact is such, therefore, as to expose Western Europe to the risk of a rapid and irreversible defeat in the event of a 'conventional' conflict. To avoid defeat we should have either to match the conventional capacity and political intransigence of the Warsaw Pact, or else to develop a strategy that would permit us to fight on far beyond the point of initial weakness. Since we cannot do the first, we must prepare for the second.

While a short combat would favour the Warsaw Pact, a long combat would turn the balance against it, by reason of the very truth to which the 'Brezhnev doctrine' refers. The East European armies are manned by our natural allies, who would sooner fight against the power which coerces them than against the West. The longer they are exposed to war, the more disaffected they will become with its purpose, a purpose which runs counter to everything that they inwardly desire.

What is to be done? The first step – but it is surely only the first step – is to take seriously the suggestion by Lord Hill-Norton and others (Letters, 29 March) that we begin now to restore our home defences. A standing army, however expert, can operate for long only from a secure base. A Britain without effective civil defence and without a force able to secure it against invasion would not have time to discover who its real allies are.

It is the belief that we may have the capacity to make that discovery which has offered the major deterrent to Soviet expansion. By virtue of the Brezhnev doctrine, the Soviet Union has gained many subjects. But it has also begun to recognise that it has no real allies at all.

19 April 1983

The Life of the Market

New York has asked to be celebrated, and what man or woman who knows the city can refuse? Some love it for its vitality, some for its charm; some for its modern offices, some for its Victorian factories; some for its culture, some for its vulgarity. A place that is loved for every reason is loved for none in particular. It is a mirage, whose pleasant prospect derives from our own subjective craving. By its universal permission, New York lends zest to appetite and gratification to every small desire. It counts nothing human alien to itself and makes only negotiable demands. You can take or leave the city, but it is adamant that you should take it of your own free will. Hence, behind the bustle and boldness of New York, the visitor experiences a rare kind of tranquillity. This New York peace is of special interest, now that the term 'peace' has been captured by people with a motive to conceal its meaning.

New York peace is founded on conciliation. It arises because people actively pursue their own advantage, while propitiating those who are similarly minded. There is a common principle which urges the citizen to agree terms, even with his opponent – indeed, especially with his opponent. Everything that happens, happens by agreement. And therefore a lot happens. The social structure is bent towards agreement, about matters not previously considered or decided. People move through the streets primed for agreeable encounter. They make rapid contact and as rapidly detach themselves, their hands and faces mobile with excitement.

American courtesies are largely to be explained by this public pursuit of agreement. We may complain of the manners which permit the instant use of Christian names, the immediate revelation of personal details, the frank discusssion of everything that could conceivably become a term in some hypothetical contract. Even preliminary gestures can seem to us impertinent or insincere. Surely, we think, the airline hostess cannot mean it when she tells us to 'have a nice day'.

And of course there is a sense in which she does not mean it. Only God could *mean* 'have a nice day' to all and sundry; but in God's voice, these words would express not conciliation, but a most terrible command. American courtesies are never commands: they are preliminaries to an agreement. Hence the hostess does not tell us to listen to the safety instruction. She does not even ask us. She says: 'We of United Airlines should like to *share* some important information with you'. In other words: 'I bring you a gift of knowledge; how will you respond?' The American instinct for contract immediately answers: 'With my second best attention. Terms agreed.'

What I have just described might be expressed more pompously as 'the phenomenology of the market'. It is life experienced through the pursuit of rapid contract. Honesty is at a premium; so are openness, activity and the rights of man. That peace is one of the consequences should not surprise us. For no transaction occurs without the consent of the parties. One may feel cheated; but never coerced, oppressed or terrorized. People can squeeze you, freak you or even gross you out; but they cannot try to get on your back without being thrown out for the jerks, finks and weenies that they are. When Milton Friedman exhorts his countrymen to get the state off their backs, he merely reminds them of the fundamental principle of American existence: nothing is to happen except by agreement.

Friedman is not the only economist to have praised the market for its efficiency, for its equilibrium, for the 'tacit knowledge' that it contains. But even if he is wrong – even if the socialists are right in their defence of a 'planned' economy – that would not alter my conviction that the market is the most acceptable mode of distribution. It is the means whereby peace is made real among strangers: and that is its value.

We should not worry if the market in equities or real estate does not appear quite like that. Those are merely the dubious outgrowths of a minutely thriving organism. Ask yourself why auctions, cattle marts, fairs and street markets are so attractive. Ask yourself why people flock to them, even when they have nothing to buy or sell. Ask yourself why these places have the character of festivals, in which expressions and gestures convey the highest animation and social readiness. The answer is simple. They are places where we enjoy the spectacle of multiple agreement, places where strangers co-operate, regardless of their individual interests and aims.

Of course the market is imperfect, as is every human thing. The socialists may be right, that it elevates freedom over justice and means over ends. There is hardly a moralist who has not been offended by the profound amorality of the market: by its ability to transform every object of human affection into an object of exchange. To make the market economy into the corner-stone of politics is indeed to simplify human existence beyond recognition. But to ignore its true merit – as the most widespread and immediate experience of human peace – is to take a step in a dangerous direction.

It is, I believe, no accident that those political systems which have abolished the market have also come to understand the term 'peace' in a novel way: not as the ability to accept and conciliate one's opponent, but as the ability to silence him forever.

26 April 1983

A Visit to Laputa

On reading that researches into the family by the Centre for Policy Studies had been partly responsible for the Prime Minister's recent creation of a Minister for Children's Play, I recalled a passage in my connoisseur's edition of *Gulliver's Travels*:

> 'I came at last to the Academy, which is but an unassuming Structure, with neither Forecourt nor Garden. The Warden received me with great Kindness, and showed me into the first Laboratory, where sat a Man of meagre Aspect, staring fitfully into a Glass of Malmsey Wine.

His Clothes, Shirt and Skin were all of the same grey Complexion, and, although the Warden did assure me of his Merit, as the Author of diverse Treatises on the mental Life of Flowers, he had about him such an Air of melancholy Dejection, as wholly to discourage my Hope that he would be able to enlighten me.

After a long Silence, during which the learned Doctor remained motionless, I made bold to reveal the Purpose of my Visit, and to beseech him to inform me whether he had yet discovered the Principle whereby men form themselves into lasting Families, and so guarantee the Future of their Kind. He told me, he had been thirty Years employing his Thoughts about the Question, and had concluded that the Principle was no different from that to be observed in Flowers, which grow naturally together in Societies, and reproduce themselves by sending abroad Pollen upon the Legs of Bees.

He did assure me that Families result from a natural Affinity, caused by the Proximity of Men and Women, and that there should be not the slighest Difficulty in rearing Children skilled in all the Virtues of Society, were the invisible Animules which distribute human Pollen to be trained to fly only towards the Person intended to receive them. He explained to me an ingenious Device, which I was not skilful enough to comprehend, whereby these Animules might be induced into small glass Chambers, and so conveyed by learned Doctors unto the Recipient, who would infallibly conceive. By such Improvements, he said, it would be possible completely to determine the Number, Character and Nurture of the unborn Generation, so removing the element of chance which had hitherto impeded human Progress, and he lamented only that Her Majesty had so far received his Ideas with Scepticism, arguing that since she herself had conceived without the aid of his Appliances, she did not see why her Subjects should require them.

I went next into another Laboratory, but hastened back, being overcome with a most horrible Stink. My Conductor pressed me forward, conjuring me in a Whisper to give no Offence, which would be highly resented. The Researcher of this Chamber was the most ingenious Scholar, who for many Years had been employed about a singular Operation, whereby he sought to extract the Wisdom from ancient Treatises of Education, by seething them in Vinegar and Gall. He assured me that one small drop of this Tincture would instil into the most obdurate Youth that compliant Disposition which would fit him for the Uses of Society. I saw him try the Experiment on a rough Boy, dragged from a neighbouring Closet, who, upon tasting the Concoction that was forced between his Lips, fell down in a Swound, from which he seemed likely never to recover.

I visited many other Apartments, but shall not trouble my reader with all the Curiosities I observed, save only two, which seemed to contain particular Instruction. I was highly pleased with a Gentleman of large and jovial Aspect, who described himself as a Political Philosopher. He insisted that I share his Wine, and showed himself most ready to answer my Inquiry, arguing that since Things are known only by their Names, my Puzzlement could be overcome simply by altering the Usage of the Word that had prompted it. He therefore proposed an ingenious Device, which he called the "one person Family", an Institution likely to prove so agreeable to those subject to its Regimen, as to endure through every Change in the political Body. This Doctor therefore proposed, that all Benefits received from the Treasury should henceforth be known as "Family Allowances", and all taxes as "Family Dues", by which simple Improvement, he did assure me, the Institution of the Family should prove as lasting as the natural Avarice of Mankind.

In another Chamber I encountered a Projector who, by the Dignity of his Robes, I assumed to be a Man of great Consequence. He received my Inquiry graciously, and told me that he had been engaged for many Years in the most exacting mental Labours, about the very Question that I proposed, and that, in his considered Judgement, Children could be brought readily to accept the Burdens and Duties of Society, provided only that suitable Facilities were provided for the Development of their native Ingenuity. He particularly mentioned the furtive Kiss, an Action whereby the Young learn simultaneously to conceal and to disclose their amorous Intentions. It was a singular Misfortune, he said, that there were so few Localities in which the furtive Kiss could now be practised, although he flattered himself, that a more noble exalted Theory never sprang in a Man's head, than that which recognised in this Action the true Seeds of mature Ambition and moral Constraint. But he assured me with Pleasure that Her Majesty had greeted his Ideas most warmly, averring that an Experience which had so awoken the Spirit of Inquiry in herself, could not fail to provide a similar Benefit even to the most obdurate of her Subjects. Furtive kissing, she assured him, contributes alike to Initiative and to Responsibility, the two most precious Virtues upon which the Future will be founded. And the learned Doctor told me that a Proclamation had that very Day gone forth from the Palace, in which he was named as Minister of the Furtive Kiss.'

3 May 1983

The Forward Path of Socialism

The visitor to the 'socialist' countries comes away with the overwhelming impression of having travelled backwards in time. The smell of coal fires, the sight of trams and steam trains, the decaying, uncared-for buildings, the empty shops, the queues of people in drab imperfect clothing, the sense of an overbearing public concern which gathers people up and robs them of initiative: all this returns the visitor to a distant experience, a confused memory of ration books and Pathé newsreels.

Above the scenes of conquest stand huge crumbling slogans: for socialism, for peace, for progress. But what a strange kind of progess is this! And what a strange kind of peace in these unsmiling faces! One would rather had said they belonged to a people still at war; that the oppression, the privation, the fear of the forties had remained, along with all their visible décor.

The reader of *Renewal*, a tract composed by the Labour Shadow Cabinet, comes away with an impression that is not dissimilar. The grey, unyielding sentences roll through his mind like a phalanx of panzers, bombarding him with grievances from another age. He is back in the world of the wicked capitalist motivated by 'greed' and cynicism, of the oppressed 'working class' struggling for 'trade union rights'. The battle for the health service has still to be won, the 'class system' to be overcome, education to be freed from privilege and from a syllabus unsuited to our progressive times.

'Social control', 'public ownership', 'a planned evolution' towards 'democratic socialism' – these are still the major purposes, and still, in muted form, are heard the condemnation of 'bellicose' America and the propitiatory references to the Soviet Union, victim of so many unjustifiable threats.

The Labour Party promises us much: an end to 'unacceptable' unemployment; an education that suits people for the needs of society (whether or not for needs of their own); an increase in investment in public transport, in medical facilities, in housing, in prison accommodation; a united Ireland (the Labour Party apparently has ways of getting the Unionists to want this); an 'irreversible' transformation whereby power is taken from the hands of unscrupulous individuals and placed in the 'care' of 'society'. For reasons which the authors neglect to mention, 'society' will then use this power for the benefit of everyone, including even the Unionists.

The most striking feature of these chapters is that, with few honourable exceptions, the authors punctuate their vague and unreasoned promises with the most violent invective against something called now 'monetarism', now 'Thatcherism'. This enemy is never clearly defined. But we are to make no mistake about its evil purposes. It alone is responsible for the present unemployment. It has 'engineered' an 'unprecedented rate of industrial decline' (Merlyn Rees). It has destroyed more of British industry than the Luftwaffe (Peter Shore). Perhaps it *is* the Luftwaffe, in some new invisible form. At any rate, it is a 'cold, blind, unrelenting callousness', a 'cold, stunted suburban imagination', operating a 'vast, lumbering, amorphous propaganda machine' (Michael Foot).

And its effects are not felt only by the unemployed. Brynmor John reminds us that 'the greatest blot on our society is the way we treat children and their parents, whether employed or in receipt of social security'. In plain English, we are *all* in the soup. There is no salvation for any of us, short of the 'irreversible' transformation that we are promised, when we shall at last be rid of the monetarist oppressor.

I suppose there are some who feel a certain nostalgia for this kind of language, and who long to hear again its bracing tones. But is it a language worthy of the Labour Party? I doubt it, and not only because this 'monetarist' enemy is so elusive and so abstract a fiction. As our authors remind us, the Labour Party is a democratic party, committed to parliamentary government. Despite Eric Heffer's assertion that 'socialism and democracy are indivisible' – a phrase which would call forth the fervent agreement of Comrade Ponomaryev – the Labour Party admits that non-socialists may sometimes have a right to rule. A democratic party is destined to govern people at least half of whom disagree with it. It is committed to accept that no change that it initiates is or ought to be 'irreversible'. It is surely a poor beginning to its election campaign that it should describe its opponent as the enemy of a people who elected her and who are likely to elect her again.

It is one of the major claims of this 'enemy' that not everything which happens in the public sphere is the responsibility of government. Some bad things just *happen*, not because they are intended or desired, but because they cannot be prevented by any reasonable measures. The statist mentality of the Labour Party is such that it cannot really accept this claim. All public happenings, it believes, are really actions of the government. The state *already* has that vast and unassailable power over human destiny that the Labour Party wishes on it. This is no doubt why the authors feel no compulsion to give either coherent theories or detailed policies. Since everything that has recently happened is the 'doing' of the monetarist enemy, it is enough to 'do' the opposite. If anyone asks 'how?' one answer alone is given: by increasing public expenditure. And if anyone again asks 'how?' he will not receive an answer, for it is he who must pay.

10 May 1983

Reform in South Africa

It is in very bad taste to praise South Africa. However, since such errors of taste are still legally permissible, I propose to indulge them: not, indeed, for the fun of it (for it is not fun to offend well-meaning moral sentiment), but for the sake of truths that have been declared unutterable. It is hard to do justice to these truths in the space of this column; but I shall try.

The policy of apartheid was founded on a myth: the myth of the voortrekkers, who laid claim to a supposedly unoccupied territory and who brought with them a religion, a language, a civilisation and a legal system of their own. According to the story, their descendants live by hereditary entitlement, won against the assaults of other peoples who, jealous of their achievements, have repeatedly tried to capture the land which the Afrikaners made their own. The Afrikaners are therefore entitled to confine these 'other peoples' to the territories from which they originally sallied forth in search of unjust profit.

The myth is not really credible. Moreover, it depends upon ideas of what constitutes a 'people' which are, to say the least, atavistic. However, these very same ideas prevail throughout Africa, providing the principal fund from which African feelings of legitimacy are drawn. It is only a kind of racism – an expectation that whites should think in a more civilised way than blacks – which causes us especially to condemn the Afrikaners for espousing them.

It goes without saying that apartheid is offensive. It was adopted, however, as the lesser of two evils. The Afrikaners believe that black majority rule has, in almost every case, led to the collapse of the constitutional government which they brought to South Africa, and upon which their freedoms and privileges – perhaps even their lives – depend. And it did not seem so very bad to deny to blacks a vote which they would, when in power, promptly deny to themselves.

Let us not defend that self-serving reasoning, but only look at the facts. Throughout South Africa the Roman–Dutch system of law prevails intact, and with it an independent judiciary which cannot be coerced by the government. Hence much of the apartheid legislation, being repugnant to natural justice, has entered into conflict with the structural principles of adjudication and so proved inapplicable

This has been especially important in the founding of the black townships, such as Soweto, where people have acquired through the courts precisely those rights of residence of which the government has sought to deprive them. The government, being constitutional, is committed to the reality of judicial independence – and in this it differs from almost every other African government south of the Nile.

We should not be surprised, therefore, if the resident of Soweto has, despite the disdain with which he is treated, rights that transcend those granted to the citizens of Mozambique and Angola, even though the citizens of these states enjoy a political equality for which the resident of Soweto longs in vain.

By the same token South Africa has been able to maintain levels of press freedom which are foreign to its neighbours. Embarrassing characters like Bishop Desmond Tutu are able to speak, to publish and to broadcast their views. Ask yourself what has happened to the opposition voice in Angola or Mozambique, and you will see that this freedom too is a precarious achievement, unlikely to survive the urgent demand for equality which most easily succeeds by reducing all citizens to a level of equal impotence.

Naturally those facts do not justify apartheid. But they are facts nevertheless, and anyone with a genuine concern for rights and freedoms ought carefully to attend to them and to the comparisons which they suggest. Our natural horror of racism – at least in the evident form of apartheid – causes us constantly to overlook real achievements and virtues; it also causes us to overlook evils. Thus the voortrekker myth ignores completely the destiny of those 'peoples' – the largely Muslim Indians and the coloureds – who have no patch of *bantu* earth to which they can be restricted. The coloureds in particular – people of mixed ancestry, partly descended from Malay slaves – were treated with inexcusable high-handedness by the legislation which disenfranchised them. The only thing that distinguishes these people from the ordinary Afrikaner is their 'race': the mythical substratum of ethical existence. In every respect material to that idea of a single 'people' by which the Afrikaners have sought to live, they belong with those who excluded them – far more, indeed, than do those whites of English or Eastern European descent who share the important privileges.

Their language is Afrikaans, their religion Calvinism, their worship that of the Dutch Reformed Church; their history, attachments and institutions are all South African, and their social and political expectations arise from the common experience and common aspirations of that place. Surely, therefore, it is a major constitutional advance that the South African government is at last proposing to undo the legislation which deprived these Afrikaners of their native rights. To take this step is to begin the long task of destroying the myth upon which apartheid is founded.

17 May 1983

In Praise of Privilege

In the minds of many Labour politicians the principal social disorder is privilege, and a Labour victory, either now or in some future election, would certainly initiate a renewed persecution of those who are thought to possess this elusive quality. Hatred of privilege is, I believe, the true reason for the desire to abolish the House of Lords (Britain's most harmless institution) and for the hostility towards private schools and private medicine. What, then, is privilege, and why is it bad?

There are two kinds of privilege: one the product of freedom, the other the product of power. The first kind is a necessary consequence of association. Suppose John, William and Mary have a common interest in mountaineering. They form a club, so as to buy equipment and furnish expeditions. In due course William retires, bequeathing his equipment to the club; John and Mary invite other members. Naturally they consider only those who will be suitable companions. Hence conditions of membership soon emerge. The club is successful, buys itself rights and offers unique advantages to members. It continues, long after the death of John and Mary, a living memorial to their association. What was once a bond of mutual affection has become a body of rules, an institution, a system of privilege. Existing members will seek to limit the number of entrants and to secure advantages for their friends and children. Such little systems of privilege are the inevitable result of free association and can be prevented only by force.

The second kind of privilege is a consequence of command. An officer can command his troops only if he can call upon a habit of obedience, established by some hierarchy of power. Such hierarchies exist wherever there is leadership and government, although they differ widely in the kinds of sanction which they exercise. They are necessary; but they are also resented, and will inevitably be resented unless subjected to a code of honour.

A person must command only that which is permitted by his office. Otherwise he abuses those beneath him. When the code of honour is scrupulously observed, we think of the officer as in a position not of privilege, but of authority. If he abuses his office, for personal gain, then his power becomes a source of privilege. It is this kind of privilege which is most resented. For, unlike the first kind, it is inherently unjust.

The universal experience of 'actually existing socialism' – the socialism imposed wherever possible by the heirs of Lenin – is of the abolition of the first kind of privilege and its replacement by the second. The process – announced by Lenin as the 'withering away of the state' – might be better described as 'the withering away of society'. The misdirected zeal with which Leninism tore down every social institution was also applied to the building of the Communist Party – the most terrifying hierarchy of command that the world has ever known. Every office in this hierarchy presents opportunities for corruption, and the resulting system of privilege has a scale and scope that defy description. It is contemptuous of honour and hostile to freedom, especially to the freedom of association. It has abolished altogether those more genial privileges which are the condition of civilised existence. Anyone who wishes to know what is hateful in privilege should therefore look at the socialist states.

The privileges denounced by the Labour Party belong largely to the first kind. They result not from a hierarchy of command, but from a society rich in institutions, based in voluntary association, in charity and in the endeavour of creative individuals who have wished not to dominate, but to unite with their fellows.

Consider the public schools. These were established by charitable men and women who wished to form societies dedicated to learning and religion. The resulting institutions are not, and were never intended to be, state institutions, and they have no coercive powers. Their members are chosen according to criteria that have evolved over centuries, through successive glosses upon the original intentions of the founders, modified as ever by the natural human instinct to offer favours to friends. The ensuing privilege is spontaneous and irrepressible. Whatever happens to 'state' education, such schools will continue to provide education and also to produce lasting association between those who have attended them.

A society which permits free association permits this kind of privilege. It is not obvious that such privilege is harmful, or even that it is widely resented. It is exclusive, but only in the way that families are exclusive: by including less than everyone. And people are more disposed to accept 'exclusiveness' now that they have seen what follows from its abolition. For it is evident that small voluntary institutions are better able to do what they purpose to do than the substitutes offered (and usually controlled) by the state.

In order to curtail social privilege, therefore, we must curtail the freedom to associate. We must follow in Lenin's footsteps and erect a system of control that will be sufficient to abolish man's natural propensity towards institution-building. We then replace association by coercion, and the privileges of society by the far more threatening privileges of the state.

24 May 1983

Limiting the Commons

Many ardent believers in democracy are dismayed by the prospect of a landslide victory for Mrs Thatcher. They argue that a government needs strong opposition, in order to control and limit it and in order to moderate its zeal. Without strong opposition, they fear, a government may be tempted to run riot.

At first sight this is hardly a democratic argument. It seems to imply that, when the people are most united in their choice of government, then are they least likely to be governed well. The 'people's choice' is to be trusted only when it is so much in conflict with itself as to be largely ineffective. On further reflection, however, we can see that the belief in democratic election, as the sole ground of legitimate government, can lead precisely to this paradoxical position. The paradox issues from two premises. First, good government is limited government. Second, both government and the force that limits it should be democratically elected.

Hence the power of the government must be limited in the Commons, by pressures exerted through the elected representatives of the people.

The conclusion follows; but only one of the premises is true. It is true that good government is limited government. But it is not true that limitation ought to be exerted only in the Commons. For a variety of reasons, we tend to exaggerate both the power and the prestige of the Commons. We tend to ignore the extent to which it feeds off other institutions, without whose co-operation it could not function as a representative chamber. It matters very much that a great many of its members are ignorant, unintelligent and personally ambitious. It matters too that they are no longer drawn from a class which feels no need to use the *Commons* for the purposes of social gain. But these things – while deplorable in themselves – would matter far more were the House not subject to limiting pressures from institutions more civilised than itself.

Two such institutions are particularly important for our future. Both have legislative powers; both have dignities which support those powers and which save them from the appearance of arbitrariness; and both have a representative function. One is the House of Lords, the other is the Judiciary. Neither has elected members; and their power depends precisely on that.

Causes that cannot be heard in the hubbub of the Commons may yet be heard in the Upper House. Individual grievances, for which the careerist politician has only half an ear, can be heard in court and may find redress through a judicial process responsive to the call of natural justice. Common law judges, armed with the rules of equity, are also legislators. When statutes hastily drafted and mindlessly applied, have driven the individual into a corner, he may yet call for judicial aid. The resulting judgment – as Lord Denning has most vividly illustrated – is more likely to remedy his grievance than any acts of the ignorant politicians who created it.

The Commons has, in recent years, shown itself jealous of all rival modes of representation. We therefore have reason to fear its power. A landslide victory for Labour would certainly be dangerous for the cause of limited government. The Labour Party seeks to abolish the House of Lords; and meanwhile it would surely do all in its power to remove its legislative powers. Moreover, the party has shown itself disposed belligerently to question judicial decisions whenever its legislative intentions are thwarted by the operations of natural justice. How much more likely is this to be true when the party is increasingly influenced by people for whom judicial independence is a merely 'bourgeois' ideal, to be overthrown in the interests of a more 'democratic' social order.

The present government has been willing to listen both to the Lords and to the judges. On several occasions it has introduced legislation which has been overturned in the Upper House. It has quietly accepted the result, without threatening to use the iniquitous Parliament Acts, which give to the House of Commons powers which match its arrogance. Nor has this government shown the slightest tendency to put pressure on the judiciary, even though ministerial intentions have been thwarted more than once – and to the embarrassment of the minister in question – by the courts.

A landslide victory for the Conservatives in the Commons would therefore not be the anti-democratic disaster that many prophesy, for the very reason that the Conservative Party is, to this degree, anti-democratic. It is prepared to concede legislative and representative functions to offices that are not filled by democratic election. It is prepared to recognise that there may be more wisdom in traditional institutions than meets the democratic eye, and that the urgent clamour of the hustings may not be the best or most serious expression of the political temper of the nation.

31 May 1983

The Elgin Marbles

When the seventh Earl of Elgin, who was then ambassador to the Sublime Porte in Constantinople, persuaded the imperial court to give him permission to study and restore the ruins of Greece, long years of neglect had taken their toll of the monuments. Lord Elgin's painters showed the condition of these ruins to the world and so stimulated the desire to protect them. Soon, prompted by such romantic philhellenes as Lord Byron, Greece achieved her independence and the ancient monuments were given official protection, as symbols of a rediscovered identity. By then the marbles which Lord Elgin had taken from the Parthenon were safe in the British Museum, bought for considerably less than he had spent in saving them.

Miss Melina Mercouri, the Greek Minister of Culture, is not the first person to accuse Lord Elgin of wrongful appropriation, nor is she the most flamboyant. In Byron's poem *The Curse of Minerva,* the pillaged goddess laments her temple in bathetic words:

That all may learn from whence the plunderer came,
The insulted wall sustains his hated name:
For Elgin's fame this grateful Pallas pleads,
Below, his name – above, behold his deeds!

This was the most highfalutin expression of a considerable public outcry. The ambassador, who was accused of dishonesty, rapacity and theft, eventually succeeded in justifying his conduct, and a Select Committee of the House of Commons, appointed in 1816 to inquire into the desirability of purchasing the marbles, exonerated him from the charges – although of course it could hardly have recommended purchase otherwise.

To whom, then, do the marbles belong? The question has three answers: legal, aesthetic and moral. The firman which came from the Porte to Lord Elgin authorising him to erect scaffolding around the Parthenon also allowed him 'to take away any pieces of stone with old inscriptions or figures thereon'. He had not originally intended to remove the marbles from Athens, but did so when he became convinced that their Ottoman custodians would simply neglect or abuse them. He brought them to England, and no objection was raised by the Ottoman authorities.

Was Lord Elgin the legal owner of the marbles? Probably. If not, then the rightful owner was the Sublime Porte, which laid claim to the Acropolis as a public building of Athens. In which case the marbles now belong to the legal successor of the Porte. Some international lawyers would say that this is Greece, on the grounds that Greece has succeeded to all territorial rights which the Ottoman emperor previously asserted over the Greek dominions. Others would argue that the true successor is Turkey, on the grounds that Turkey has succeeded to the movable property of the Ottoman Court, which had exerted continuous and exclusive control over the marbles for a century and a half. Until this legal question is decided, the marbles must clearly remain in the benign custodianship of the British Museum.

In fact nobody cares very much about legal ownership, since most people recognise the *ad hoc* character of international law, which is more concerned to prevent conflict than to establish rights. The other arguments therefore prevail. The aesthetic argument tells us that the marbles belong with the Parthenon and are integral to its beauty. When we consider the symbolic importance of the temple and all that it represents by way of history, civilisation and artistic achievement, we can only feel outrage that it remains disjoined from its necessary parts.

The argument is powerful. But what force does it have when we are told that the Greek government seeks possession of the marbles merely in order to exhibit them in another museum? How much more painful will the dismembered Parthenon appear when its missing organs lie bottled beside it, protected from the corrosive breath of tourists by screens of transparent plastic? Far better to keep them in the quiet, seedy galleries of the British Museum, in rooms calculated to intimidate the ignorant and to bore the merely curious.

What then of the moral argument? The marbles, we are told, are part of the patrimony of Greece and belong by right to the modern republic, heir to Athens and to the achievements of Athens. But what is the modern Greek republic? A fragile democracy which grew upon roots transplanted from Europe. The patrimony of Athens exists only partly in marble form. The meaning of those marbles is to be found in literature, in law, in institutions, in the public spirit which caused the Athenians to immortalise themselves in verse and stone. Who is heir to that spirit? Who adopted that literature, those laws and those institutions? Of whom could it be said, during the long years of darkness when Greece did not exist as a nation, that the public spirit of Athens animated their conduct so that they were, in the words given to Pericles, 'free and tolerant in private things, in public obedient to the law'? Surely this public spirit animated Lord Elgin, just as it animated those who questioned him and the House of Commons which finally took his part.

To return the marbles to Greece is to return lumps of stone to people who have not been – as we have been – guardians of their meaning. George Seferis, perhaps the greatest of modern Greek poets, acknowledged the grief and anxiety that such a belated inheritance entails:

> I awoke with this marble head in my hands
> which exhausts my elbows, and I know not where to put it down.
> It fell into my dream as I emerged from it,
> and now our lives are joined; it will be hard to break apart . . .

The marble head which afflicts Seferis spoke clearly and cheerfully to Lord Elgin, who encountered it not in a dream but in that wakeful enthusiasm which is the undying spirit of ancient Greece.

7 June 1983

In Praise of Bourgeois Art

The two most potent post-war orthodoxies – socialist politics and modernist art – have at least one feature in common: they are both forms of snobbery, the anti-bourgeois snobbery of people convinced of their right to dictate to the common man in the name of the common man.

Fortunately the common man is, or aspires to be, a bourgeois. The last thing he wants is to be governed by egalitarians. After all, he has his life to lead, his children to raise, his identity to establish. Once he woke up to what was happening, therefore, he rejected the pretensions of those who sought to make him equal to his neighbour. We may now look forward to a welcome period of bourgeois equilibrium. But the more important question remains: can our culture recover from the post-war fads as readily as our politics? Can natural bourgeois man regain the right to his own tastes, or will he be for ever put upon by modernist aesthetes?

The Royal Academy's summer exhibition is naturally crowded with derivative paintings. But they mostly derive from nothing more recent than Vuillard. A few abstracts glare out in ferocious primary colours; but their stares are not reciprocated. The favoured images are quiet, comforting and figurative: a tree in a field; two cups in a shaft of sunlight; a face by a window. Many are miniatures; some are confined in Baroque or Renaissance frames – a welcome recognition of the truth that painting is furniture. Most are wonderfully old-fashioned.

One in particular captures the attention: a large acrylic by Robert Lowe showing middle-aged people emerging from a classical doorway. A sharp light punctures their features and seems to bake the wall behind them; they stagger under its impact and threaten to fall out of the picture towards you. The faces are unmistakable: fathers and mothers, whose mediocre sorrow is also our mediocre guilt.

The painting is intensely disturbing: its very figurative intentions – carried out with the most meticulous technical perfection – seem to distance us from its subject. These parents are helpless and alien; and the most troubling thing is that the painting which creates them also threatens to pitch them into our arms.

Lowe's painting is a metaphor of lost bearings. It also vividly illustrates the difficulties which now beset the figurative painter. In 'the age of mechanical reproduction', we are told, the image does not bring us closer to its subject, but rather distances us still further from it. We are also told that Cubism destroyed the conventions of figurative art and initiated an irreversible movement towards the abstract ideal. No wonder, then, that you bourgeois are so unsettled by painters like Robert Lowe.

Actually none of that is true. In retrospect (at the Tate) the Cubist works have the quaint character of period pieces. They are lyrical, poignant, good-humoured. Objects seen through the distorting lens of Cubism remain warm and cheerful, happy to dress up in their angular disguises. There is no denial of the figurative here, but merely an abstraction from it. The enterprise is very like that of Turner, whose abstracts are really the peeled-off surfaces of figurative designs. The beauty of the result is a beauty of implication, whereby the profoundest thoughts are uttered in the lightest idiom.

What is popularly called abstract art is no such thing – and it is certainly nothing like Cubism. Instead of abstracting from the given image, the modernist *constructs* an image *de novo*, out of the abstract matter of shape and colour. Such art – which elevates garbled ideas over intelligent vision – is an art of skeletons, a fleshless remainder that can never be better than inoffensive.

The growth of the abstract industry in fact initiated a disastrous process of diseducation. It became possible to believe that an artist need have no figurative skills whatsoever. Schools began to abandon life drawing, anatomy, art history; in short to destroy discipline in favour of a fantasy of free expression. A new generation of students emerged, exemplary in their pristine incompetence and with eyes as untrained to see the world as their hands were unskilled to depict it. It is not surprising that this new generation, in a desperate attempt to recover its bearings, flies to photography (art's natural enemy – see the photo-realists at Fischer Fine Art) or else announces its incompetence as a new kind of skill – as in the 'New Image Painting' *(aliter 'Bad Painting')* visible at the Marlborough.

Once permitted, educational incompetence becomes sovereign. Natural bourgeois man cannot use his only weapon, the vote, in order to destroy it. A nice illustration is provided by the epicentre of sculptural modernism, St Martin's School of Art. There the brave director of sculpture, Tim Scott, has tried to introduce courses in anatomy; he has required his students to understand materials, to represent the human form, to discipline their eyes and hands. As a result, the Council for National Academic Awards has decided that this course is too illiberal, too authoritarian, to be taught. *O tempora, o mores*!

14 June 1983

The Hereditary Principle

In discussions of political principle – where there are many questions and few answers, and where no answers are universally satisfying – the major issue is always one of onus. Who bears the burden of proof? Whoever does so will labour under a singular disadvantage and can seldom unsettle his opponent.

The question of onus, however, is as disputable as every other. In recent years socialism has begged this question in its own flavour, high-handedly assuming that inequality and privilege must be justified and that, unless they are justified, socialism has right and reason on its side. The correct answer to socialism is: prove it. Prove that there is something wrong with inequality and privilege. And, more importantly, prove that you have something better to put in their place.

It is irrational to discard an existing social order until one is fairly certain of a better one. For this reason, the question of onus ought generally to be decided in the conservative's favour. He defends not what might be, but what is, and the proof of his politics lies here and now, in the concrete details of political existence. It is not complacent to rest one's faith in the actual, since the actual constantly jolts one into a sense of its imperfection. Far more complacent, indeed, to rest satisfied with the ill-sketched utopias of the left, which could be rationally pursued only if we were persuaded that they conceal no evils greater than the goods which make them so attractive.

When the conservative wishes to restore something, however – be it hereditary peerages or capital punishment – he cannot be quite so secure in his conviction that reason is on his side. A search for principle must be undertaken. The practice of granting hereditary peerages has never been abolished, but merely neglected. To resume it is at least to rouse curiosity, and probably to rouse indignation as well. The tired old arguments will be rehearsed, concerning the 'irrationality' of hereditary entitlement and the likelihood that political power and social privilege will pass unhindered into the hands of a psychopath or a mental defective. Personally, it has always seemed to me far more likely that psychopaths and mental defectives should gain power by democratic election. But to argue at this level is not to argue seriously.

If a citizen were rewarded for services to his country with a gift of property, he would naturally feel aggrieved if told that he could not pass it to his children and that he must either spend it in his lifetime or return it to his sovereign. What kind of a feudal liberty is this, he would complain, that pretends to reward me with a gift that I cannot freely bestow? When peerages first became hereditary, it was partly because barons had come to regard them as property and to resent the feudal habit of dictating their inheritance, regardless of the claims of family and kin. Conversely, the hostility to hereditary peerages has coincided with hostility to hereditary property. There has been a general shift in moral perception which requires all a man's goods and all a man's evils to be the upshot of his own activity and to be enjoyed within the space of his lifetime alone.

Those who object to inherited property often argue that a society in which some have this advantage is 'unfair', and that 'unfairness' is an evil. Their arguments, I believe, are spurious. Moreover, the consequences of accepting them would be singularly unattractive. Having no capacity to establish a durable household, every wage earner would turn his attention to immediate consumption and neglect to provide for the future. The resulting society of profligates would present a moral spectacle of the utmost bleakness, devoid alike of prudence and filial trust. The dangerous absorption of our energies in this 'getting and spending' can be halted only if there is saving which traverses generations and which binds the future to the past without thought for any particular person's profit.

Such genuine saving is possible only if there are ambitions which reach across generations – ambitions not for oneself, but for one's children and one's children's children. In short there must be objects of pursuit which are also hereditary entitlements. Wealth can be one of these – but why not honour? After all, this too can be subject to profligate waste; this too can be made cheap and purposeless by someone who sees it as no more durable than himself.

Hereditary honour has indeed been one of the ways in which societies have encouraged saving. By acquiring such honour, a man acquires the motive to lay up store for the future and to pass on to his successors an honourable estate. Hence it was socially beneficial that hereditary honour and hereditary wealth should be united.

In societies where wealth is privately owned – and where it will therefore accumulate in the hands of those most skilled and most interested in acquiring it – the hereditary principle has acted as a major safeguard of the national wealth: a guarantee that present resources remain unsquandered. Where the major wealth of a society is vested in the state, and is therefore at the disposition of bureaucrats with no permanent interest in its preservation, the nation is at the mercy of profligates. Thus arise the debt-ridden economies of the socialist world – economies which barely survive from day to day and which would collapse overnight were it not for the loans extended by deluded capitalists.

To reject hereditary honours is therefore to reject one of the principal motives for economic stability. It is to take a step in the direction of the spendthrift society, in which wealth is created for instant use and in which the purpose of durable things cannot easily be perceived.

21 June 1983

In Praise of Bourgeois Music

From the moment that Elgar fitted out his Edwardian hymn tunes with the harmonies of Wagner and the rhythms of Brahms, it was clear that modern English music was to be music for the people. There followed the greatest period of our musical culture, in which giants like Elgar, Tippett and Britten existed alongside countless secondary talents. All have been greeted with enthusiasm, by a people for whom concert-going is a necessary social occasion and for whom a repertoire of old music is incomplete without a constant addition of new.

It is partly because he has been so conscious of this support that the modern English composer has written intelligible music. His work is the result of an unspoken bargain with the private man. The very same individual who sings in the village choir or plays tuba in the colliery band, who writes to his local paper on hearing the first cuckoo or to his MP on hearing his neighbour – this familiar, eccentric, Thermos-carrying creature, with his violent antipathy to officialdom and his paradoxical love of royalty – has been the spiritual guide of the modern English composer. For it is from such exemplary material that music festivals are made.

True musical culture is an amateur activity. It is made, sustained, enjoyed and criticised by amateurs, all of whom have their private tastes and accomplishments, which they willingly pool in a common pursuit of excellence. Benjamin Britten at Aldeburgh and Peter Maxwell Davies in Orkney – such figures are magnets to which amateurs are drawn, fructifying the composer with the matey affability of his tribe. We should not be surprised if the resulting art so little resembles the solitary practices of a recluse like Messiaen or a snob like Boulez. There is a real contrast between the musical laboratory at the Centre Pompidou, where the arcane tinkerings of the initiated ring out in holy stillness, and the cheerful bustle of Aldeburgh, where natural bourgeois man rubs shoulders with his fellows, mixing in his conversation Bach and rood screens, Stravinsky and elderberry jam.

Nor should the political significance of the example escape us. Here is a paradigm of free association, from which an institution has grown. The Aldeburgh Festival sprang from the energy and wealth of a successful composer, and from the free co-operation of those who admired him. Such an institution could be neither generated nor conserved by the socialist state, which would destroy both the wealth which created it and the freedom through which it endures.

Natural bourgeois man is surrounded by enemies, in music as well as in the other arts. The history of modern music displays, however, just how far he is willing to compromise, to stretch to the limits the understanding with which nature endowed him, in order to honour his obligations towards the composer. Anti-bourgeois snobbery therefore tries to push music beyond the limits of comprehension: the art of sound becomes an act of defiance towards the ordinary musical ear. The anti-bourgeois may be a genius, or a charlatan, or a bit of both. But in either guise his strength is dedicated to a deviant idea of music, in which intelligent hearing is abolished by sophistical thought.

If we wish to support music, we must first support the musical amateur, since he is the social condition from which musical culture derives. Hence we must support the principle of musical intelligibility. Many young English composers understand this, and have therefore tried to emancipate the new music from the demands of a spurious originality.

A recent concert at the Barbican (that indestructible monument to the folly of modern architecture) celebrated the fortieth anniversary of the Society for the Promotion of New Music. It was fitting that this most English of institutions should uphold the bargain between the modern composer and the private man. The piece which dominated the programme – a new chamber work by Robin Holloway – was not only genial and melodic: it began and ended unequivocally in D, with so many intervening periods of tonal harmony as to set up a familiar resonance in the ears of bourgeois man. It was a pleasure to see the looks of intense concentration and solemn knowingness that had greeted the preceding cacophony suddenly giving way to simple-hearted smiles.

The looks returned, however, when the heroic London Sinfonietta, under Oliver Knussen, began to puff and writhe through a morass of

Ferneyhough – the composer selected by anti-bourgeois critics as sufficiently abrasive to merit unqualified praise. The score, patterned with subsidiary cross-rhythms and mounted on the most unnatural and acerbic harmonic progressions, is an object lesson in obscurity. It was truly painful to observe the immense wasted effort of a band which, had it been improvising, might at least have consoled itself with a common rhythm. Such is the folly of modernism that, in order to denigrate the ears of bourgeois man, it must injure the ears and exhaust the energies of our most brilliant musicians, and hence, by destroying performance, destroy itself.

28 June 1983

Standards in Schools

A country's educational system is one of its most important assets, the outcome, in our case, of centuries of institution building. Without flourishing schools and universities no society can transmit the knowledge upon which its existence depends. After national defence, therefore, the first priority of government must be to maintain what is valuable in education and to withdraw support from everything that tends to its destruction.

No government can be trusted to perform this task unguided. Government is the forum where powerful interests compete, and powerful interests may neither understand educational attainment nor esteem it. Only a society rich in autonomous schools and colleges can provide the necessary standard against which the officially sanctioned 'education' may be judged. This, I believe, is the most important reason for defending private education. Without it we must take the minister's word for it that this or that state-controlled institution is a place of education. And in such matters, what is the value of a minister's word? Those who wish to defend standards in education, therefore, ought to give their support to private schools.

It is somewhat surprising that the present government has not proposed to help these schools in the most direct way available – by allowing fees to be charged against income tax. The measure is reasonable; it is also just. For the parent who pays fees to a private school makes a double contribution to the state educational system. Not only does he support the standards on which the system depends; he also pays, through the rates, for its upkeep. Should not the state be prepared to reward his public utility? Some may say that he can afford this double expenditure, because he is rich. But that is neither relevant nor generally true.

Whatever help the government may offer to the private schools, however, it has a far greater duty to the schools that are in its care. It is a received idea that the state must provide education for the children of those who lack the means or (what is, to be honest, more usual) the desire to pay for it.

Since the early nineteenth century governments have tried to respond to this conception of their duty. By a slow process of imitation and adjustment, the grammar schools triumphantly vindicated the effort and began to compete with private schools for the scarce resources of Oxford and Cambridge. Those of us who benefited owe an enormous debt of gratitude to those institutions, which successfully offered education to the people, while ensuring that it was education, and not some specious substitute, that the people received.

Small wonder that we should have greeted the 'experiment' in comprehensive education with dismay. Our detractors have an explanation for our dismay: we had to work for our advantages, they say, and therefore strive to keep them to ourselves. But that is a misrepresentation. In fact, we feared that our advantages would never again be made available, except for cash.

Time has justified that fear. There are of course many good comprehensive schools, and many good teachers discharging as best they can the obligations of their profession in circumstances unpropitious for the transmission of learning. And it would be shortsighted to blame their difficulties on the comprehensive system alone – as though there had been no general loss of culture, no general withering away of the long-term view of things sufficient to undermine the desire for knowledge.

But we must also face the facts. And the facts – presented to us by John Marks, Baroness Cox and Maciej Pomian-Srzednicki in a report published last Thursday* – are far from reassuring. Not only is a clever child likely to do better in examinations at a grammar school than at a comprehensive, but *any* child, even one who is destined for the secondary modern, has a better chance of doing well in the old system of selective education than he has in a comprehensive. The authors show that selective systems obtain about a third more O-levels nationally per pupil, and about 50 per cent more in areas for which the mixture of social class matches the national average. They also show that the average pupil in secondary modern school comes close to the average pupil in a comprehensive, and may often excel him in some subjects, including the basic subject of English. Given the obvious fact that secondary modern schools contain only the less able children from a given area, the conclusion must be not only that a bright pupil will have a better chance in a grammar school, but also that a less bright pupil will have a better chance in a secondary modern.

The result could have been predicted, by anyone who did not have an ideological need to disbelieve it. The authors of the study recognise that examinations are not everything and that their results are open to a variety of interpretations. At the same time, national examinations are one of the few independent tests of scholarly performance. They provide a criterion whereby parents may have advance knowledge of the academic character of the school to which their child may go. The authors argue that parents ought to be allowed to choose their child's school, on the basis of its academic record. For if schools are to retain standards, they must have some interest in doing so. If that interest does not take the form of fees, it must take the more elusive – but more dignified – form of popularity.

5 July 1983

**Standards in English Schools,* National Council for Educational Standards, 3 Arnellan House, Slough Lane, Kingsbury, London NW9.

In Defence of Bourgeois Man

It is with some reluctance that I return to the defence of natural bourgeois man, but letters appearing in *The Times* require me to explain myself. To place the destiny of art and politics in the hands of such a creature, to make him sovereign in government and arbiter in taste – what is this but philistinism? Culture exists not to console the bourgeois with his own image but to enlighten him with the sight of what is godlike and strange.

Once he is released from the bondage of self-consciousness, once the downward-turning eye of the cultural modernist ceases to transfix him, our bourgeois will swell with complacent self-approval, fill the world with inanities and finally stop up the well-springs of art. So, at least, we are told.

The wiser artists of the *fin-de-siècle* saw through that nonsense. They recognised the important truth which the Marxists had tried to conceal: this 'bourgeois' is none other than the city dweller, the agent of commerce and social interaction, the maker of laws and the architect of culture. Civilisation is but another name for the *bürgerliche Gesellschaft* of Hegel – the organism which was born in the city states of the ancient world and which has survived, despite the vigilant animosity of the snob and the underdog, into our own distempered times.

Almost all that we know of law, institutions and religion, of art and morality, owes its existence to 'civil society', and the fine-eyed disdain of the modernist aesthete is itself no more than one among its abundant offshoots. With the evaporation of the mythologised 'class struggle' we can see that the town and its people have a unity and a universality that no temporary antagonism has been able to destroy. It is this unity and this universality that we mean, or ought to mean, by 'culture'.

Culture is a system of communication. There is no private culture, any more than there is a private language. Every work of art, however personal in its inspiration and however novel in its form, is an act of communication, which deserves its status only to the extent that it finds or creates an audience. There can be successful experiment in art because the response to art is flexible.

It has been a singular virtue of our 'bourgeois' society that, in every age, it has found the means to sustain and enjoy social and aesthetic experiment. Even when spat upon by the modernist and the revolutionary, our good citizen has done his best to receive whatever message has been aimed at him and to respond with the good humour that his need for tolerant community requires.

It is interesting that the greatest work of modernist literature – James Joyce's *Ulysses* – celebrates, in the character of Leopold Bloom, the affable decencies of natural bourgeois man. Bloom's bubbling consciousness is an irrepressible stream of city culture, in which religion, art, science and morality flow together in the channels marked out by a meandering amateurism. Bloom is the inheritor of a common consciousness, seeking always for the little outlets and opportunities through which to pass it on. Hence the tragi-comedy of his encounter with the snobbish modernist, Stephen, when artist and audience pass each other like ships in the night.

Each is the poorer for this failure, but as Joyce makes clear, neither is to blame.

What, then, must the modern artist do? Surely he cannot compromise in the one major demand of his existence – the demand for authenticity, for the new bottles in which the old wine of human experience is to be served? And if bourgeois man has lost his tolerance towards innovations, is it not time to join with the minor modernists in repudiating him?

But there is a crucial distinction to be made between innovation and originality. The second, unlike the first, can never break with what preceded it: to be original, an artist must also belong to the tradition from which he departs. To put it another way: he must violate the expectations of his audience, but he must also, in countless ways, uphold and endorse them.

Let me remind the reader of the great drama which Wagner pitched in the idealised 'civil society' of his imagination. The C major melody of the Mastersingers, which represents the achievements of bourgeois culture, is the embodiment of rules and forms, of strictures and principles – of a thousand obstacles to the free flowering of the artistic spirit. It is also the record of a former popularity, and of the collective participation in an intelligible tradition of song. But the tradition must be renewed: no longer is it in touch with the spirit which Sachs – poet, labourer and citizen – divines in Act 2, as the scent of elderflower wafts over him. The little questioning phrase accompanying his meditation foreshadows the new melody, the prize song of Walther, which finally sweeps away the clouds of melancholy and wins the hand of Eva.

The melody succeeds not because the rules have been changed or their guardians persuaded, but because it has found an audience. It has stirred the people of Nuremberg, those good amateurs, into a spontaneous recognition that this song – unlike the clumsy academicism of Beckmesser – is no mere novelty, but an original expression of the live tradition to which they belong. There then recurs that wonderful moment, heard already in the overture, when the prize song and the theme of the Mastersingers are played together and, lo and behold, they harmonise.

Walther is wedded to his originality and seeks to reject the laurel of the masters. But Sachs, in prophetic words, reminds him of what had made his achievement possible – of the true German culture, the culture of the town, which by providing his audience, had also secured his prize. I remembered this moment – for which Wagner has so often been criticised as a proto-fascist – when I read Alfred Brendel's letter (30 June) comparing me to Dr Goebbels. I realised then that you do not have to be a genius in order to be misunderstood.

12 July 1983

On Representative Democracy

The House of Commons has now silenced the demand for hanging, until the next horrible crime revives it. Parliament has thus provided, at the outset of Mrs Thatcher's second term of office, an opportunity to reflect on the meaning of representative democracy.

In decisions like this, when a Member's vote runs contrary to the wishes of his constituents, the good parliamentarian will invoke Burke's famous distinction between the representative and the delegate. The delegate is a slave, bound by the opinions of those who appointed him. The representative is a free man, bound only by his conscience. Since he was elected for his conscience, then it is his conscience that he must obey. Hence there is no absurdity in a representative parliament which defies the wishes of the electorate.

That is all very well, so far as it goes. But it does not go very far. We all know that representatives obey the party whips first and their consciences only when the whips command them to do so: in other words, only when the government is largely indifferent to the outcome. Last Wednesday's vote is a very good indication of what then ensues. Whatever government is in office, and whatever the feeling of the nation as a whole, the decision will be dictated by those who control the channels of communication. The Leninists have always said so; if they are wrong, it is in their belief that under 'bourgeois democracy' the channels of communication are controlled by the 'forces of reaction'. On the contrary, they are controlled by the semi-educated, the self-consciously enlightened, the would-be teachers and reformers – in short by that congeries of decent left-liberal sentiment which is the main observable mark of a university education.

Certainly Fleet Street has managed to retain a seasoned core of robust prejudice and is still able on occasion to give credence to left-wing outbursts against the 'capitalist press'. But Fleet Street is a dying institution, no more fitted to our times than a monastery or a gentlemen's club. Television, by contrast, is vigorously controlled by the radical middle classes, dedicated to endowing every left-wing play group, from Greenham Common to the GLC, with the honours and dignities of an heroic struggle.

Furthermore, it is a mistake to assume that the media are politically important. Their very nature as a majority interest makes them ineffective in a battle of ideas. Of course, it is useful to control them. But it is far more useful to control the universities and the professional societies – for these channels, while narrow, are more firmly connected to the instruments of power. Ideas which gain currency among professors, lawyers, doctors and literati soon gain currency in parliament. For the main purpose of parliament is to represent the professions. Without the co-operation of the professions, constitutional government could not be carried on. The rule of law can be sustained only with the co-operation of lawyers; the executive can act only by grace of administrators; the opposition will remain loyal only so long as it represents the same education, and the same *Weltanschauung*, that moulded the character of those in power.

Hence whenever, by some accident of fortune, a member should come forward who is prepared to defend the sentiments of the people against the enlightened scepticism of the professional classes, he is at once denounced as a 'populist'. It is not very clear what this term means, except that the populist is in some obscure way the enemy of democracy. Such a person threatens the structure of parliament. He promises to bring the workings of government to a standstill by making it too directly answerable to the wishes of the governed. It is certain that he will meet with the concerted opposition of the professionals, and almost equally certain that he will be overcome.

The value of representation is two-fold: that it enables politicians to be jettisoned from office by those who are not politicians, and that it provides a legitimate and vociferous opposition. It thereby embeds in the heart of government an internal limitation to its power. It is by virtue of this fact that fundamental freedoms are preserved and the rule of law kept at a safe distance from executive command. Those virtues have no special connexion with democracy; but, in the conditions of modern government, democratic election is one of the best ways to secure them.

But now a note of warning. No government, however enlightened, can continue to guarantee the freedom of the governed if it does not also have their loyalty. Without that loyalty it must depend on the police for its power. Certain popular sentiments are so fundamental to the experience of society that a governing class which refuses to be influenced by them loses the goodwill of those upon whom it calls for its entitlement. Those sentiments are rare but hardy; they arise not from opinion or ratiocination, but from the immediate moral understanding which resides in life itself.

When such sentiments come before parliament, the whips at once renounce their claim to dictate to the nation. They rule that conscience must rule; and by 'conscience' they mean the enlightened scepticism of those whose experience has been sufficiently comfortable to permit the luxury of hesitation. The result is the moral nonsense of last Wednesday's vote, and the inevitable weakening of popular allegiance.

19 July 1983

Waging War on the Individual

On 14 July a Turkish diplomat, Dursun Aksoy, was gunned down in Brussels. On the next day a bomb went off in the Turkish Airlines kiosk at Orly, killing seven people and injuring many more. In both cases, according to the newspapers, Armenian groups 'claimed responsibility' for the outrage.

As a matter of fact they did no such thing. The Armenians in question wished categorically to assert that they were in no way to be blamed for these deaths, that what had the appearance of cold-blooded murder was in fact justified retribution, that the crowds at Orly, like Mr Aksoy, were not the innocent victims of atrocity but 'legitimate targets' in a war of just revenge.

This revanchist excuse for bloodshed expresses a peculiar and horrible corruption. But like many forms of moral corruption, it has its origins in sentiments that are inescapable and pure. Those who feel proud of their country may feel rightly proud; and yet they assert, through their feeling, a certain responsibility, which links them equally to their ancestors and to their descendants. Those who accuse a nation of injustice, or praise it for its virtue, likewise acknowledge an idea of collective liability, without which, indeed, it would be impossible to understand either the present world of politics or the past history of mankind.

It is a small step from these innocent-seeming ideas of collective identity to the sinful thoughts which animate the Armenian revanchist. For him, the collective responsibility of the Turkish people is born individually by every living Turk. The individual is blamed for actions in which no living individual had a hand, and becomes the butt of an anger which no single person could either soften or deserve. When broad feelings towards a collective become so narrowly focused, their violence is annihilating. The victim is stripped bare of every right, for he is a mere symbol of collective guilt. He becomes an abstraction, who has already ceased to exist in the eyes of his pursuer and who therefore calls in vain for mercy.

Revanchism is one of many depraved habits of thought which have proved useful in justifying murder. All such habits share the feature to which I have alluded: they turn the individual into an abstraction, so that he may bear responsibility for collective faults. He ceases to be a human being and becomes instead a type, like the racial degenerate of Hitler or the 'class enemy' of Lenin, Stalin and Pol Pot.

Terrorists often claim to be fighting wars, and to be doing no more than is necessary in war. This is nonsense. War is certainly the natural expression of collective resentment; but it occurs between organised groups and is fought openly, against a collective enemy. It is possible to fight a war with undiminished respect for the rights of the enemy individual. Indeed, that is the duty of every soldier. But the terrorist must disregard this duty and disobey the law of war. His feelings towards the individual are abolished by his loathing of the group, and it is this – rather than his cowardice, cruelty or intemperate hate – that constitutes his true moral corruption.

There can be collective responsibility only where there is collective agency – that is, only where a group exists which can be praised or blamed for its collusive actions. The worst crimes in history have been committed against groups which, because they could not act collectively, could not reasonably be resented. Hence the obnoxiousness of racism. 'Races' are not agents, and cannot bear collective responsibility for the faults or actions of their members. People act collectively only through institutions, and whatever a 'race' may be, it is not an institution, since no one may join or leave it.

The primary institution in international politics is the state, and it is the state – rather than 'the people', 'the race' or 'the nation' – which bears the burden of collective blame. This last fact is evident to students of international law and would be equally evident to everyone, were it not for the fact that the state is too cold, too legal and too inhuman a thing to attract the full fury of human resentments. How much more satisfying to punish a people, or a race, than to punish a legal fiction!

The Armenian revanchists claim that, during the strife which preceded the final dissolution of the Ottoman Empire, large numbers of Armenians living in central and eastern Turkey were massacred by Ottoman Turks. The facts are disputed, and some of the Armenian claims may be exaggerated. But suppose they are right. Who is to blame?

The answer, I believe, is: 'No one living'. And that answer is the only one that can be rationally supported. The modern Turkish state, which deliberately turned its back on the old Ottoman Empire, no more existed at the time of these events than the individuals who are now gunned down in pointless retribution. And yet the Turkish state is the only collective agency which could possibly bear the guilt.

Of course such thoughts can do nothing to soften the sentiments of the revanchist, which are too necessary to his identity, and too enjoyable in themselves, to be modified by reasoned argument. But they should perhaps lead us to ask ourselves who is really behind his action? Who really stands to gain from crimes which jeopardise the lives and property of the Armenian Turks and which paralyse the efforts of Turkey to retain effective diplomatic relations with its allies? Certainly not the Armenians who have settled abroad, into lives which are far more comfortable than anything that they might presently enjoy in Turkey.

26 July 1983

On White Burgundy

Of all the conflicts that have shaken the civilised world, that between claret and burgundy has probably been the most beneficial. It is at once easily resolved and endlessly renewable. It begins in pleasure and ceases in sleep, passing meanwhile through a glorious interlude of belligerent intoxication. Language, literature, history – all are brought to bear on this vital disputation, which has absorbed the after-dinner energies of countless politicians and businessmen, so stilling for a few precious hours the dangerous projects of production and reform.

Men need conflict. The essential requirement of civilisation is to provide matter for conflicts which, while instructive and agreeable to those who are engaged in them, can do no conceivable damage to those who are not. The present conflict is one of the most educationally valuable that I know. What could better engage the learning of the classicist than the rival claims of Château Ausone and Mercurey, the one named from the estate of a Roman poet, the other from the temple of a Roman god? What could stir the English speaker's sense of history more effectively than Château Talbot, named from the great Earl of Shrewsbury; Haut-Brion, which might really be O'Brien; or the sheer enigma of names like Boyd-Cantenac and Lynch-Bages? What could more poignantly remind us of the voice of poetry, than the great names of Burgundy – Vougeot, Chambertin, Meursault, Chambolle-Musigny les Amoureuses (a wine that generally lives up to the promise of its name)?

Beneficial though this conflict has been in the annals of our history, however, it is also to be regretted. For it is only the red wines of Bordeaux and Burgundy that can be fruitfully compared. The white wines are eclipsed by enthusiasms which largely disregard them. As a result one of the highest achievements of western culture has been shrouded in ignorance. I am referring to white burgundy, without whose assistance it would be impossible for a philosopher to compress his thoughts into the measure laid down by the editor of *The Times*.

Naturally, anyone who encounters Le Montrachet will know that he is in the presence of the greatest white wine that mere mortals could make – at least he will know this if he is fortunate enough to taste vintages like that of 1969. Most amateurs would also admit that there are white wines made in the Côte d'Or – Corton-Charlemagne, Bâtard-Montrachet, Meursault–Perrières – which, while not strictly comparable to Le Montrachet, deserve to be drunk with the same bellicose gratitude for the human condition as inspires and refreshes the conflict between claret and burgundy. Two important facts, however, are not generally understood.

The first is that white burgundies are incomparably better value than reds. The rich white wines of Auxey-Duresses and Santenay, or the minor domaines of Meursault, can sometimes be obtained for as little as £6 a bottle. Should you be seeking for red wine, then at that price you must certainly choose claret. The second and more important fact – more important, that is, for those concerned not merely with the survival but with the spread of civilisation – is that truly great white burgundies exist which almost anyone can afford. These wines are grown not in the Côte d'Or, but to the north of it in Chablis and to the south of it in the Côte Chalonnais.

The essential characteristics of good white burgundy are three: a flavour as full and rich as is compatible with disciplined dryness; a bouquet that is neither sharp nor flowery, but rounded and heady, with a lingering suggestion of mouldy vegetation; and a dry, nutty after-taste, which returns after many hours, enriched with associations like the memory of a passionate kiss. These three qualities are rarely combined in a single experience, and it is arguable that only the Chardonnay grape can really unite them. It is the use of this grape, rather than the strict criteria of geography, that leads me to describe Chablis as a white burgundy.

The lesser wines of Chablis are of course well known for their crisp invigorating attack. But is is not widely appreciated that, in remarkable years like 1978, the wines of Chablis fill out, acquiring the three dimensions of taste which I have mentioned and becoming equal at their best to the very greatest products of the Côte d'Or. Already those designated *premier cru* manage to combine the pebbly foretaste of Chablis with some of the lingering after-taste of the more southern vintages. But for a little extra money (the sum may be no more than £7 a bottle) the *grands crus* – with dour peasant names like Bougrots – can be obtained. Such wines equal the best products of the Côte d'Or, and in a good year may even surpass them. Unfortunately the widespread ignorance of their merit, which causes them to be so usefully underpriced, makes their manufacture far less profitable than justice requires. Hence the future of these great wines is increasingly precarious. I therefore urge the readers of *The Times* to lend full-throated support to this vital component of our culture.

While the English drinking public has begun to appreciate the white wines of the Mâconnais, and to realise that St Véran and Mâcon-Lugny are sometimes the equals of Pouilly-Fuissé, it has yet to discover the treasurers that lie to the north of that region, in the Côte Chalonnais. True, Montagny is now a familiar name. But how often does one encounter a white Rully, a white Buxy or a white Mercurey, whose Clos du Petit Clou can can easily be mistaken for a minor Meursault? The greatest of these wines sell for less than cheap Champagne and provide, by contrast, a grandeur and fullness of experience which may redeem even the vile dog days of a London summer.

9 August 1983

An Invitation to the Dance

Holidays, like birthdays, weddings and temporary farewells, are points of transition and renewal. Hence they are occasions for dancing. Every summer people gather in Mediterranean resorts and, to the sound of violin, guitar, bouzouki or electric organ, begin to shuffle off their coils. Timorous at first, they steadily gain inspiration, and step out with unpractised movements and a kind of stumbling courtesy. By a miracle of pre-established harmony they begin to move to a common pulse, and gradually their faces suffuse with smiles.

So it is, at least, in the south, where the habit of social dancing – dancing which needs no lustful motive, which extends equally to the very old and the very young, which permits man to dance with man, woman with woman and child with child – has not yet disappeared.

In the north, however, dancing has virtually ceased to exist as a social occasion. What passes for dancing is in fact a lonely parody of the sexual act, a formless vibrating of the body accompanied by vacant expressions and wild movements of the hands and arms. The participants do not touch but stand isolated in the solitude of their feelings, jerked by the music like puppets on a string. The dance relies for its excitement upon a constant heightening of the tension in this string, as lights flash and noises throb in a ghastly simulacrum of battle.

The distance between a bop and a minuet reflects the immense distance between cultures. In the first each dancer is free to stimulate himself in his preferred way, without reference to his nominal partner. Such a dance lends itself perfectly to the temper of a society that fears accomplishments and which believes that each person has an equal right to consideration, regardless of his social competence or personal charm.

The minuet, by contrast, is exclusive and disciplined. It is also social: each dancer must obey the formation and from time to time change partners so as to dance with someone whom he did not choose. He must confine his seductive gestures to those little nuances which are all the more pleasurable for their resemblance to the innocent smiles and touches of the dance. The excitement lies in the co-ordinated movement, in which a shared skill provides the foundation for a common pleasure. Hence the minuet is a truly liberating dance, containing a vast store of social opportunity, freed from the imperatives of sexual desire.

To bop with someone to whom you are not attracted is a desultory experience, since the meaning of the act has been removed. It is scarcely surprising that the practice of asking different partners to dance has disappeared, and dancing itself become confined to the sexually eligible. The revival of Scottish country dancing did little to arrest the decline, and when finally the Viennese waltzes and polkas had dashed the legitimate expectations of the ugly and the aged, it was firmly established that dancing is an affair for the young couple alone. The history of modern dancing is the result of two forces which a society of isolated couples cannot resist: the fear of competence, which necessitates the discovery of dances which have no recognisable steps, and the fear of social affection, which requires that bodies set in motion by music should not be touched but merely displayed.

Perhaps, you may say. But why go on filling space that might have been devoted to the burning questions of politics? The answer is simple: if you do not understand dancing, then you will never understand politics. Dancing is the paradigm of political fulfilment. People who step together in a dance are at one with themselves and their fellows. Their action is also response, and they move in a collective movement, with no purpose beyond the present pleasure. The uselessness of dancing is precisely why we value it. The person who joins the dance extinguishes purpose and is content, for the moment, to be. The meaning of the dance is the dance itself.

Dancing therefore reminds us of the fundamental truth of our condition. The purpose of life is life itself. This is the truth that Keats perceived in the figures of the Grecian urn, and which he summarised in such paradoxical words. It was also perceived by those who devised the old social dances. They saw that the revelation of the sublime purposelessness of human existence must be carefully prepared, that it must be given a full and generous social context, freed from the tyranny of sexual excitement and decked out in the costumes of peace. The dance then becomes a symbol of all that matters in our political condition.

True politics maintains a social order in its own self-made equilibrium; it eschews those 'final solutions' and 'irreversible shifts' with which fascists and socialists threaten all that is merely actual; it renounces the desire to establish the kingdom of heaven and interferes in the rhythm of ordinary life only so as to teach the steps of the dance.

These steps must be complex and varied, so as to break down the aggressive isolation of the sexual bond and to generate a public life that is something more than a congeries of private intimacies. The highest forms of politics exhibit the order and beauty of the minuet; the lowest forms resemble the disorderly solipsism of the jive. But even in its lowest form politics is to be preferred to that other thing which is not politics but war – the reckless pursuit of purpose by those in the grip of an idea.

16 August 1983

Impossible Partners

The purpose of dancing is the dance. The purpose of chatter is the chat. Human life presents countless such social occasions, in which we renounce our business and find pleasure in the present moment alone. All time not spent in dancing or in conversation is wasted time. For these moments contain not the means of human existence but the end. The dancer and the talker are at rest – but actively at rest, rejoicing in their social condition and at one with their fellow men.

The most valuable relations are also those, like friendship, which have no further purpose. The opposite of friendship is not hatred, but crime. The criminal is the man whose purposes take precedence over every opposing claim. He is the man prepared, through force, fraud or annihilation, to discount the freedom of the other who stands in his way. He is the true enemy of peace, for he destroys the trust which makes conversation possible.

States are more like people than they are like anything else: they exist by purpose, reason, suffering and joy. And peace between states is also like peace between people. It involves the willing renunciation of purpose, in the mutual desire not to do, but to be.

Peace is endangered, therefore, not by the weapons of the peaceful, but by the actions of the purposeful. There exist states, just as there exist people, whose lives are structured by a purpose and who cannot accept another's freedom as an obstacle to its fulfilment. The overriding aim is so urgent that neither the freedom nor the existence of another body politic can deflect it.

If the purpose is also international – involving transformations beyond the frontiers of municipal government – then peace has already been put at risk. We know this from Iran and Libya. But we ought also to have known it from the Soviet Union, a state founded upon a consuming international purpose, which has never ceased to impose its preferred political order upon unwilling recipients, whether in its own domains or in the domains of clients and neighbours.

Criminal law exists in order to deter the over-purposeful. But international law, which lacks the supreme coercive power of a sovereign authority, cannot exert any comparable influence. It is obeyed only because states agree to be bound by it. Of course all states appear to be bound by international law, since there is value in sustaining this appearance. But states with a ruling purpose cannot really be bound: they cannot be bound 'in their hearts'. For their hearts are ruled by something other than law, something which discounts law whenever it conflicts with the overriding idea.

States which accept international law do so because it is the universal shadow of a principle by which they already live. Thus Canada and the United States, each of which is governed by a rule of law, find no difficulty in co-existing, despite long-standing disagreements over territorial waters and disputed islands. No troops amass on their common border; no threats are made, or sanctions imposed. For a legal decision will suffice to regulate the conduct of the parties.

The mark of the purposeful *polis* is that it cannot be governed by law, that actual law is a pretence which vanishes just so soon as the ruling purpose is questioned or compromised. Such states are never truly at peace, since they are never at rest. To converse with them is dangerous; to cease to confront them yet more so.

Consider the Helsinki accords, established in order to reduce the tension in Europe. The 'agreement' was twofold: to reduce military preparedness and to extend human rights. Our naive politicians imagined that this agreement was genuine, and took comfort from the fact that it was given quasi-legal status by the Soviet state. What a joke! Of course it was convenient to pretend to the agreement and to dress it up in the bourgeois trappings of legality. Western eyes were closed for a while to the renewed build-up of armaments.

Moreover, a brilliant new method was acquired for identifying trouble-makers. The brief pretence of legality encouraged the bravest and best of the citizens to come forward, to associate, to attempt to secure obedience to this novel law which seem to grant essential freedoms. No more economical way could have been discovered of persuading the next inmates of the Gulag to give themselves up.

And for some unaccountable reason we are still discussing, still attempting even to 'renew' this 'agreement' that has so endangered us. Is it not time that we woke up, time that we realised that we should feel bound by agreements only towards those who are able to respect them?

23 August 1983

On Judicial Independence

Last week several air force officers, arraigned before the High Court of Zimbabwe on charges of sabotage, were acquitted, after a long trial in which the defence plausibly claimed that the accused had confessed under torture. The verdict, composed and justified according to the most scrupulous legal practice, was a model of judicial rectitude, and Mr Justice Dumbutshena deserves the highest praise for his courage and integrity in delivering it. Besides doing credit to himself, however, Mr Justice Dumbutshena does credit to his country: he shows – what otherwise might be doubted – that it is quite possible for Zimbabwe to govern itself by a rule of law.

Or is it? No sooner that the verdict been issued than the officers in question were rearrested, under a warrant issued by Dr Ushewokunze, the Minister of Home Affairs. This warrant permits the retention of the former accused for an indefinite period, without trial. In other words, the state has chosen to declare that it will not be governed by the decision of its judges and that it has its own ways of dealing with those who have aroused its displeasure. This blatant mockery of the judicial process is not the first instance of its kind in Zimbabwe. Nor will it be the last. In countless ways Robert Mugabe's government has expressed its impatience with constitutional niceties and its determination to have its own way, regardless of law.

Judicial independence is not a luxury. On the contrary, it is the cornerstone of constitutional government. It has now disappeared from most of central and southern Africa, and from the communist states: this fact alone should suffice to remind us of its political importance. Without judicial independence no citizen has the legal means to oppose the state should it choose to attack him. Nor can the state perceive opposition to its executive commands as other than treasonable. When the Polish government finally decided to crush Solidarity, it was after the union had called for an independent judiciary: the state then realised that is was being asked to take opposition seriously, by granting it the mantle of law.

When an independent judiciary exists, the state lends its sovereign power to upholding the decisions of the law courts, regardless of their content. The judge, through his verdict, is able to set the state against itself and so to limit its power. Without judicial independence the power of the state is limited not by the law, but by some other and less accessible factor – such as the power of a party, faction or pressure group. This second kind of limitation closes government to the ordinary man. He can no longer really protect himself against the powers that be. If he does not have the luck to belong to an influential faction, then his rights may be disregarded whenever they hamper the executive command. Indeed, in the absence of judicial independence there are no real civil rights, but only indeterminate privileges, available to those with the influence to obtain them.

Virtually all modern states have 'constitutions'. That is to say, they have pieces of paper which are so described and which purport to specify the procedures of government, the rights of the citizen, the powers of the executive and so on. These documents are all lodged in that haven of mendacity, the United Nations, where they bear witness to the extraordinary power of paper over the modern intelligence.

In fact, without an independent judiciary these pieces of paper are meaningless. What is the significance of a document stating my rights against the state, when there is no judge to whom I can appeal to enforce it, except one who is controlled or overruled by the executive power whenever it has an interest in the outcome? It is clear that a state with a written 'constitution' but without an independent judiciary – a state dedicated to the idea of 'people's justice' on the Soviet model – does not really have a constitution. Conversely, one like the United Kingdom, which lacks a written constitution but possesses an independent judiciary, is for that reason alone constitutional.

A developed legal system, with elaborate commmon law rights and supported by a system of natural justice, was the most precious legacy of our empire. If it were still permissible to defend colonisation, I should justify it in terms of this bequest and at the same time contrast the colonisation of Africa with the Soviet 'colonisation' of eastern Europe, which has advanced not by the generation but by the destruction of law.

Of course, judicial independence is difficult to achieve, since it requires that the power which appoints a judge must also be prepared to yield to him. Maybe we should not expect a new country like Zimbabwe to sustain such nuances. Perhaps only a long history of public spirit and civic virtue will enable the citizens of Zimbabwe to rediscover this precious inheritance. Meanwhile, however, we ought to allow ourselves to see in such as Mr Justice Dumbutshena just what the government of Zimbabwe stands to lose. In threatening to discard judicial independence, Zimbabwe threatens not only to discard what is most valuable in its colonial inheritance, but also to exclude the most virtuous of its citizens from power.

6 September 1983

Intolerance and Paedophilia

We should be thankful for paedophilia, because it vividly reminds us that sexual acts between consenting partners are sometimes wrong. Not just wrong, but also despicable. But how difficult it is to say it.

Few of us, in our hearts, doubt that the pursuit of children for sexual purposes is morally intolerable, and few of us would regret the introduction of the severest laws, not only to prevent it, but also – what is now more urgent – to stifle its attempts to gain a public audience. For if you go on long enough, if you raise every question and cast doubt on every unexamined answer, you can begin to justify anything. You can make any moral aberration seem like a persecuted 'alternative', provided only that you deal adroitly in the language of rights and freedoms and get yourself advertised in some official handbook for the disadvantaged.

It is uncertain how far the Paedophile Information Exchange has gone in its attempts to gain the sympathy of the tolerant. But if it is true, as the organisation apparently claims, that it can now be contacted through the Citizen's Advice Bureau, then it is surely time that the wishes of the intolerant – who in this matter constitute the overwhelming majority – were respected. The morality of tolerance is all very well in its place. But towards some acts you can become tolerant only by becoming insensible. No society can survive in a state of moral insensibility. It is therefore imperative that the rights of the intolerant, and their freedom to suppress what outrages them, be respected.

Paedophiles must be prevented from 'coming out'. Every attempt to display their vice as a legitimate 'alternative' to conventional morality must be not refuted, but silenced. For in this area it is sufficient to allow the question to be asked, 'Why not?', for the tolerant to rush in with their easy sympathy, and the battle for common decency is lost.

Why not, however? Why is it, in the end, that the sexual pursuit of children disgusts us? The answer, I believe, will awaken us to the most important, but also most neglected, moral truths. We are disgusted by paedophilia because we subscribe, in our hearts, to the value of innocence. We ardently believe – although we seldom declare it – that our lives as sexual beings are divided into two distinct periods. There is a line between the sexuality of the child and that of the adult which we cross never to return. Everything that happens before we cross that line is crucial to our subsequent development. So too is the existence of the line.

The memory of innocence exerts a powerful influence over our sexual conduct. It causes us to see the act of love not as something which happens to us – like hunger or thirst – but as something that we choose, with our full personality. This is the true meaning of modesty: that we withhold ourselves, except from that to which we give ourselves entirely. Only the modest person is capable of passion. For only by so damming up the sexual impulse do we ensure that, in surrendering to it, we also surrender ourselves. Modesty is therefore the virtue which frees us for commitment, and its highest form – virginity – is rightly prized as a component in the unpolluted readiness for love.

Children are boundlessly curious, and about nothing more than about sex. The force which most effectively limits their curiosity is shame, and all who have concern for their children's future know the importance of shame as the greatest single obstacle to premature experiment and the necessary prelude to adult love. We hate paedophilia since we hate whatever removes the sense of shame and, with it, the safeguards of childhood innocence.

But in that case we should also hate much else that is inflicted on our children in the name of enlightened good sense. Consider 'sex education', that insidious propaganda devoted to freeing the sexual act from its moral overtones, to liberating our children from guilt and to dressing up in surgical neutrality what can be neutrally regarded only by the childish and the insensible. To tolerate this outrage is also to connive at the loss of innocence, and so to lay aside responsibility for our children's future emotions.

13 September 1983

Life in the Country

Readers of *The Times* are now familiar with the summer sufferings of journalists. Your average hack is not a bad lot: hard-working on the whole, devoted to his family, moderate in his opinions and with a talent for friendship and conversation. If he has a fault, it is a relish for literature and a consequent preference for imagining what he prefers not to see.

His world is therefore full of disappointments, and none of them greater than the countryside. He knows as well as the next man that the way to renew his appetite for home is to take a couple of weeks in some man-made nightmare like the Costa Brava. But when the time comes, his imagination gets the better of him, he hires a cottage in a country spot, packs up his Thompson and his Kilvert, and sets off in search of rural tranquillity.

There follow days of insufferable agony. Tractors roar in his ears from morn to night; harvesters trundle past, pushing before them great tidal waves of clatter; the night air is rent by the lugubrious howls of dogs and the endless baaing of sheep lost in the ditches; the evening stillness is shattered by the sound of shotguns; and all Sunday morning the church bells beat against eardrums which – with the sole exception of the journalist's – have long since ceased to respond to any such disturbance.

Pollution, on a scale that defies the urban imagination, invades every pore. The air about his cottage is thick with diesel fumes and the vapours of sewerage; the smoke from the burning stubble creeps through the cracks of ill-fitting doors and window-frames, and black flecks of charcoal settle onto every exposed surface, blotting his hands, lungs, shirt and copybook.

After the fresh vegetables, fresh fish and wholemeal bread of London, what stomach can take comfort in the tray of tired old turnips in the village shop, the bags of impossibly strong onions, the sad brown cauliflowers? What nature-lover, pampered with the products of Greece and Italy, can easily tolerate the exorbitant price exacted by the local chemist for a phial of olive oil from which every memory of life has been refined away? What healthy carnivore can stomach the inexplicable piles of flesh in the butcher's window, looking less like the result of dissection than the aftermath of bombardment; or the pies and sausages wrapped in industrial Cellophane, and the white flakes of fish flesh buried deep in a crust of saffron-coloured breadcrumbs?

Nor can the weary city-dweller refresh his eyes and mind with sights of natural harmony. From the cottage he overlooks an appalling bungalow, with green tiles, metal-framed windows and a sky-blue swimming pool, built by the farmer in order to escape from the dingy Elizabethan manor in which he had spent such miserable years. The hilltops are blackened by regiments of sombre conifers and the valleys have lost their hedgerows, churned by a phalanx of tractors into a sea of mud, unalleviated by any contour except the occasional string of barbed wire.

In this God-forsaken place the journalist naturally begins to yearn for the clean air, the fresh invigorating food and the urban tranquillity of Notting Hill Gate. He remembers the quiet beauty of the London streets, the soothing classical facades, the unspoilable parks and gardens and the natural orderliness of civilised living. He rages against the farmers for their wanton spoliation of the gifts of nature. And then, in quieter mood, he looks round for a remedy.

What the countryside needs, he reflects, is planning – proper, efficient, comprehensive planning, such as we have at home. Our towns are protected (he imagines) by conservation laws, building regulations, planning inquiries, laws against dirt, pollution, ugliness and noise. We need to extend this same rigorous concern for the environment to the countryside, to be as alert to the imperatives of rural conservation as to those of town planning.

The argument is seductive, and never more so than when it flows from the eloquent pen of Simon Jenkins. But we must ask the crucial question. Who is to be in charge of this planning? We soon find the answer. Our journalist in fact wants the countryside to be planned by urban intellectuals, as an instrument for their leisure. He would like it to be the plot for a perfect literary guidebook.

Now imagine what would happen to our cities if we trusted their design to farmers. The farmer comes to the city in search of company, bustle and display. And what does he find? Only the endless solitude of city life, the impassable distances between places, the remoteness of every desirable thing, the slow-moving, time-wasting jostle of the crowds.

If he had his way he would change all that. The city would be a place of shopping precincts, served by wide roads, with people heaped in tower blocks above bright halls of entertainment full of one-armed bandits and obscene video displays. Such a London was in fact emerging in the 1950s and '60s. For at that time the typical English parliamentarian, planner or architect was either a bumpkin himself, or had fallen under the influence of some pernicious author, such as Lawrence or Le Corbusier, who told him to think like one. The result might have been ecological catastrophe, had not our decent feeling for the quiet life of the town not reasserted itself.

Our culture is of course deeply rooted in the love of the countryside: take this away, and precious little of English literature would remain. However, the true experience of the country is an experience not of leisure, but of labour, and it is the rhythm of country labour that inspired the idylls of Constable, Eliot and Hardy. To plan the country as a leisure ground is not to protect the experience which those artists convey to us, but to extinguish it. It is far better for urban man to remain at home, in the peaceful haunts of his own devising, than to roam abroad menacing the noisy innocence of the peasantry and telling them that they may go about their business only according to rules devised by someone who has no active part in it.

20 September 1983

The Pestilence of Pulpit Politics

The National Conference of Roman Catholic Priests, which met recently in Birmingham, was attended by 93 clergymen. Since there are more than 5000 Roman Catholic priests in England and Wales, it cannot be said with any certainty that the assembly was representative. Nevertheless it was vociferous, and the opinions of the vociferous count for much in this world, even if, as one may hope, they count for nothing in the next.

The increasing predominance of conferences in pastoral affairs is part of the process whereby the Roman Catholic Church has been transformed from a prescriptive authority, whose currency is faith, to a debating chamber, dealing in the inflationary coinage of opinion. It is inevitable that such a body should begin to turn away from what matters in religion, the eternal verities, towards what, *sub specie aeternitatis*, matters least of all – the affairs of this world, which can be the subject of opinion only because they lie outside the domain of faith.

The National Conference therefore followed in the footsteps of the National Pastoral Congress of 1980, and the Bishops' Conference of England and Wales, in devoting time and energy to secular causes. And Cardinal Hume himself exhorted those present to involve themselves 'much more in the institutions of our land, in neighbourhood organisations, trade unions, local government and parliament'.

We must remember that a certain kind of politics is, for a priest, an easy way out. It is far more agreeable to exalt oneself through compassion for what is anonymous and abstract – the working class, the victims of capitalist oppression, the Third World – than to work humbly in the ways of charity, which obliges us to help those concrete, knowable and often unlovable individuals whom Providence has placed in our path.

Not only is it more agreeable, it is also more gratifying to the ego. The attention of the world is more readily captured by the man with a cause than by the man who merely attends to his duty. There lies the origin of the modern heresy, which sees true religion in large-scale worldly enterprises and which exhorts us to fight oppression in Chile, racism in South Africa or nuclear weapons at home – in short, to perfect the unfinished work of Providence – rather than to save our own souls. It is significant, indeed, that the causes chosen by those in the grip of this heresy are precisely those which further the interests of the world's most militant atheist power.

Addressing the National Conference, the chaplain to the University of

East Anglia argued against the obligatory fast on Friday, on the ground that, because young people did not see the sense of it, this practice was an obstacle to his apostolic work. One would have thought that his duty was to *make* them see the sense of it. Besides, young people seem to be magnetised by those religions, however eccentric in doctrine or rococo in performance, which try to control their eating habits. But the chaplain's complaint eloquently captures the apostolic incompetence of a Church dedicated to secular affairs.

Man knows that he is not self-created, and he knows therefore that he owes a debt of gratitude, which can be repaid only by obedience. But obedience to what? Until he answers that question, he lives in a state of anxiety; it is the central tenet of Christian doctrine that the answer lies in faith. With faith a man may at last do with an easy heart what he otherwise does only hesitantly: he may fast and pray. Someone who does not see the sense of such activities is someone who is not yet in a position to believe. Someone who does see the sense of them sees also that they are performed not only for the sake of others, but also, and principally, for the sake of oneself, that one may be reconciled with the power to whom one's life is owed.

The strength of the traditional Roman Catholic Church was two-fold. It offered a definite and authoritative system of answers to life's questions, worked out over centuries of discussion and inquiry and delivered in a language that spoke directly to the individual heart. It also rehearsed, in sublime ritual, the mystery of man's condition and the universality of the Church which promised his redemption. This certainty and self-containment were the grounds of its success. For no convert can be won by a religion which compromises with his doubts and hesitations, or which puts secular causes in the place of individual salvation.

No doubt the majority of priests realise that. No doubt they accept that their duty lies towards the individual sinner, for whose sake they must renounce so many of life's pleasures – including the pleasure of trumpeting abroad their virtuous concern for peace and social justice. The true priest works quietly, outside the publicity that gravitates to those of little faith.

The oral instructions offered to his flock by one such priest have recently been recorded and transcribed by a group of his friends. *We Believe* is a remarkable document, written with warm emotion and lucid intellect. It completely demolishes the secular superstitions with which the faith of Rome has recently been confounded, and presents a doctrine sufficiently complete and sufficiently rich in implications for the individual life as to make conversion possible. It does, indeed, what all apostolic writing must do, and what so much modern Catholic literature refrains from doing: it presents belief to the unbeliever. My thought on closing the books was: if this were true, as it is beautiful, then it would suffice.

27 September 1983

From the House of the Dead

Enoch Powell is surely right: we *did* over-react to the shooting down of the Korean airliner. For we treated this disaster as though actual human beings were accountable for it. We assumed, as we assume again and again, and always to our cost, that the Soviet system is one of rational decision-making, in which living, feeling creatures make choices for which they are subsequently held publicly liable. Until we learn that that is not so, we shall be the victims of our own generosity, which leads us to interpret inhuman dangers in merely human terms.

If such an event happened in the West, there would be the following consequences: an outcry would be sent up by the media; the parliamentary opposition would join in, as would many members of the governing party, forcing the leadership to take action at the highest level. A public process of recrimination would be initiated, designed to discover the culprit and to punish him. The state would accept responsibility for its military arm and admit moral and legal liability towards the victims. Compensation would be claimed, sued for and awarded; apologies would be offered; and, most important of all, steps would be taken to ensure that the episode did not recur. Such a process is rational, scrutable and, above all, human. It is also the essential manifestation of self-correcting government.

It is important to realise that not *one* of those consequences could occur in the Soviet Union. All channels of communication are controlled by the state, and no journalist dares raise his voice in protest. There is no parliamentary opposition, and indeed no legal opposition of any kind. Nor is there any serious possibility of expressing publicly one's disagreement with the party line. In short, there is no public opinion in the Soviet Union – not, at least, in the proper sense of that expression, according to which it denotes a corrective pressure on the powers that be.

No process of recrimination could be publicly initiated or conducted, nor could it be ascertained with any confidence who the culprit was, or under what instructions he had acted. The state could not assume legal responsibility, since it cannot be bound by the decisions of its law courts, nor would any individual be so foolhardy as to stand up and accuse it before a judge whose decision it controls.

No one is in a position to offer apologies sincerely, since no one is in a position to ensure that the episode will not recur. We are faced not with an institution of human government, but with an impersonal machine which cannot adjust itself according to the logic of rational choice. Its logic is the logic of fear – a fear so ubiquitous that, when a recent member of a Russian delegation to Edinburgh University gave utterance to a human doubt about the Soviet action, he left the country cravenly protesting in the loudest possible terms that he had been tricked into expressing it. No doubt he is now being treated professionally for his temporary mental disturbance. But we should not be blind to the truth that he revealed.

But surely, you will say, the Soviet system is controlled, in the end, by human beings? Surely there are people at the top who have the power to respond to circumstances and to make the necessary adjustments? After all, what was our visitor afraid of, if there are not people somewhere with an interest in shutting him up and with the power to do so?

It is true that, on state occasions, a few old men shuffle on to the balcony of the Kremlin and raise their hands in zombie-like salutation. It is true that, when foreign statesmen visit, an unsmiling mask called Andropov is carried forward and sometimes reaches towards them an unsteady palsied hand. But can we be sure that these bodies are really alive, that the voice which speaks from their dry stiff faces is still the voice of a feeling creature, with responses of its own? I do not think so. Even at their most energetic, these bodies career about the stage of world politics as though controlled by a sightless mechanism. Energy is not life. And it is not life that distinguishes the ruined Andropov from the sprightly Gromyko who, like a headless chicken, struts about in pursuit of immutable purposes, unaware that the soul has fled.

When the missile was fired, the air was alive with orders. But whose? They vanished at once, like a chorus of spirits from *Faust*. No sooner was the deed accomplished than the process of oblivion was set in motion. The machine was beginning to fabricate evidence and counter-evidence, as each person, afraid for his neck, passed his story to his immediate commander. A collective and contradictory excuse eventually reached the Kremlin. Those at the top, acting from the same fear as those beneath them – for the system may strike at any time, without respect for rank – deliberated over whether to accept it. If they did so, it is not because they believed it to be true – truth can no more play a part in their calculations than any other concept derived from the honest interplay of human emotion. The excuse was accepted as the most likely propitiation, offered to a machine that daily threatens to destroy the power of those whom it raised into eminence.

The impersonality of the communist state is not easy to understand. The huge dangers with which its subjects are daily confronted seem to come from nowhere, while threatening everyone who accepts responsibility for his own existence and so dares to be a man. Franz Kafka described the workings of this machine in a prophetic book, the moral of which many of our statesmen, including Mr Powell, have yet to learn. When they have learnt it, they will also know why *The Castle*, along with every other work by Prague's greatest writer, is no longer published in the country of his birth.

4 October 1983

The Myth of the Working Class

We are poorer for the lack of an effective opposition in the House of Commons, and therefore we all should hope that the Labour Party will now rise from its knees and begin to search for political opportunities. However, it has got used to being on its knees. Indeed, it finds the posture rather consoling.

The cause of this habit of genuflection is the worship of an idol: the Labour Party never ceases to abase itself before a peculiar fiction called the working class. It believes itself to have been created by the working class and to stand now in a privileged relation to it, protected and authorised by a deity from whom all legitimacy ultimately flows. But this idol is dead, and what the Labour Party takes for the odour of sanctity is in fact the stink of divine putrefaction.

I borrow that phrase from Nietzsche – Mr Kinnock's least favourite author – because it so perfectly captures the rotten sentimentality of Labour thinking, which seeks to persuade itself that the party was the product, and not the producer, of the fiction by which it lives. The Labour Party is the party of nostalgia. It harks back always to the 'heroic struggles' of the factory era, and to the days of the Depression, when it seemed to be fighting a holy war against the enemies of the working class. It continues to describe its ambitions in terms of 'struggles', 'fights' and even 'crusades', as though seeking to emulate the barbarians who spread murder and pillage through the peaceful lands of Islam in the name of a God whose purposes they so imperfectly comprehended.

There is a good form of this nostalgia, which grows from the love of one's history. British socialism has been imbued with our native sense that the source of legitimacy lies not in the future, but in the past. This longing for community with generations that have gone before provides the Labour Party with its human face.

But it is a human face stiffened by sanctimonious holiness. It too often confronts its opponents not with criticism, but with moral abuse. It too often exhorts us to worship its idol, or to kneel before incomprehensible abstractions such as equality, social ownership and social justice. It is vast in its ambition, but fertile less in positive suggestions than in a vitriolic pursuit of objects and institutions that it might destroy. That, indeed, is the normal course of sentimental emotion, which hides the unreality of what it loves in a hatred for what is real.

The working class once existed. There was, once, a definite social entity, consisting of largely propertyless people, with sufficient community of interests and powers to be sensibly described as a class. Historians and novelists have made us familiar with its situation and caused us to sympathise with its distress. Only ignorance or callousness could lead us to despise the aspirations, or to resent the achievements, of this class.

The British Labour Movement – which pressed with such extraordinary civility and open-mindedness for the representation of the working class in parliament – attracted the sympathy equally of socialists, liberals and Tories. Its resolute attachment to an ideal of human dignity proved, in the end, to be its greatest weapon, forcing its opponents to confront it with terms and tactics which, by their very nature, promised victory to itself. The critical period, however, is the one which followed, when the representation of the working class was so firmly established both in and out of parliament that the Labour Party could eventually claim to be one of the natural parties of government.

The working class then proceeded – by the very anti-revolutionary process which had brought it to power – to do what Marx and Engels had predicted that it could do only by means of revolution: it proceeded to abolish itself as a class. The objects of the Labour Movement had been accomplished, and the socialist ideology with which they had been decorated began to seem irrelevant. The worker no longer felt that community of interests and powers which had been the vital cement of his class. He was no longer a unit in a 'class struggle' but an individual, intent on making his way in the world.

The Marxists had predicted the increasing 'proletarianisation' of the middle class. What happened, in fact was the *embourgeoisement* of the worker. The modern worker is a property owner, with access to medical care and education. He stands poised on the brink of opportunities that may raise him up or throw him down. At the same time, although he may fall, he cannot fall far. He can survive, as increasing numbers do, without working, devoting himself all day (provided the Labour Party does not win another election) to the 'hunting, fishing and literary criticism' which Marx and Engels wished him to enjoy. Like all middle-class people, he is deeply suspicious of factions and cartels, among which the trade unions – which impinge most heavily on his life – are the most immediate objects of his resentment.

The Labour Party, which clings with such fervent nostalgia to its vision of a 'class solidarity' expressed through trade union power, is wholly out of tune with the sentiments of this emancipated worker. Indeed, one can fairly say that Labour is the most reactionary of the major political parties, in that it seeks to impose a dead social order upon a society that has become inherently resistant to it.

Perhaps it perceives that this can be done only by force – the kind of force which sustains the 'dictatorship of the proletariat' behind the Iron Curtain. If that is so, then at least one of its recently declared policies shows an element of realism: its policy of unilateral nuclear disarmament.

11 October 1983

The Folly of Local Government

The Conservative Party's White Paper on local government has aroused considerable opposition. Since most of this comes from officials and employees in local government, the paper is probably a step in the desired direction. For it is party policy to curtail local government, and therefore to arouse opposition from those engaged in extending it. I doubt that the Conservatives have thought of a more popular policy since the Factory Acts. The only problem is that, now as then, the proposals do not go far enough.

The White Paper speaks of transitional periods and transitional costs, of 'functions transferred to the lower tier', of 'joint boards' to be set up to administer what was previously the business of the metropolitan county councils. To transfer functions is to preserve them; what is required, however, is that the apparatus which created these functions be destroyed, and the functions themselves along with it.

Can this be done? That it must be done is evident to any observer of human nature. The ordinary middle-class Londoner, who bears the principal burden of the rates, is at the limit of his patience. Unlike so many whom he is compelled to support, he has chosen to take responsibility for himself and his family. He is therefore a target for all arbitrary taxation. The politicised playboys of the GLC, like the assiduous sinecure-seekers of Nalgo, regard him as fair game. And he feels their inroads into his hard-earned profits as a deep injustice. Of course, he welcomes the services of the police, the dustmen and the street-cleaners. But to the extent that he does so, he believes that they should be provided either privately (as may be advisable in the case of refuse collection) or else nationally, as is appropriate in the case of the police. The thought that they are controlled by the very same Mafia to whom he pays his rates fills him with outrage.

For consider how the remaining 80 per cent of his rate bill is spent: on the ILEA – to whose schools he would never dream of sending his children if he could help it; on the social services – which, far from confining themselves to natural measures of charitable relief, are dedicated to the task of creating an empire of ungrateful dependants; on the local planning department – with its tyrannical power both to compel work and to prevent it, and with its purely arbitrary relation to any moral or aesthetic standard comprehensible to the ordinary citizen.

All this appears to our ratepayer as a forced redistribution of money that is rightly his. His own encounters with town hall bureaucracy will have convinced him, moreover, that he is no more than the despised victim of the tyrants whose livelihood he provides. When, year after year, the rates rise at twice the level of inflation, to the point where he is compelled to part with more than a month's salary in every year or else face imprisonment, his anger becomes irrepressible. Do not ask whether he is justified; just look at the facts. Unless central government takes radical action, our ratepayer will do what the middle classes do only reluctantly, but with devasting effectiveness: he will organise himself to defy the law. And he will succeed. The result will be a catastrophe for local government, which will be immediately bankrupted, and which will never re-emerge from the ensuing chaos in its original form. In order to protect local government, therefore, the national government must at once abolish every part of it that is not absolutely necessary. Sections of local government must be simply eliminated – including most social service, planning, advisory, cultural and para-educational departments. While this happens Nalgo will of course go on strike. That is in itself a good thing, provided that the strike can be made permanent. In order to provide for that possibility, it will be necessary to prepare other arrangements for the control of sanitation and the police, in the hope that employees will eventually emerge who are willing to work in the revised and diminished town halls of the future.

Meanwhile, however, the single greatest cause of the disaster of local government must be removed. I mean the elected councils. Local elections in the United Kingdom suffer from two defects which make the councils morally incompetent in local matters. First, by subjecting themselves to a vote, the councils gain legitimacy for edicts which are tantamount to legislation. Thus, despite their universal incompetence in matters of law, government and administration, the councils issue proclamations which have the force of law. Second, they become the practice ground for aspiring politicians, who stand in the name of the major national parties and who become subject to the discipline of an informal whip, enacting at the local level fantasies of reform and revolution which they are powerless to impose on the nation as a whole.

If local elections are to be preserved, then it is at least clear that no national party should be allowed to participate in them, and that candidates who run for them should be subsequently debarred from parliament. Far better, however, to abolish elections altogether, and to return to local government on the medieval model – by the sovereign's command. If attendance at council meetings were a duty, like jury service, imposed upon citizens of sufficient public standing for a limited period and with no prospect of reward, then the result would be precisely what the Conservative Party is seeking. Local government would begin to dwindle at once, and the quantity that would eventually remain would be just sufficient to ensure that the local community, upon which the officers depend for their public standing, flourishes according to its local condition.

18 October 1983

Bourgeois Man on the March

Left-wing historians wax emotional over the 'class solidarity' which grew from the miseries of the Industrial Revolution, and which – according to their version of events – was the principal impulse behind the Labour Movement. I should like to pay tribute to another kind of solidarity which also has its origins in the Industrial Revolution, but which has proved more durable –the solidarity of the brass band.

The brass band movement is as old as the Labour Movement and indeed, at the outset, hardly distinguishable from it. The Besses o'th' Barn Band, for example, was already active in 1821 and acquired its present fame after 1880, when the great Alexander Owen came to it from the equally old and equally famous Black Dyke Mills.

Most of the bands originated in works and collieries, and the instruments were purchased with money contributed by the players themselves. They have remained associations of musical amateurs, with all the catholicity of taste and variety of achievement that that implies. But they are also more than associations, for they have gathered to themselves an extraordinary social ambience which is unmistakably British in its subdued pageantry and phlegmatic togetherness.

The brass band movement, like the Labour Movement, has been associated with non-conformist religion (and with the Salvation Army in particular), with temperance, self-help and trade union rights. It bears the imprint of the industrial proletariat. Unlike the Labour Movement, however, it has not made a fetish of its origins and so has experienced no difficulty in transcending them. It endures as a remarkable institution of popular culture, recruiting its members from every trade and every social class. The Black Dyke Mills Bank numbers among its players a joiner, a teacher, several students, an engineer, a stores manager, a wool buyer, an organ builder and tuner, a telecommunications engineer, a school caretaker, an export manager for a firm of sanitary goods, a carpet warehouse owner and a retired director of a manufacturing company. That mixture is by no means untypical.

The aesthete will look down on such fertile forms of association and on the musical culture which they generate. For it is a culture wholly without 'authenticity', a culture of transcriptions, medleys and arrangements, much of it based on hymn tunes, marches and popular song. It draws upon the common fund of musical, religious and moral experience, from which non-conformist religion shaped the social order of the industrial towns. How could such a congeries of old-fashioned decencies measure up to the exacting standards of high art?

It is true that the bandstand is frequently wearisome and seldom very subtle. But it is worth noting that the brass band movement has done more to spread the works of high art than has ever been done by the cavillings of aesthetes. Take Alexander Owen. When leader of the Besses o'th' Barn he arranged some of the most advanced music of his time for the benefit of his instrumentalists and their audience – including the Prelude to *Tristan und Isolde,* together with some further 20 minutes of music from what was, to contemporary ears, the most difficult of all modern scores. The brass band movement has also produced its own school of composers, and – with all due respect to the editorial injunction which tells me not to use 'bourgeois' as a term of commendation – it is certain that names like Derek Bourgeois, Gilbert Vinter and Eric Ball will achieve an honourable and lasting place in our musical history.

Ball, who celebrates his eightieth birthday this month, is a fine example of the tradition which he sustains: a Salvation Army man, motivated by sincere and cheerful religious emotion and with an ear nurtured on the works of Elgar and Parry, who has poured a public spirit of Athenian proportions into the copious vessels of the movement and enriched it with music which, for its feeling and craftsmanship, deserves a place in the classical tradition from which it descends.

The historian of the Labour Movement would do well to attend the National Brass Band Festival, which takes place annually at the Royal Albert Hall in London, about the same time as the Labour Party conference. The audience, brought in coachloads from the towns and valleys of industrial England, is bound by a consuming common interest. The object of this interest is not material, but cultural. It is also competitive – competitions having been an essential part of the movement from its beginnings.

This element of rivalry both unifies the crowd and lends tone and gravity to the impresario who addresses it. The event transcends all narrow class identity, to make contact with a tradition of worship and song which aims to be the common property of mankind. And the whole occasion is imbued with a quiet, serious patriotism, a conscious sense of national identity, which finds culminating expression when the audience finally rises to sing the hymn which conveys the meaning of their movement: Parry's setting of 'Jerusalem'.

The lessons for the Labour historian are many. Socialist orthodoxy to the contrary, solidarity is not impeded but fostered by competition. It is a feeling not of class, but of history. It grows not from shared material circumstances, but from a common culture. It expresses itself not in the sentimental worship of a vanished era, but in a loyal and sober attachment to the country and its institutions. How far this is from that hysterical affirmation of class solidarity which, at every Labour Party conference, throws up its hopelessly divided cries for unity and then peters out in a rendering of *Auld Lang Syne!*

25 October 1983

Peace and Pfitzner

How can the 'peace movement' be cured of its ruling illusions? How can it be brought to see that peace requires not the absence of weapons, but the absence of war; that war exists just so long as enmity is not deterred; and that enmity – towards our freedom, our institutions, our customs, our religion and our ideals – has existed unaltered since 1917?

I do not know the answer to those questions. But I do know that 'peace' means something more than the absence of war, and that, without that something more, the constant threat of war induces an unbearable longing for peace, a longing so great that men will throw down their weapons under its influence, believing that fate will not harm them, who intend no harm.

That is a religious belief, and the error of the 'peace' movement, as I see it, is to have transferred onto the world of human relations a sentiment that attaches properly only to God. If God exists, then indeed he can do no harm to those who intend no harm. But 'harm' is not, in God's eyes, what it is in ours. For God intends our death: the death of each of us individually, and (who knows?) perhaps the death of all of us together. A human being guilty of such an intention is indeed the enemy of peace. But that is because men are motivated differently from God, and because the peace of God is something other than the peace of man.

For us, 'harm' has an earthly meaning and includes such catastrophes as sickness and death. There is a certain impiety in supposing that we can guarantee that men will not produce those harms by renouncing the intention to deter them. For this is to base our attitude to other men not in a recognition of their partial evil, but in an illusion of their perfect good. It is to suppose that we should exchange provisional trust for absolute faith and so make man, not God, the object of our worship.

Idolatry of the merely human is a normal feature of modern experience. It need not be dangerous, even if it is always faintly ridiculous; it becomes dangerous only in the face of genuine human enmity, for then it threatens peace. Men need peace, and of both kinds. They need the partial peace of human co-existence, and also the absolute peace of worship, in which they are reconciled to their condition. The old liturgies provided the language through which an image of that absolute peace could be briefly entertained. The cause of peace – of true peace – is therefore inseparable from that of liturgical tradition. The peace of the liturgy is a peace of reconciliation, which is granted only because we are permitted to see ourselves, for a moment, outside human conflict, set like a jewel in God's ring:

Nun schmiede mich, den letzten Stein
An einem deiner tausend Ringe,
Du Gott – und ich will guter Dinge
Und friedvoll sein.

Having touched on the theme of the opera from which those lines are taken, I can now turn to what concerns me: the work itself. How is it that this, which combines one of the greatest scores of our century with the most poetic of modern libretti, should have been presented only once in London during the 65 years of its existence, and then by a company of adventurous amateurs? How is it that a work of art that touches on the most vital issues of our time – the survival of religious and political traditions, the meaning of the liturgy and the need for a more than human peace – should remain so neglected? I refer to Hans Pfitzner's *Palestrina*, the sole work of genius by a composer who matched, in this opera, a chaste and noble musical style with poignant and perceptive drama.

I am not blaming the opera houses. I have the greatest respect for all that they have recently done. Thanks to their efforts – and the efforts of the English National Opera in particular – we know that Janáček, Berg and Britten are the virtual peers of Verdi and Wagner. We have been brought face to face with powerful and demanding works, such as Szymanowski's *King Roger* (whose stupendous score just manages to survive the deflating effect of its mawkish libretto) and Schoenberg's *Moses and Aaron*, an opera that likewise suffers from its composer's total lack of literary judgment. But if such things can be attempted, why not *Palestrina*? It surpasses them in majesty and mystery, and in addition, it confronts the modern listener with issues about which he simply *has* to care, if he is to exist critically and consciously in his times.

Pfitzner's hero lives, as we do, in a period of spiritual conflict. He has lost his strength and inspiration, and cannot hope either to understand or to emulate the new musical styles that threaten the rule of polyphony. It is also the time of the Council of Trent. The liturgy that had, until then, survived unattended can now survive only because human consciousness takes note of it. Palestrina remains loyal to his tradition, and finally achieves both the liturgical renewal that is politically required of him and the inner tranquillity which is his heart's desire. In the delicate movement of this private drama, Pfitzner shows a small attempt to bring an end to vast human conflicts. The attempt is successful, but only because it has the more than human peace of the individual as its primary aim, and because the individual in question refuses to renounce the tradition and experience that created him.

We Europeans, who wish never again to know the reality of war, should take a lesson from this work of imagination. We should see that peace is created only in the human soul, but also that the human soul must work to preserve the institutions which contain it. Perhaps – whether or not inspired by such a philosophy – some commissar of the opera house will now help us to judge whether it is true.

1 November 1983

In Search of a Crown

VIENNA

The Josefplatz is enclosed on three sides by the dirty white facade of the old Hofburg, whose plain doors, lifeless windows and dusty stucco give it the appearance of a blackcloth for amateur theatricals. To the casual passer-by this is the least interesting space in Vienna, noteworthy only as a reminder of the modest style and provincial shabbiness of the Habsburg crown.

Behind one of these doors, however, lies the greatest secular interior in Europe: J. B. Fischer von Erlach's Hofbibliothek, a composition at once bursting with vitality and totally at rest, integral in its conception and also intimate and craftsmanlike in every tiny part. Behind another door is the Spanish Riding School, where horses are made to prance and posture for no other reason than the sheer wonder of it. A third door conceals the official apartments, while a fourth opens every Sunday into the West Porch of the Augustinerkirche, where whosoever wishes may participate in the true liturgy of the Roman Church and hear its meaning echoed by choir and orchestra in the life-giving language of Haydn. To someone who knows what these doors conceal, the Josefplatz is full of meaning: this shabby box is the outer wrapping of a stupendous culture, in which religion, learning, architecture and music are mingled inextricably, along with the sublime futilities of horsemanship and the petty tragedies of kings.

On 26 October I surveyed this scene from the first floor apartments of the Palais Pallavicini, where cream marble walls, gilded mirrors and Venetian candelabras compete for space above a teak and satinwood parquet. 26 October is a significant day for Austrians, being the anniversary of the departure from their territory of the Soviet 'liberator'. Certain things still testify to the ten years of occupation. There is the Red Army monument in the Schwarzenbergplatz, for example, known sarcastically as the Tomb of the Unknown Father – a hideous mass of Stalinist kitsch, which the Austrians are obliged by treaty to conserve. There is also the intense feeling of relief and gratitude which is rehearsed every year on 26 October and which now forms the substance of Austrian patriotism.

Despite the pressure of modern history, which has confined Austria against its inner logic within the borders of a nation state, Austrian patriotism remains cosmopolitan. In the gorgeous salon of the Palais Pallavicini, the Anton Gindely Prize – awarded each year for historical research into the Danube monarchy – was being presented. This national occasion, attended by burghers, *hofrats*, herr professors and herr doktors, is taken very seriously. For the Gindely Prize is a symbol of faith in Austrian history and in the cultural and political identity which, despite the unutterable catastrophes of our century, unites the citizens of Vienna with all those whose ancestors were once ruled from the shabby palace on the Josefplatz.

One of the two recipients was of Polish extraction and was to be rewarded for a book about Stanislaw Madeyski, a statesman from the Polish region of the Habsburg Empire. Two musicians had been commanded; they were also Polish, and played only Polish music, including Szymanowski's self-consciously folkish nocturne for violin and piano. The address was given by a Polish professor named Bartoszewsky on the topic of 'Patriotism Today'. It is difficult to imagine such an expression of patriotic sentiment outside Austria; to imagine, say, a gathering of Spanish dignitaries, assembled for a national festival, in which a prize is presented to a Dutch-born author for a book about a Dutch statesman and in which the ears are assailed, first by difficult Dutch music, and then by a lecture from a Dutch professor on the international character of the patriotic urge.

Professor Bartoszewsky touched every Austrian heart, however, as he described the difference between the nationalism which nearly destroyed Europe and the patriotism which has so far preserved it. For the nationalist the individual is nothing, and the people everything; for the patriot the individual is everything, even though bound by an indefeasible duty to his people, place and time. Listening to this Polish spokesman for Habsburg values, I felt how far the work of restoration had proceeded, how much of that old reverence for local custom and general law had been revived and how premature was the title of the great book – *Die Welt von Gestern* – in which Stefan Zweig lamented what he supposed to be its final passing.

The prize-giving began, and the Austrians took over. Their nervous humour, and their sly digs at political rivals, showed that they were party men, for whom Austrian patriotism is a matter less of sentiment than of policy. True patriotism lies above politics, and no mere party can appropriate it without destroying it. In Austria, however, despite all the efforts of restoration that have raised laws and institutions still breathing from their temporary grave, it is the party, and not the country, that is the major focus of public life and attention.

The Palais Pallavicini bears a name redolent of Habsburg catholicity. Confronted by its empty rooms, the visitor is impressed with a sense that they speak for the whole of Austria: refined, liberal, tolerant, but belonging to no one. Austrian culture cries out for the spirit of ownership. It wishes above all to belong to someone – someone other than, and higher than, a political party. Only then will patriotism find its true focus. Every Austrian knows this, but he has been persuaded to deny what he feels; persuaded to think that monarchy is somehow outmoded, atavistic, the enemy, rather than the only begetter, of cosmopolitan ties.

It is surely time for the Austrians to cast off those Enlightenment superstitions and to do what their still living institutions require. Besides, they have their opportunity. Otto von Habsburg is an astute and experienced politician, an intelligent observer of European politics; he even writes for the *Salisbury Review*. What more could they want?

8 November 1983

Law and Force

Forget about Grenada. Whatever happened, the issue of principle remains: should the United States be prepared to act in defiance of international law when its long-term interests are threatened by obeying it? Its enemies will continue to fabricate the occasions; how then should the United States respond? I believe that the answer is obvious. However, because what is obvious to me may not be obvious to others, I shall give my reasons.

Consider, for a moment, not international law, but the ordinary domestic law of a state. Two things make it possible for a society to be governed by law: the disposition of the state to enforce the law, and that of the citizens to obey it. The importance of the second condition is not always recognised. The erection of an impartial machinery of justice (whereby the state enforces the law against all malefactors including, where necessary, itself) will not suffice to secure a rule of law. The state is rendered incompetent by widespread disobedience, and the machinery of justice will work only when malefactors are rare. A rule of law requires a society of law-abiding citizens. The law does not create those citizens.

They exist by virtue of their 'public spirit', and a public spirit may take centuries of civilisation to acquire.

International law must be understood on the analogy with municipal law: for we have no other model for it. There will be an international rule of law only if there is a power to enforce it and a general readiness to obey it. It is obvious that, in present conditions, neither requirement is satisfied. The power of the United Nations is a power not of coercion but of influence, and the influence is steadily declining. Half of the members of the UN cannot obey their own laws, let alone laws made for them by others. Hence the institution has – and with reason – become so discredited that it cannot really influence the conduct of those nations which are disposed to violate whatever law they choose.

The second requirement of the rule of law is also absent. The member states of the United Nations are not, on the whole, 'law-abiding citizens' of an international polity, and their good opinion is not always something that an honest person should seek or value. A substantial number of the delegates who sit at the United Nations General Assembly represent not the people of the nation whose name they bear, but cliques of gangsters (very often military men) who obtained power by force, and who have no intention of relinquishing power by any legal process. Other states are ruled by the successors of such cliques, who have crept steathily to power in the manner of Mr Andropov, to enjoy at the threshold of death a mouthful of the bitter fruit of tyranny. Most of these ruling cliques have silenced opposition within their borders, and devote their diplomatic efforts to silencing opposition beyond them.

For such states, law is a facade, and diplomacy (to parody Clausewitz) war by other means. Such states could not rule by law: for to accept the rule of law is to limit your power, by placing in the hand of the ordinary citizen the only thing that can protect him from dictatorship. Of course these states *pretend* to rule by law. But in any real conflict with the individual the law is brushed aside, usually by a judge acting under instructions from the dictatorship. Law becomes an exercise in propaganda; but when real interests are threatened, either at home or abroad, it is at once replaced by force as the only principle of political movement.

A state that is not governed by law in its dealings with its own subjects cannot be governed by law in its dealings with other states. In the last analysis, it is only public opinion at home that can compel a government to abide by the precepts of international law, and where this opinion is silenced, the compulsion is no longer felt. The United States is subject to the power of public opinion, spontaneously generated by its domestic rule of law. Its principal enemy – the Soviet Union – is not ruled by law, but by force, without legal opposition and without the kind of public opinion that would compel it to obey international legislation. Soviet policy towards the United States is inimical, based on ideological aversion and on a domestic need for the 'objective enemy', through whom to justify the privations suffered by the Soviet people. Cuba has its own reasons for hatred of the United States. But it is no more bound by the constraint of law than is its ally, and no more susceptible than is its ally to the correcting pressures of legal opposition and public opinion.

To imagine that you can always deal with such states through the medium of law is to give way to a dangerous fantasy. Law is not an independent influence on their behaviour. There is not, within the structure of their domestic government, that responsiveness to law which would enable them to respond also to the law of nations. In any crucial encounter they cast all such niceties aside; and we must, when dealing with them, be prepared to do likewise, or else weaken our defences to the point of danger.

We all wish for that 'perpetual peace' in which conflict between nations is resolved by law and never by force. But when the most aggressive nations cannot respond to law we must – if we are to achieve the precarious peace which is alone achievable – confront them at the deeper level of genuine enmity. We Europeans, who created the idea of international law, are disposed to believe that the world can be governed by a mere idea. We thereby fall victim to our perennial illusion, which is to believe that the principles whereby we live apply beyond the boundaries of the civilisation which created them.

15 November 1983

The Turks of Cyprus

In order to maintain peace within its disparate territories, the Ottoman Empire often granted legal protection to languages, religions and customs other than those of the Sultan. When the Ottomans captured Cyprus from the Venetians in 1581, their first act was to restore the autocephalous Cypriot Church and to confer upon its patriarch those powers of government which he had previously been accustomed to enjoy. Henceforth the Greek orthodox religion and Christian customs were dominant in Cyprus, and when the empire began to collapse and its various communities struggled to find an identity outside it, it was inevitable that the Greek Cypriots should nurture the idea that their territory – which has never been a Greek possession – is nevertheless 'essentially' Christian and 'essentially' Greek.

Had the British not stepped in and incorporated the island into another foundering empire, the Cypriot Turks (a largely peasant community, dispersed across the land in unfortified villages) would have gone the way of the Cretan Turks, none of whom survived the territorial enthusiasm of their Greek-speaking compatriots.

The *megali* idea – the idea of a pan-hellenic state, embracing all those communities and territories where Greek was the common tongue – persisted in the minds of the Greek Cypriots. When Archbishop Makarios stepped by democratic election into the hereditary privileges of the patriarch, it was with the promise of *enosis* – of union with Greece. It cannot be denied that, in the minds of many Greek Cypriots, *enosis* also meant the expulsion of the Turkish 'foreigner'. We know what the armed struggle for *enosis* meant to our unfortunate troops on the island. But we tend to ignore the fact that it continued long after independence in 1960.

The constitution adopted in 1960 provided for a 'bi-communal' state and was guaranteed by the three interested parties – Greece, Britain and Turkey – each of which had the right to intervene unilaterally in the event of a breakdown of the treaty between them. This right was finally exercised by Turkey in 1974. A 'bi-communal constitution' is not a federal constitution, since it does not recognise the separate legal personality of either community. It merely stipulates that so many offices in the government, administration, police, judiciary, etc. must be filled from each side. During the years leading up to 1974, when Greece was ruled by a military dictatorship, Turkish civil servants received no salaries, Turkish judges found themselves unable to enforce their judgments, Turkish villages were deprived of services and Turkish government officers were subjected to intimidation.

In short, the constitution was put aside in favour of *de facto* tyranny of Greek over Turk. Appalling massacres of Turkish villagers occurred, and while Archbishop Makarios dissociated himself from the worst of these crimes, he proved unable to prevent them and indeed often seemed quietly to condone them. Finally he was himself deposed by the vile terrorist Nikos Samson, whose accession threw the country into civil war.

The immediate effect of the civil war was to drive Turks in thousands from their homes and to subject them to the risk of genocide at the hands of the Eoka fanatics who now controlled much of the island. These fanatics were aided by large contingents from the mainland Greek army, which had been installed illegally during the previous years. After the Turkish intervention those Turks who could escape to the North were able at last to find refuge from danger. For the first time in more than 20 years the Turkish community had the prospect of safety. Moreover, as a result of the intervention, Makarios was returned to power, the rule of law prevailed in both North and South, the military dictatorship in Greece was toppled and democracy was restored in the country which fondly imagines itself to have invented it.

During subsequent negotiations, the Greek Cypriots refused to contemplate any solution that recognised the legal personality of the Turkish community: the Turks were to remain a minority, protected by a bill of 'minority rights' and thereafter dispersed among the people who had tried to murder them. The assumption that the Turks would even consider something so mad is a fair expression of the contempt in which the Greek Cypriots hold their fellow islanders. The government of Mr Spyros Kyprianou is elected by Greek Cypriots only; it presently withholds all foreign aid from the Turkish community, imposes rigorous sanctions designed to deprive the Turks of commerce and livelihood, and has deliberately hampered all arrangements that could prove advantageous to the Turkish minority, even when they are also advantageous to the Greeks. And yet this government claims to 'represent' the Turkish Cypriots and to have a right to their allegiance.

The UN, moreover, agrees that it does, and has pronounced the new government of Mr Rauf Denktaş 'illegal'. But it is said that our own government had a part in the pronouncement. One can only hope that the Turkish Cypriots will not see this as yet further evidence of the conviction that the territories mentioned in Homer ought now to be governed from Athens, or the still more atavistic idea that legality is a Christian invention, whose edicts must be accepted unquestioningly by the 'barbarous' Turk.

22 November 1983

Left, Right and Wrong

In the French Estates General of 1789, the nobility sat on the King's right and the 'third estate' on his left. Probably nothing else that those troublesome people did has proved more damaging. Henceforth left and right were to name the two exclusive and exhaustive political options, the two poles of an axis upon which every political opinion must ultimately be made to lie.

Then came the communists with their deafening propaganda. To left was added 'communist', and to right 'fascist'. And the extraordinary thing was that it worked! I constantly come across people who show no other signs of being mentally retarded, and indeed who are as intelligent and well-educated as is necessary for the conduct of everyday affairs, who nevertheless solemnly subscribe to the view that on the 'far right' of political opinion lies fascism, and on the far left communism. What masterly propaganda that makes communism no more than a distant point along the road on which you have already embarked, just as soon as you have recoiled from the 'fascist' enemy!

The effect of this is to obscure the real similarity between those purported opposites. Fascism and communism both involve the attempt to create a mass popular movement and a state bound together under the rule of a single party, in which there will be total cohesion about a common goal.

Both demand the elimination of opposition, by whatever means, and the replacement of ordered dispute between parties by clandestine 'discussion' within the ruling elite. Both involve taking control ('in the name of the people') of the means of communication and education, and both involve subjecting the economy to a central command. Both movements regard law as defeasible and constitutional constraints as largely irrelevant, for both are essentially 'revolutionary', governed from above by an iron discipline.

Fully realised, fascism and communism are forms of military government, involving the permanent mobilisation of the entire populace, which can no longer perform even the most peaceful-seeming actions – eating, walking, praying or meeting – except in a spirit of war. There is a difference however. Whereas fascist governments have come to power with extensive popular support, and occasionally renounced power in favour of constitutional government, communist governments have almost always gained power by a coup d'état, and have never peacefully relinquished it.

Such facts destroy the two equations which are so fundamental to current journalese: 'fascist = far right', 'communist = far left'. Far more pernicious than these equations, however, has been the reasoning of those who hold that the 'far right' is to be identified in terms of specific 'fascist' attitudes – in particular attitudes towards race and national identity. This disease of the intellect, which puts the 'free association of ideas' in place of argument, leads to such absurd conclusions as that the National Front is 'on the extreme right'. It also leads to the idea that politicians who advocate immigration controls, repatriation or whatever are to the 'right' of those who do not. Since this reasoning is almost invariably conducted by those for whom it is morally impossible to *be* on the right, it has the effect of closing the mind to all rational discussion of one of our most important political problems.

If I had to decide the question, I should say that the National Front – an egalitarian and populist movement, hostile to constitutional government and to traditional authority, fired by ideology and by a spurious search for a common purpose – is more on the 'left' than on the 'right'.

But I hesitate to use the labels. After all, where do *I* stand? I believe in the welfare state, in a government ready to participate in the nation's economic life, in strong and representative trade unions active in pursuit of their members' interests, in liberal laws of assembly and association. That puts me on the 'left'. However, I also believe in private ownership of the means of production, in authoritative government, in immigration controls, in autonomous institutions organised around traditional values and customary usage, in a law dedicated to upholding the moral values of the community with whatever severity be required. That puts me on the 'right'.

Let us change the subject. There is a distinction which is far more important and far more pertinent to our current political situation than that between 'left' and 'right'. This is the distinction between governments which recognise opposition and those which do not. That is the distinction that aligns, for example, Nicaragua with the Soviet Union and Turkey with the West. For *us*, the major purpose of politics is to make opposition possible, by providing the framework within which it can be accommodated and where possible resolved. For *them*, the first purpose of politics is to root out opposition and silence it, to achieve that 'unity about a common purpose' which is equally the goal of fascism and communism, and which sets each movement at variance not only with constitutional government, but also with itself.

6 December 1983

Fantasy and Imagination

Having refused to watch *The Day After*, I feel particularly qualified to pass judgment upon it. I am one of those who has the habit of passing judgment, so as to know in advance which experiences I would rather not have. Nor am I alone. Shocking though it may seem to the enlightened, there are millions of people who, on no first-hand evidence whatsoever, have decided never to see a video nasty. Indeed these ignorant and prejudiced people may even be in the majority; at least I hope that they are.

The Day After is, by report, a particularly disgusting video nasty, larded with the moralising cant that one must expect from people who let their thoughts dwell upon the image of human suffering. That it should have been banned goes without saying. There is no more excuse for displaying a realistic picture of nuclear catastrophe than for displaying a realistic picture of a pregnant woman being cut up with a chain saw, or a live child being slowly disembowelled by hungry cannibals. Those who have no ability to imagine such things when required (and we must imagine the effects of nuclear war if we are to make wise political decisions about it) have no imagination. And nothing is more dangerous than to provoke mass hysteria in the literal-minded.

There is nothing human – not even death itself – that cannot be taken too seriously. And a person without imagination can take anything too seriously. His emotions, once deflected from the realities of daily existence, are out of his control, for imagination alone could permit him to control them. Where imagination is dead (imagine) fantasy triumphs. Fantasy consists in a morbid fascination with unrealities, which secretly transforms itself into a desire to make them real. Imagination is a form of intellectual control, which presents us with the image of unrealities in order that we should understand and feel distanced from them. In imagination we dominate; in fantasy we are dominated.

Anyone who wishes to know what pornography is – and *The Day After* is, I assume, pornography – ought to study the distinction. When Dante takes his reader through the miseries of hell, what he describes is worse than any nuclear holocaust. He describes a world without hope, a world of ceaseless torment unrelieved by unconsciousness or death, a world (and this is worst of all) denied the redeeming gift of love. But Dante does not invite us to fantasise, to dwell morbidly on these images with the lustful hunger of the masochist. He invites us to imagine the torments of hell and, in imagining, to distance ourselves from what we read. We must work to extract his meaning, and the imaginary object which we discover through his verses excites in us feelings which, however powerful, are only imaginary. We remain in control of ourselves, and although we are moved, it is with a calm and collected emotion, whose main ingredient is compassionate understanding. What is most horrible in Dante's hell is not stated, but implied, and presented to us through a veil of artistic conventions which serve constantly to remind us that we look upon these scenes from a point of view outside them.

Even Goya, in his engravings of the horrors of war, subjects his images to a discipline that neutralises the morbid passions of the merely curious. His powerful lines and contrasts, and his psychological intensity, transform everything that he pictures. A butchered body ceases to be a disgusting relic and becomes instead a symbol of man's hatred of himself. You cannot appreciate Goya's meaning without also stepping back from it. That is why you can live happily with these engravings hanging beside you on the wall.

Every critic, and every true artist, knows why, in the Greek tragedy, the actor wears a mask and the horrible events take place off stage. These devices are designed to stimulate the imagination by destroying fantasy, which is its greatest enemy and rival. Works of imagination say to us: this is not true, but it concerns you, so understand. Works of fantasy say: this is real, real, real, and you are in it, whether or not you understand. The video nasty employs no conventions comparable to those of the Greek stage. Its pornographic quality consists in its utter dedication to the realistic portrayal of scenes which prey upon our morbid emotions and acquire a horrible power over us. Those things which most overwhelm us in reality – sex and violence – are the natural subject of fantasy. People in the grip of sexual and violent fantasies are people who have lost control of the centre of their experience. Such people are dangerous to themselves, and dangerous to those around them. That is why pornography – which is the deliberate stimulation of fantasy – is evil, and why it should not be permitted.

It is hard, in a liberal democracy, to persuade people of truths which condemn the guilty pleasures of millions, and which imply that a government is failing in its duty by not exerting strong powers of censorship. But a liberal democracy will not last long when its subjects are prey to violent emotions which they can neither understand nor control. And even if it could last in these circumstances, it would not be worth it.

The question raised by *The Day After* is the question of human happiness. What is the value of liberal democracy, if the cost of living in it is that we surrender our brief lives to morbid terror? We are not here for long, and there may be no other world to which we are proceeding. And because we are weak, would it not be better to be protected from those grim temptations which threaten the little happiness that we may here achieve?

13 December 1983

The Education of the Judge

The English legal system is rooted in common law, and decisions made by judges have led to an accumulated weight of tacit legislation which parliament could overthrow only by destroying the basis of its own legislative competence. Some regret this fact, arguing that judges, since they are not elected representatives, ought not to make law. Others welcome it, arguing that judges, because they are not elected representatives, are competent to make law. No man becomes a judge merely by standing at the hustings and shrieking out his identity with a political party. To become a judge you need to know the law and to have acquired long experience of its application in the concrete circumstances of human conflict. To become a member of the House of Commons you need no qualifications whatsoever.

At the same time, no judge can take the overarching, long-term view of things which we expect (and occasionally receive) from parliament. It would be not so much optimistic as irrational to wish (with Professor Hayek) that all laws should issue slowly and piecemeal from repeated applications of judicial reasoning. Although modern statutes are often hastily drafted, crudely debated and ignorantly understood, it would be absurd to try to govern a modern society without a powerful legislative body able to dictate statutes to the courts.

But the dangers are obvious. How is parliament to be controlled, and by whom? It is not enough to say: by the electorate. The electorate has a narrow choice between two or three major contenders, and is hardly likely to vote a government out of office for just this or that piece of legislative nonsense. Besides, by the time of an election, the damage may be done. Habits form quickly in politics and, as the history of industrial legislation displays, rights once granted to powerful bodies cannot easily be removed.

The obvious answer is that parliament must be responsive to judicial criticism. One of the major virtues of the House of Lords is that it contains the highest judges in the land, who may influence the upper house to reject ill-considered legislation or to introduce appropriate amendments. But valuable as this influence has been, it cannot suffice to correct the major defect of the House of Commons, which is its tendency to neglect the detail of human conflict in order to achieve a synthetic perspective, often guided more by ideology than by a concern for truth. The real test of law is in the courts, in confrontation with the human reality. Hence parliament must listen to criticism such as was offered on 6 December by the Court of Appeal in its judgment of the Dimbleby case. It was persuasively argued that the 1982 Employment Act contains a serious intellectual flaw which, properly exploited by management, would deprive unions of a power that they ought to have: the power to carry on a dispute with an employer who has tried to slip out of it by changing his legal identity.

Given the importance of judges in determining the character and conduct of our political process, how should a judge be educated? It is a wise principle of English law that High Court judges should be chosen not from the ranks of solicitors, whose long-standing personal relation with their clients must inevitably conflict with the objective responsibility towards the law, but from the ranks of barristers, whose duty is to put the law on trial before the facts of human conflict, by making the best possible case for a particular judgment. And it is a further wise principle of our law – though one that is constantly threatened – that the two legal professions should be kept as far apart as is compatible with their constant need to co-operate.

The problem is therefore subsumed within another: how should a barrister be educated? I do not mean after qualifying, when experience is his master, but before qualifying, during the years when he acquires his 'formal education'. There has been a tendency in recent years for the Bar Council, and its educational arm, the Council for Legal Education, to believe that the main ingredient in a barrister's education should be *law*. In 1981, therefore, following the report of the Ormrod Committee, it was decreed that nobody should read for the Bar who has not obtained either a degree in law or the diploma in law offered by the City University and the Polytechnic of Central London as a postgraduate qualification. After all, if a degree in law is worth anything, it is to a barrister, and what better qualification could he have?

This short-sighted view neglects the prime fact, which is that the education of the barrister is also the education of the judge. Common law judges are legislators, with a refined and far-reaching political function, who must be able to perceive both the deadness of dead legislation and the vitality of new legal solutions. Our common law owes its strength to the creative genius of judges who, by obeying their own doctrines and principles, have generally proved more competent to untie the knots of human conflict than has parliament. The greatest recent example of this creative genius – Lord Denning – began by reading mathematics at university, and displays in his judgments the broad education and culture which, by helping him to enter imaginatively into the conflict before him, have given substance and direction to his strikingly novel interpretations of the law.

How then should a barrister be educated? He needs imaginative understanding, literary competence and common sense – gifts which some have thought to be acquired through study of the classics, some through the 'practical criticism' of the Leavisites, some through philosophy, some through history, but none, so far as I know, through law.

20 December 1983

Against Economics

Ebenezer Scrooge, Dickens' most noble character and the only one to struggle with true fortitude against the sentimentality of his creator, is finally overcome by literary devices (ghosts in particular) against which the innocent fiction has no defence. He too goes under, is caught up in the welter of false sentiment and renounces the identity which he had so carefully established over years of financial management. For Dickens, Scrooge is unlovable, tyrannical and mean. Had his portrait been written by a friend, Scrooge would have appeared sparing in his affections, but true; gruff, but decent; and with a commendable sense of economy. The currency of Scrooge's feelings is never debased, for, in sentiment as in finance, Scrooge puts saving before spending. He is therefore the true provider of sudden indulgences, the modest, anonymous, self-sacrificing worker whose labour is squandered on the feast days of the poor.

Of course Scrooge has his faults. One cannot deny that there is a certain poetic justice in the horrible transformation which turns him from an honest citizen into yet another ardent sentimentalist, anxious to impose his charity upon those in no position to resist it. Scrooge's major failing, and the one expressed equally in this tragic reversal, is his single-minded devotion to economics, his lack of that balanced judgment which refuses to elevate means over ends or to regard housekeeping as the sole purpose of home.

Scroogism proves corrosive of individual life; it also proves corrosive of politics. Dickens' contemporary, Marx, argued that political action is but an offshoot of economic transformation, and that laws and institutions are to be understood largely in terms of their economic function – in terms of their ability to promote the development of economic forces. He thereby endowed Scroogism with the pretensions of a science. Of course the Marxian theory of history is a myth. The only problem is that people are disposed to believe it. And then they suffer the same kind of reversal as was suffered by Scrooge.

Consider modern Europe. To the east of the Elbe, where Marxism is the official creed, governments are occupied in refuting Marxism, using political force to fetter the economy. To the west of the Elbe, where Marxism is officially scorned, governments are occupied in confirming Marxism, by subordinating all major political decisions to the laws of economic growth.

Whichever way we look, Marxism is triumphant. Among the ruling class in the East it is believed as theory, with disastrous consequences for economics. In the West it is imposed in practice, with disastrous consequences for politics. Two budding disasters will illustrate my meaning: the Turkish 'guest workers' in Germany and the European Community.

Within a decade or so, West Berlin, if present demographic trends continue, will be a predominantly Turkish-speaking, Muslim city, inhabited by Anatolian peasants fiercely attached to customs that have as much relation to Berlin as an olive has to a fir tree. How did this happen? The answer is simple: practical Marxism. A political decision with incalculable consequences was taken *for economic reasons alone*, to maintain the level of economic growth without which the German Christmas would not be its usual orgy of self-indulgence. The political continuity and social harmony of the nation were exchanged for a sausage. Millions of innocent Anatolians were simultaneously encouraged in expectations that cannot be fulfilled and placed at the mercy of a people who have not shown themselves particularly lenient to ethnic minorities. Perhaps a solution can be found: *insh Allah*. But the eventual cost will be higher than any temporary benefit.

But it is to the EEC that we must turn for the greatest example of the follies of practical Marxism. To establish a trading partnership – and one rightly perceived by the Third World as a dangerous protectionist cartel – it was decided to remake the entire politics of Europe. New political institutions, new laws, new councils, courts and even a weird kind of 'parliament' were established – all for the sake of trade. To secure the economic benefits which the EEC promises, a government must do what it cannot do legitimately: it must limit its sovereignty over the people to whom it is answerable, and so make itself unable to answer them.

It began badly enough, with the disappearance of our traditional money, which was anathema to the spirit of accumulation. The dozen, which can be divided by two, three, four and six, had to give way to the decade, which can be divided only by two and five, and which is therefore resistant to the natural impulse of human generosity.

This small change was the first of many: the European Parliament tells us that intolerably heavy lorries must shatter our villages. The judges of the European Court of Human Rights tell the citizens of the Isle of Man that they should renounce a form of punishment that might have improved the complexion of many a parliamentary backside. Posturing social democrats in the Council of Europe dictate politics to Turkey and morality to the world. Anonymous bureaucrats play with the economic map of Europe as though it were a game of Monopoly. And so it goes on. No one knows how the process can be stopped without losing the economic benefits, and we are told that the benefits are essential to our survival. So that as soon as we ask ourselves – as a result of this or that high-handedness – in the name of what are we dictated to by these second-rate politicians and unanswerable bureaucrats, then we find no answer but this: in the name of economic growth, which is the master of our destiny and against which we have neither the right nor the political opportunity to complain.

The crisis over the European budget now allows us to question the wisdom of Scroogist government. It may prompt our leaders into recognising that politics and economics are of equal importance, and that to subject the first to the second is to surrender our destiny to forces that we can neither understand nor control.

27 December 1983

Peace Studies

What is the government doing to counter the effects of socialist policies in education? Sir Keith Joseph did eventually take a stand against the campaign of vilification recently directed at the National Council for Educational Standards. But not before the socialist establishment had filled the channels of communication with unscrupulous propaganda, designed to impede rational discussion of the council's latest report.

The government seems determined to abolish the GLC, and yet it is willing to retain the only section of it that does lasting damage: the ILEA, surely the most militantly politicised of all our 'educational' institutions, dedicated to 'equality' at whatever educational cost.

Far worse than these two examples of a continuing hegemony, however, is the movement to introduce 'peace studies' into our schools. This subject – if it can be so called – shares an important feature with various other pursuits that incorporate the word 'studies' into their name: women's studies, for example, black studies and gay studies. This is that you can be fairly certain of the ideology of those who promote them.

In serious subjects, such as Latin, English and mathematics, all ideologies are represented and none prevails. In women's studies, however, you can be certain that a majority of the teachers are feminists, convinced of the need to 'redress the political balance' to the benefit of a 'disadvantaged' sex. Anyone who dares to suggest that the ideology of feminism might actually be false will be denounced by them as a 'reactionary', perhaps even a 'fascist'. The question of the truth of feminism is vast and complex. The purpose of inventing 'women's studies' is not to discuss the question, but to beg it, by making feminism into the *premise* of an academic discipline.

'Peace studies' is similarly concerned to beg the only question that it could conceivably answer: the question of how peace is secured. I happen to believe that there is no way to preserve peace in Europe without matching the armaments, and blocking the expansionist policies, of the Soviet Union. That belief of mine is based on reasoning, the major premise of which is the nature and history of the Soviet Union. Take away the premise, and I should certainly arrive at a different conclusion. I may be wrong; but I know that any person who sets out to discuss this question without first considering the major premise is irrational, and that a subject which is devoted (as 'peace studies' is devoted) to preventing all consideration of its own major premise is not an academic discipline but an exercise in propaganda.

A recent report prepared by the department of 'peace and conflict research' at Lancaster University tells us that 11.8 per cent of Conservative councils and 30.6 per cent of Labour councils have peace studies on the curriculum in their schools. The political asymmetry is already significant. What is most alarming, however, is the sheer extent of peace studies teaching in our schools.

One can be fairly certain that someone advocating the introduction of such a subject is a supporter of CND, and perhaps an out-and-out pacifist. Thus the main pressure group advocating the introduction of peace studies – Teachers for Peace – declares that it 'comes under the umbrella of CND'. Its 'Dovepax' starter pack, issued to help teachers to begin a course of peace studies, contains nothing but unilateralist propaganda. Among the teaching methods that it advocates is the following, introduced into schools in the North-east by Durham Schools Against the Bomb.

One of the 'teachers' describes a line running along the middle of the classroom. This line goes from 'complete pacifism' to the opposite extreme, which is, apparently, 'belief in both nuclear and conventional weapons'. The children are then encouraged to stand at their preferred point on the line, and to suffer whatever criticism may be provoked by doing so. Predictably, the middle point on the line (and therefore the point of safety to which the pupil will naturally gravitate) is defined as that of the 'unilateral nuclear disarmer'.

The aim of propaganda is to teach people to think in one-dimensional terms, and so to reduce all problems, however complex, to a simple for and against, left and right, them and us. In a democracy, the clever propagandist defines his preferred position as the centre between two extremes. All he has to do is to persuade his victim to accept the spectrum, and he can then guarantee the result that he desires. Such is the nature of the campaign that is now being fought in all seriousness in our schools. It is a campaign not for new forms of education, but against the very idea of education, a campaign to replace teaching by indoctrination. And its aim is transparently political. Only government action can defeat such a campaign, and yet once again the government hesitates to act. Once again, therefore, a ploy to undermine educational values seems likely to succeed.

3 January 1984

A Feast of Fibich

There are many reasons for visiting Prague: it is, for example, one of the most beautiful of European cities, and its setting is unrivalled. However, there is a special reason which – in an excess of New Year generosity – I have decided to disclose to the readers of *The Times*, hoping nevertheless (like a man opening his best wine for the benefit of teetotallers) that it will leave you unmoved. The reason is the second-hand music shop in Myslíkova Street.

Behind a dirty window papered with dust-jackets and record sleeves lies a single room, with an adjoining sanctum. The shelves that line this room are piled high with bound editions of the classics: piano sonatas, opera scores, chamber music of every kind, lieder and folk song; even (just occasionally) the full score of a symphonic masterpiece. Anyone who wishes to re-live the musical culture to which these shelves are so vivid a memorial will have an additional reason for browsing in them, and for negotiating a purchase or two with the good-natured set of grey overalls that resides in the inner sanctum. For in the centre of the left-hand wall he will find arrangements for piano duet of most of the major classical symphonies.

In the age of mechanical reproduction the symphony, boomed out from the radio or gramophone into every living room, has decisively changed its character. It is no longer what it was for our ancestors, who *played* these works at home, sensing the musical logic of Mozart and Beethoven in their fingers as well as their ears. When they heard these symphonies in the concert hall, it was against the background of a musical understanding acquired at the keyboard, and with a profound sense of the distinction between harmony and colour. Now that every performance can be fixed forever on disc or tape, composers have ceased to observe that distinction, and a dimension of musical significance has been lost. Imagine a piano transcription of an orchestral extravaganza by Stockhausen!

It was in this shop that I came across the works of the world's most unjustly neglected composer: Zdeněk Fibich, disciple of Dvořák and Wagner, friend of the poet Vrchlický and last of the true Czech romantics. A little volume of his pansies *(Nálady, Dojmy a Upomínky)* fell from the bundle of music that I was struggling with; bending to retrieve it, my curiosity was aroused by the fact that the piece confronting me was numbered 168. The volume turned out to contain 50 items in half the number of pages. Each piece seemed packed with ideas, and none was longer than a few bars. Intrigued and sceptical, I bought the volume, imagining that it would sound like the conversation of a man who speaks only of difficult matters in dark images, and who in addition never finishes a sentence.

On the contrary. These pieces, abounding in modulations and transitions, justified their every move, in a style that is both melodic and logical. Like a Chopin prelude or a Beethoven bagatelle, a Fibich pansy comprises the exact and completed statement of a musical idea and echoes in the mind like a well-turned epigram.

Discovering that Fibich was also the author of many orchestral and chamber works, I returned to the music shop in search of them. I found only a few dusty operas, which I bought in an equally sceptical frame of mind, now believing Fibich to be a miniaturist who could never sustain inspiration through an evening of drama. Wrong again. I began with his last opera, *Dargun*, written to a libretto by his beloved pupil and mistress Anežka Schulzová. Here was the melodic invention and harmonic clarity of the pansies, but drawn out with true Wagnerian breadth and with a dramatic understanding hampered only by Miss Schulzová's grisly libretto. Hastening to the record shop, I learned that there is no recorded version of *Dargun*, and indeed that only one opera of Fibich's is currently available: *Šárka*, in what I discovered to be an excellent version by the Brno opera.

Since acquiring the records, I have not ceased to ask myself why *Šárka* is never performed. Not only is it a work of unremitting musical craftsmanship, with beautiful melodies and sublime climaxes; it is also the only opera that goes to the heart of the great fantasy issue of our time – the issue of feminism. Miss Schulzová's libretto places on stage, in a series of hair-raising sado-masochistic images, the conflict of the sexes, exaggerated to the point of total war. Her heroine, a kind of masochistic version of Kleist's Penthesilea, leads a band of maidens to war for the sake of women's rights, and then betrays them for the sake of a man. She kills herself, at last, in a fit of intolerable remorse.

Fibich sustains all this with remarkable equanimity, in a firm musical language that rises to every climax, however melodramatic. And the sound of the distraught Miss Schulzová, bewailing the state of woman while cradled in the fatherly arms of her protector, is extraordinarily moving. For there is something profoundly true in her despair, and something equally true in the warm melody with which Fibich seeks to console it.

10 January 1984

In Black and White

Readers have sometimes written to ask me where I stand on the issue of race. The question that they mean to ask could perhaps be posed in the following terms: are you a member of the white racist establishment, an upholder of white majority rule, advocating policies of cultural hegemony designed to deny the validity of black culture and black experience and to sustain power structures from which black people are permanently excluded?

I can now provide these readers with an answer. The plain and simple truth of the matter is that I am black. I am also the defender of a minority culture. I was helped to discover these truths, as I was helped to find the correct terms in which to pose my readers' question, by an ILEA publication on *Race, Sex and Class*, subtitled *multi-ethnic education in schools*. This offers the following definition:

> 'Black' is used to refer to both Afro-Caribbean and Asian people. The term black emphasises the common experience which both Afro-Caribbean and Asian people have of being victims of racism, and their common determination to oppose racism. Other groups who, together with the black communities, are usually referred to as 'ethnic minorities' also suffer varying degrees of prejudice and discrimination. These include Chinese, Greek Cypriots, Turkish Cypriots, Turks, Vietnamese, Moroccans. In a similar way, though not always to the same extent, some white ethnic groups, such as the Irish and Jews, experience prejudice and discrimination. In using the term 'black' in this paper, it is not the Authority's intention to exclude any minority group.

It was that last phrase which comforted me. I belong to what is, I suppose, the most persecuted of all minority groups in our society, the group most often discriminated against and excluded from the structures of power, the object of the most persistent and immovable prejudice on the part of those who do not belong to it – I mean the group of educated people. Therefore I am 'black'. Discovering this enabled me to read the ILEA's pamphlet in a changed frame of mind. Is it really true, as is there maintained, that blacks are systematically discriminated against and excluded from positions of power in our system of education? Could someone belonging to my minority group, for example, ascend to a position of influence in the ILEA?

The answer is surely No. For the ILEA is deeply hostile to education. No educated person would, when attempting to understand the effect of culture and ancestry upon educational achievement, classify 'Afro-Caribbeans' and 'Asians' together. He would recognise that such a classification merely abolishes a fundamental datum – the datum that, while members of the first class tend to do less well than white children, members of the second class tend to do as well or better.

No educated person would base his historical overview of the British public school system on a sociologist's thumbnail sketch, according to which the main aim of the system was to 'produce an establishment schooled in the history, traditions, values and norms of colonial and imperial Britain'. An educated person would not assert unequivocally that the idea that European civilisation has shown a peculiar propensity for discovery, inventiveness and achievement is nothing better than a myth, nor would he accept the extraordinary caricature of British history upon which the ILEA bases its assertion that, by the end of the nineteenth century, 'racism as an ideology had become institutionalised in British society'.

He would be wary of anyone who advocated constant review of textbooks and teaching materials with a view to replacing those 'which display a negative cultural bias', as he would be wary of such generalisations as the following: 'There is, rightly, among the black communities and other ethnic minorities, an implacable opposition to racism' – as though belonging to an ethnic minority diminished, rather than increased, a person's natural xenophobia.

An educated person is likely to defend educational values and not lightly to cast them aside in response to this or that fancy, conceived in brains oppressed by sociological jargon and stirred by political enthusiasm. He is likely to reject the ILEA's criticism of the 'competitive system of public examinations' and the view that schools should become 'multi-cultural' – where this means placing equal emphasis on Shakespeare and reggae music; inventing a 'multi-cultural' history for Britain; teaching children in their 'mother tongue' and not in English; being prepared to dismiss everything that he knows to be worthwhile for a child to learn, in the interests of an 'equality' which would be worth nothing even if we could achieve it. Above all, he would not assume that a teacher who endeavours to communicate the culture which is expressed in his language – and who is aware that there is no greater mental discipline than to understand the achievements and institutions of the civilisation into which one was born – is a 'racist', actively seeking to exclude 'blacks' from privileges whose value he rightly seeks to explain to them.

Such a person, however, will – by virtue of his membership of the educated minority – meet with the most virulent hostility and prejudice from the uneducated. And when the uneducated control education, as seems to be the case in London, his chances of promotion are negligible.

17 January 1984

On British Philosophy

The *Guardian* has recently published a series of articles purporting to describe the state of British philosophy. The philosophy taught in our universities is described as insular, pedantic, hostile to the 'New Ideas' which circulate in France, ill-written and largely incomprehensible. The writer seems to have little understanding of the subject, and it occurred to me that the newspaper-reading public might benefit from a short reply.

The vice of which Martin Walker accuses us is named after a Frenchman – one M. Chauvin, whose admiration for Napoleon caused him to reject out of hand any criticism of his country and its emperor. Until becoming acquainted with French intellectual life, I imagined that Henry James's judgment of Paris as the most provincial of modern cities expressed nothing more serious than pique. Subsequent experience has taught me otherwise.

Consider literary criticism. English literature departments in Britain have recently been shaken by controversy over the relevance or otherwise of 'La Nouvelle Critique'. Have French literature departments in France ever been shaken by controversy over Leavisism, for example? Have they ever responded to the impressive critical achievement of Empson, Eliot, C. S. Lewis, Ivor Winters – to say nothing of Arnold, Coleridge, Hazlitt and Lamb? Actually, hardly any modern English or American criticism has been translated into French; little of it is read in French universities and none of it is taught there. Compare the reception of English criticism and philosophy in France with the reception in Britain of Lacan, Foucault, Barthes, Althusser and Derrida, and you will see at once how tolerant we have been of literature much of which is utterly worthless and all of which is closed to serious influence from outside.

But my subject is philosophy. The main influence on post-war British philosophy was an Austrian: Wittgenstein. His work grew upon foundations laid by a German (Frege) and an Englishman (Russell). In Cambridge I was taught to study those thinkers and others in the tradition to which they belonged. Nobody forbade me to read Sartre and Heidegger, although it is true that their relevance to the issues which we were taught to consider was, at the time, only dimly perceived. This concentration upon a small range of authors is not a vice, but a virtue. It is a direct consequence of the fact that, in a British philosophy department, the student is taught to consider not authors, but intellectual questions. Philosophy is taught here as it was taught by the four great teachers Socrates, Aristotle, Aquinas and Kant: not in order to drop names at literary parties, but in order to discover the truth about difficult and important questions. Hence, as soon as it was realised that the works of Husserl and Heidegger are, despite appearances, relevant to those questions, they began to be studied. And it is a proof of the openness of Anglo-Saxon culture that they had already been translated – long before Wittgenstein was being published in Germany, and long before Frege had even been mentioned, let alone translated, in a French intellectual journal.

The primary purpose of a university education in the Humanities is to teach the student to read a book. If you can read one book, you can read many. But if you learn to glance at thousands, you will probably never learn how to extract the meaning from a single one. The important thing is to acquire intellectual discipline, to learn how to distinguish genuine questions from spurious phantoms, valid argument from sophistry, words rightly used and to true effect from empty bombast and stultifying pedantry. I was taught for two years without being required to read a single work of philosophy published before this century, and only then did I turn my attention to the founders of my subject. Nevertheless, having read widely in the recent French, German and English literature on the philosophy of Kant, I am persuaded that only the last has made a serious contribution to the subject. And it has done so by rediscovering the spirit of Kant himself – the spirit of dispassionate concern for true conclusions and valid arguments.

There is, in any subject, a vast distinction between the first-rate and the second-rate, and inevitably what is second-rate will be pedantic, derivative and ill-written, in the manner of much British philosophy. But let us consider an example of what is first-rate. A student who is taught philosophy of language in a British university will be made to grapple with the extremely difficult and far-reaching arguments of Frege (a German), Tarski (a Pole), Quine (an American) and Grice (an Englishman). He will emerge from this – if he is any good – with a changed view both of language and of reality. And one consequence will be that the amateurish speculations of Saussure, Jakobson, Hjelmslev and the structuralists will seem to him to have little or no force. Were French and German universities to teach this kind of discipline, the Nouvelle Critique might never have existed. But the very cultural isolation of those establishments – their separation from all true ideals of liberal education – prevents the deficiency from being remedied.

Why then does Mr Walker complain so much? Reflecting on this question, I was struck by a peculiar fact. The philosophers considered by Mr Walker are almost entirely from Oxford; he himself was an undergraduate there and acquired his smattering of philosophical knowledge at the feet of the people whom he discusses. In other words, the articles provide an illustration of the very insularity that they purport to criticise, and another instance of Oxford's age-old self-obsession, its indefatigable desire to display its isolation to the world.

24 January 1984

Heath's Confused Conservatism

Mr Heath has recently come out. He ended all the doubts which grew during his years of office and which have since remained undiminished. He has declared himself a conservative. This, he told the House of Commons, is the real ground of his opposition to Mrs Thatcher in the matter of local government.

Did me mean 'conservative' with a small c or with a large one? Not the latter, surely. For it is hardly plausible to declare that one is speaking for the Conservative Party in the very act of betraying it. In view of his references to political theory, it is safer to assume that he meant the word 'conservative' in its philosophical sense – the sense in which it might be applied, for example, to the policies of Gaitskell and Eden (though not to those of Heath).

Conservatism, Mr Heath argued, is founded upon the idea that powers must be divided and balanced against one another. Centralisation concentrates power in a single body, and so destroys the balance. Any attempt to weaken local government is an attempt to concentrate power, and therefore a move towards the monolithic state which is the true enemy of conservative government and the true friend of socialism.

The argument is based on two confusions: between concentration and centralisation, and between sovereignty and power. The local councils are new inventions, and the authorities upon whom Mr Heath relies for his theory – Burke and Montesquieu – had no knowledge of them. It has been a constant theme of conservative government that the growth of local government does not so much divide power, as transfer power into the hands of those incompetent to wield it. Suppose the Mafia had offices in every county, together with the power to defy the law in each of them. That would be not a division, but a concentration of power. It would also constitute a grave threat to sovereignty. Clearly, then, the division of power means something other than its dispersion.

Montesquieu's division – into legislative, executive and judiciary – is not a division into separate governments, each with a separate regional sphere. On the contrary, it is a division of *central* power, which depends upon centralisation if it is to be effective. It is, if you like, a discomposing of the idea of sovereignty, whose three separate strands limit each other's movements as well as strengthening their common bond. Each power within the sovereign body must be centralised in order to limit the others. Imagine the judiciary reigning in the North, the executive in the South-west, the legislature in the South-east. Nowhere would then be truly governed; no power would be truly limited; no citizen would be truly protected by power, nor would any citizen be protected *from* it. Only when the three powers are joined in the knot of sovereignty do they limit and strengthen government.

Local government poses a threat to sovereignty, since it allows the accumulation of legislative and executive powers in the hands of people who are neither representative of their constituents nor obedient to the sovereign authority. They become unrepresentative from two causes: first, because local elections are little understood by those entitled to vote in them; and second, because the taxes levied by the councils come mostly from those who are disfranchised: business and central government. They become disobedient for two further reasons: because the compulsory levy of rates enables councils to engage in projects which have nothing to do with the well-being of the local community, and because the local councils have become practising grounds for aspiring politicians, who use the privileges of power in order to mount gestures of defiance towards a parliament the temper of which runs counter to their ambitions and the authority of which profoundly displeases them.

The respect of such local politicians for sovereignty, and for the division of powers invoked by Mr Heath, is well illustrated by the case of the London Transport subsidy. When this subsidy was ruled illegal by the House of Lords, the GLC mounted a campaign (funded from its own taxation) not only against the outcome, but also against the very idea of an independent judiciary, issuing badges and posters abusing the Law Lords, and calling for action to curtail their powers. Such a campaign would be inconceivable on the part of central government, for the reason that its unconstitutional nature would be immediately perceived. And it is precisely the centralisation of power in a single (but divided) body that would make that perception available.

It is the business of government to establish sovereignty over all *de facto* powers: over criminals, big businesses, trade unions, local councils, and over any other organisation that may threaten the freedom and trouble the life of the ordinary citizen. Only on that condition does it make sense for a government to divide its power. For only then does it protect the citizen by dividing itself, rather than exposing him to powers far more arbitrary, and far less easily curtailed, than itself.

14 February 1984

The Stately and the State-controlled

Wealth taxes and death duties, which produce very little revenue for the state, have many evil consequences. They transfer wealth from private to public ownership, so severing the connection between the holding of wealth and the prudent use of it. They discourage the creative and the industrious from exploiting their talents. They undermine the attempt to found a durable household, for the benefit of one's children and one's children's children. Hence they divorce property from procreation and edge us towards a future in which men will live for the moment alone, with no intelligible loyalty towards the unborn or the dead. Wealth taxes are the modern equivalent of the medieval sumptuary laws, whereby monarchs attempted to humiliate their more creative subjects. In short, they are a sop to envy and an insult to success.

There is no more vivid example of the effect of these taxes than the fate of our stately houses and the gradual extension of the dead hand of the National Trust over these once glorious living institutions. I am not the only person who groans aloud at the news of another noble pile destined to be eternally fossilised 'for the nation's sake' by an institution which, while purporting to represent the nation, is in truth the smooth apologist for the injustices of the state. For many people, when they enter these tombs from which all traces of life have been removed, shudder at the impious work of the trust in so unctuously concealing the life-destroying taxation upon which it feeds.

Consider how it happens. After centuries of prudent housekeeping, in which a beautiful landmark is maintained at no public expense and a collection of minor paintings, tapestries and furniture slowly gathered into a single place, the final crippling demand for death duties brings a family to its knees. It can escape the tax only by offering the house to 'the nation', along with all the contents and a sufficient sum for maintenance.

The family may perhaps be permitted to reside in some small portion of the museum, as one interesting exhibit among others. But it resides there as a humiliated vassal in its own ancestral domains. In this way there occurs a 'gift' to 'the nation' of one small part of the nation's life, so that 'the nation' can kill it.

The consequences are the following. The state does not gain the unjust revenue which it had sought. In fact it gains nothing. The National Trust, meanwhile, gains another liability, and proceeds to maintain imprudently and lavishly as a mausoleum what had maintained itself and many beneficiaries prudently and modestly as a house. The trust moves in with an army of experts, to dissect and catalogue the sad leavings of a life that will never again be re-established in these rooms – for gifts to the trust are inalienable. The unselfconscious muddle of a family household gives way to an 'authentic' interior, concocted by a fashionable Chelsea decorator. But it is not concocted *for* anyone: he does not paper over the traces of one life in order to prepare it for another, but rather so as to extinguish life for ever. His task is to create not a house, but a museum.

Those cupboards, chests and writing tables, those carpets and tapestries, those landscapes and family portraits, all of which were once the source of the liveliest domestic pleasure, have ceased to be the familiar companions of a daily routine. Detached from their ancient uses, placed stark and immobile in their now tasteful arrangement, they seem embarrassed and uncertain, as though stripped for a medical inspection. For the first time their minor character, their 'second best-ness', is made apparent. Gone is every circumstance that made them meaningful – the kitchen smells, the scuffle of dogs and children, the clamour of visitors and the attentive routines of ownership. These objects have fallen out of the human world of ownership into a void from which they can never be retrieved.

The country house was a source of constant expenditure and employment. It provided an endlessly renewable pattern of redistribution, whereby wealth acquired both in the country and the city could create profitable employment for the villages. And not only employment, but life, interest and spectacle. With the arrival of the National Trust, all that ceases for ever.

For a year or more – as at Canons Ashby and now Kingston Lacy – the house is closed, while the experts make their ghoulish inventory and the decorators move in to take charge of work which can no longer be entrusted to the 'ignorant' village painter. Huge sums are squandered in the act of taxidermy before the house is reopened in its new, urbanised, form. A few locals will again find employment there, but in work which no longer has, for them, the charm of historical loyalty or the satisfaction of a domestic tie.

Visitors come, anxious to see the patina of a life that was more than comfortable in a house that was more than functional. But the patina has been rubbed out, the furniture fumigated and repolished, the kitchens emptied and the stables closed. That people come is a testimony to their deep respect for the country house as an institution and a symbol – a respect that is surely stronger than the envy which our wealth taxes are designed (one supposes) to appease. That they go away so mournfully is, however, a testimony to the enterprise of the National Trust, which extinguishes one after another these little fires of our national inheritance in the ice-cold waters of the bureaucratic state.

21 February 1984

Race, Class and Politics

An attempt has recently been made to label the Conservative Party as 'racist'. I hope it may contribute to the public assessment of this accusation if I try to define its principal term.

'Racism', as it is now universally described in the English-speaking world, involves three beliefs. The first is that mankind is divided into separate 'races', defined not by common culture or common language, but by a common ancestry. The second is the belief that a person's 'race' tends to be expressed in his character, so that those who differ in their ancestry may for that reason differ in their customs, outlook, aptitudes and vitality. The third belief is that a person's racial affinity is morally decisive – in other words, that his rights and liabilities, his guilt and his innocence, are alike determined by his race.

Not all of those beliefs are equally dangerous. In fact, the first two are held by many of the critics of racism. Such critics have been known to praise the vitality and openness of African and Caribbean peoples, and to criticise the haughtiness of white Anglo-Saxons. They have sometimes attributed the excesses of communism to the 'Russian' temperament, or to an 'inherited' need for dictatorial authority. They have even been known to excuse the tribal massacres that have blighted modern Africa by referring to the 'unnatural' mixing of peoples by colonial rule.

Such ways of thinking are probably fallacious. Nevertheless, they exemplify an idea by which many people live, the idea that *'ethnos* is *ethos'*. It has been a dominant belief in human society that racial origins are a determinant of character. In all crucial decisions – marriage, war and alliance – this idea has proved one of the few points of departure from which a lasting course of action can be planned.

Neither of the first two beliefs has any tendency to confirm the third, and it is the third which is the most dangerous. Race is at best an influence on behaviour, not the moral source of it. It is the individual alone who acts, and he alone who should bear the benefits and the burdens of moral judgment. In all questions of right and duty, it is both wicked and nonsensical to refer to a person's race – whether the purpose be to accuse him or to exonerate him. To do so is to place the crucial attribute of responsibility where it does not belong: with the abstract totality, rather than with the concrete individual. The racist ignores every genuine right and obligation in pursuit of a merely abstract reckoning: he seeks to reward or punish the individual in respect of qualities which are not of his own choosing and for which he can in truth be neither praised nor blamed.

It is surely obvious that racism is an evil. Even if it were not obvious from its intrinsic nature, it is obvious from its effects. Millions have died precisely because, in the eyes of the racist, they were already dead, being of 'inferior' race, without rights, condemned by their very existence. Racism exemplifies the single most disturbing moral characteristic of the twentieth century. Ours is a century of 'mass movements' and 'impersonal forces'. Our wars are declared and fought for purely abstract causes, regardless of every individual obligation and every individual right. And in peace, as in war, our affairs are conducted in the shadow of vast, impersonal crimes.

Consider another example – that of 'classism', as I shall call it. This is distinguished by three beliefs. The first is that mankind is divided into separate classes, defined, not by common culture or common language, but by a common economic function. The second is that a person's 'class' tends to be displayed in his character, affecting his customs, outlook, attitude and vitality. The third is that a person's 'class membership' is morally decisive – determining rights and liabilities, innocence and guilt.

The first two beliefs are disputable, but comparatively innocent. But what of the third? Does it not permit just the same channelling of an impersonal, annihilating hatred as is permitted by the grim allegiances of the racist? And has it not had precisely the same devastating effects upon the conscience of our century? Consider the 'liquidation of the kulaks', in which 10 million people paid the supreme price, merely for their membership of a 'parasitic' class. Or consider the so-called 'cultural revolution' in China and the genocide initiated by the Khmer Rouge in Cambodia. Is it not obvious that, in the light of these crimes, we should be as careful to extinguish every spark of classism in our thinking as we are to 'stamp out' and 'kick out' racism?

Those last phrases belong to Labour Party propaganda and return me to the point from which I began. Whether the accusations against the Conservative Party are justified I do not know. But I am certain that many members of the Labour Party are guilty of classism when they refer with such scorn to the 'middle class', as though the great modern crimes against this 'class' have been in no way initiated by socialist habits of thinking.

When Mr Kinnock sneers at the 'middle class' commentators who do not understand his language, or boasts of the 'working class' affiliations which 'justify' his power, I feel a decided chill. Substitute 'Jew' or 'black' for 'middle class' – for after all, we are in each case considering the fate of a minority – and you will see what I mean.

28 February 1984

The Right Divine to Govern Wrong

John Stuart Mill characterised the Conservative Party as the stupid party, his own impeccably liberal opinions and policies being, he implied, far less stupid, and therefore far more fitted for the tasks of government. Mill belonged to a circle of people who believed that government should be conducted by those with intellect, education and ideas. This weird belief has shown a remarkable capacity for survival. Thus, in the United States, East Coast intellectuals groan under the yoke of the 'ignorant cowboy' Reagan as though under a barbarian conquest. In Britain too the belief has had considerable authority, and is responsible for the enormous influence wielded over the Labour Party until recently by the Fabian Society. Most striking of all is its success in the communist world, where every major leader, from Lenin to Ho Chi Minh, has justified his usurpation in terms of 'theoretical correctness', 'revolutionary insight' and 'progressive ideas'.

The belief that intellectuals have a natural right to govern is the modern version of an old superstition: that of a 'divine right' which can sanction the rule of an individual over people who do not wish to be governed by him. It is, however, far more dangerous than the doctrine of the divine right of kings. For a king, as a rule, has a hereditary title. He steps into an office the privileges of which have been steadily eroded by the flux of popular discontent, and the liabilities and responsibilities of which have been determined by a history whose influence is more powerful than his own. Furthermore, his presence on the throne is, and is perceived to be, arbitrary in just the way that human life is arbitrary.

He owes it to no personal quality, to no effort, talent or achievement, but simply to the accident of birth. Kingship therefore represents, in the eyes of the ordinary subject, the accidental quality of his own condition, and, by reminding him of the immutable facts of human destiny, reconciles him to the discipline of government. Hence government by a monarch is fairly likely to be government by consent.

Moreover, hereditary monarchy is, in a sense, the most representative form of government. Hereditary entitlement means that, by a natural process, every human type – including the lazy, the stupid, the obdurate and the insane – has a chance of sitting in the seat of power. Unqualified democratic election, by contrast, discriminates heavily in favour of the energetic, the cunning, the ruthless and the plausible. Our own system is the result of an attempt to combine the virtues, and cancel out the vices, of both arrangements. We have so devised the office of monarchy that its tenant acts not from individual impulse, but with the slow measured choice of history.

We have, in effect, created an institution that is wiser than any of its incumbents and balanced it against a parliament in which the energies of the members are rendered comparatively harmless by the oppressive weight of their official business.

It remains to be seen whether the modern republic will achieve so happy a balance – and, in particular, whether it will provide for the intellectual leader an office equivalent to that of constitutional monarch, an office which contains more wisdom than the head of its occupant. So far, the results have not been very encouraging. Consider Lenin and Stalin – autodidacts of immense range, who consciously identified themselves as men of ideas and who justified their crimes in terms of a vision which they alone knew how to realise. Consider Hitler, painter, dreamer, playwright and philosopher; or Mao, who summed up the matter with the words 'no army can resist an idea whose time has come'. Consider, finally, the Iranian intellectual whose philosophy of 'theocratic guardianship' moved him to return to his homeland after years of justified exile in order to replace the divine right of inheritance with the divine right of truth.

Such cases illustrate the dangers inherent in the doctrine of an 'intellectual right'. The king whose power is justified by divine right knows that he is answerable to a power who is, in the end, 'absolute sole lord of life and death'. The intellectual knows no such thing, but only that what he thinks is right. The intellectual justifies his assumption of power by referring to the impeccable truth or reasonableness of his ideas; hence his capacity to tolerate opposition is jeopardised by his newfound ability to silence it.

Is it not obvious, therefore, that the doctrine of 'intellectual right' leads naturally to the extinction of all opposing positions and all rival ways of thought? In other words, is it not obvious that the superstition refutes itself, by extinguishing the very intellectual light that it claims to worship?

Recently, *Le Monde* ran a series of articles entitled 'The Silence of the Intellectuals', lamenting the absence of the 'political consciousness' which had reigned supreme in the 1960s and 1970s. What has happened, it asked, to those fulminating intellects who provided such an inspiration to the left in the dark days of opposition, and who established the left's 'right divine to govern wrong'? The answer is simple. They are in power. No wonder they are keeping quiet.

6 March 1984

In Praise of Money

Almost everyone curses money, because almost everyone believes either that he does not have enough of it, or that some other person has too much. In the judgment of religion money represents the sacrifice of spiritual peace to wordly agitation; in the judgment of the enlightened moralist it represents the supreme triumph of means over ends, the 'instrumentalisation' of human purposes and the final self-alienation of man.

But money has survived these curses, and will always survive them. It bears the imprint of original sin – but only because it is all too human. Indeed, money is so integral a part of our social existence that we perceive it as a heraldic emblem of government. Caesar's head may be embossed upon his coinage, but not so deeply as his coinage is embossed upon his hand. Consider what man is without money. He must dispose of his surplus product by gift or barter. His transactions are limited, clumsy and time-consuming. He has no certain measure of the value of what is offered to him and will be reluctant to exchange his produce with those whom he does not know.

Money totally transforms his situation. It removes uncertainty, by providing a single scale of value. It permits transactions of the utmost flexibility with the widest circle of purchasers. By virtue of money, goods and services are rapidly dispersed to their natural destinations, and each man's surplus is poured at once into a common pool, from which it may be drawn off at some distant point imperceptible to the producer. Hence money focuses our economic impulses, while extending the sphere of their repercussions; under its influence, exchange multiplies quietly and peacefully to infinity.

And yet, apart from its function in exchange, money is worthless. It is a pure economic instrument: the means to almost everything, but the end of nothing. Money is the condensed residue of unspoken contracts, and its power lies in its ability to establish both the motive and the terms of ever new agreements, between ever new parties, concerning ever new matters of exchange. But there too lies its virtue. For money is 'crystallised agreement' – the sign and the consummation of social harmony.

Or at least, so it should be. Money can encapsulate harmony, however, only so long as we believe in the banker who supports it with his promise. What is this promise? To hand over a stated quantity of gold? But what is gold, if not money, whose value again depends entirely upon our willingness to accept it as an object of exchange?

To put it simply, the bank promises to sustain as best it can the purchasing power of its coinage. It does this by attaching money not to a valuable substance, but to a valuable process. Its money should symbolise not a quantity of gold, but a stake in the means of production. For it is the process of production which is the ultimate provider of everything that may be bought and sold. It is production, therefore, that is the objective guarantee of value.

But not every bank recognises the obligation to match its promises by its investments. Consider the national banks of the communist world, kept precariously afloat by massive loans from foolish private bankers in the West. The currency of the communist world is supported not by productive investment, but by price control. The result is devastating: shortages, black markets and a society rotten with secret thefts which can never be punished and with secret contracts that can never be enforced. Important transactions are now conducted by barter, or by the use of 'hard currency' from a foreign bank.

Communist regimes have even established shops which sell for foreign currency what is unobtainable for Caesar's coin. Hence, to the tacit admission that its money is nothing but an empty promise, the national bank adds an insulting display of the privileges enjoyed by the few, by virtue of its broken promise towards the many. In the money of such countries, one holds the sign and the consummation of social discord, of the haunting division between 'us' and 'them'.

If we are revolted by the meaning of those scraps of paper, however, we should be less than wholly pleased by the meaning of our own familiar quid, which has barely retained its capacity as a quid pro quo. Our money too is sustained by a national bank obedient to political imperatives. Should not the present administration – ostensibly so responsive to the need for a free economy and so impatient with the humbug of 'social ownership' – act to privatise the Bank of England? What better way to provide the bank with the incentive to honour its promise to the bearer who demands, than by freeing it to make investments not as Caesar commands, but as wisdom advises?

13 March 1984

The Morality of Commerce

Many explanations could be offered for the decline in serious sherry drinking; perhaps the most obvious is the decline of serious sherry. Less obvious, perhaps, but no less important, has been the long-term effect of King Edward VII's sale, in 1901, of 60 000 bottles of vintage sherry judged 'surplus to royal requirements' – a gesture which caused the following comment from *Queen:*

> The business capacity of His Majesty has shown itself by ordering that sale, while the memory of his august mother is most vivid among us; for there is no doubt that, allowing for a certain quantity of the liquor going to the dealers, the greater part of it will find its way to the cellars of the *vieux* and *nouveaux riches,* who will offer it to their guests as a kind of historic beverage . . . the truth is that sherry has had its day even among connoisseurs of wine, and also among better class women . . . albeit that few of the latter could have given an adequate, still less a gastronomical, reason for preferring it to the French dry wines . . . such as Bourgogne Montrachet or Côtes du Rhône blanc. . .

One assumes that the last-named wine was not the bland potion currently sold under that label, but white Hermitage, which may indeed sometimes bear comparison with the greatest dry white wine of all.

But where would one now find a bottle of serious sherry? Or, for that matter, a bottle of the best white Hermitage? The answer is discreetly contained in the records of the royal auction. A certain Mr Berry, having quietly bid throughout the proceedings, carried home in triumph, at a price too appalling to disclose, the last nine dozen bottles. Part of the royal surplus thus found a temporary home in the cellars of a wine merchant who has remained to this day one of the few reliable purveyors of the drink which the royal liver could no longer tolerate.

I hesitate to sing the praises of Berry Bros and Rudd Ltd. Those who know the discreet shop in St James's Street, London SW1, will be appalled at the risk involved in publicising its existence. Those who do not know it are probably suffering from some moral deficiency – perhaps even from a lack of interest in wine – which must surely lead to a double charge of sacrilege against the writer who would share such precious information with infidels. However, the example set by Berry's is so important that I hope to be excused, if not for my methods, at least for their meaning. For Berry's is one of the few remaining businesses conducted entirely according to a moral idea, in which personal association and respect for the merchandise take precedence over anything that might be called a 'market force'.

The family concern, at present conducted by a Mr Berry of the seventh generation and by the current Mr Rudd, presides over one of the most remarkable of London's archives, recording the weights of distinguished customers who have sat on the black coffee scales in the front of the shop. This record of the tangible presence of famous men – of their momentary translation into an equivalent in groceries – has a strangely soothing influence. Peer and commoner, genius and lunatic, judge and criminal: all are reduced to a single measure, equalised at last, in their final transition from quality to quantity. Such is the genial influence of trade.

Like any institution dedicated to the equality of its members, Berry's presents obstacles to the uninitiated. Nothing stands in the window; no advertisement beckons to the passer-by or flatters his vanity. Nor, indeed, does the shop contain anything that could conceivably be bought or sold – no wine, no cigars, no merchandise of any description; only the old black scales, a few Windsor chairs, some antique desks and a collection of dignified empties set on mahogany shelves along the wall. It has the feel of a London club: the same deeply masculine sense that a comfortable arrangement, once discovered, should never be changed, and certainly not for the convenience of strangers.

In the courtesy of the staff can be discerned an equal refusal to yield to terms that have not been approved by the existing members. On one occasion, when the assistant had just fetched my order from the cellar, a bluff character barged through the door and loudly declared his interest in acquiring large quantities of wine for investment. Without shifting his attention from the single bottle of 'Good Ordinary Claret' that I had purchased on account, the assistant explained stiffly that the firm did not sell for investment purposes and besides had not the habit of dealing in the quantities required.

Once admitted, however, the customer is treated with exemplary concern, by a firm that manages to conduct its business as though totally indifferent to profit and loss. Its respect for the customer is matched by an equal respect for the quality of what is sold. Berry's continues to bottle many of its wines and, rare among major importers, retains its own office in Bordeaux. Its modest labels have remained unpolluted by classifications and resistant to the false expertise of the speculator. The resulting list contains more true bargains than any cut-price chain store, and is chosen with a love for the matter of trade that equals the firm's love for its manner.

From time immemorial Berry's has stocked a most extraordinary white Hermitage, and it is with this vintage that I now drink a toast to the old habits of commerce, habits which, properly guarded, may still resist the market forces which elsewhere have eroded them.

20 March 1984

Utopia and Conservation

When Sir Thomas More invented the name 'Utopia' – meaning 'nowhere' – he showed more respect for the sound of English than the grammar of Greek. But his meaning was clear: the political ideal which he described is not of this world – to which one might add, 'thank heavens'.

By the time William Morris came to retrace the steps of his saintly predecessor, 'Utopia' had become a term of abuse. Morris therefore entitled his political vision *News from Nowhere*, and proceeded to give (what socialists seldom give) a description of the earthly paradise, its temper, economy and institutions. The resulting piece of pie-eyed sentimentality would long ago have been consigned to the 'dustheap of history' had its author not established an independent reputation as a phenomenal creative genius and the greatest cultural conservationist of his time.

The Institute of Contemporary Arts is currently displaying a rag-bag of photographs, reproductions, films, sketches and collages, designed to set Morris's decorative achievements within the context of his social philosophy. At the same time, a conscious attempt is made to assimilate this philosophy to movements which are flourishing now and which share Morris's ultimate purpose – the overcoming of all that is harsh and alienated in the human condition.

Beside each page or pattern by Morris, therefore, the visitor finds some record of his supposed legacy. There is one photograph of E. P. Thompson haranguing the crowds at a CND rally, another of the massed resolute faces of his listeners; there is even a series displaying the 'literacy campaign' in Nicaragua, whose main purpose, it would seem, is to teach the peasantry to stretch out their arms in clenched-fist salutes.

In contrast to those scenes of human progress, collages, quotations and pictures display the grim reality of Thatcherite Britain, whose people, oppressed by monetarism, industry, tower blocks, sprawling suburbs, unemployment and countless other social ills (including inflation, lack of industry, lack of housing, compulsory employment) live out their days in groaning servitude. Every life-giving glimpse of Morris's wallpaper is paid for by a piece of this insulting propaganda, and every poetic fragment is neutralised by some smattering of semi-literate abuse.

The intention, one assumes, is to urge the visitor to embrace the same illusion as was embraced by Morris: to believe that the evils of modern society are uniquely due to the 'private ownership of the means of production'. It would suffice to arrange the world according to socialist principles in order to usher in the golden age of dignified labour.

The modern reader of *News from Nowhere* is likely to be struck by two features of Morris's paradise which distinguish it from the average socialist utopia. First, everything is produced according to exact aesthetic principles, by the most patient workmanship and with a medieval sense of the validity of ornament. Second, nature is properly tended, resources are guarded, and noise, pollution and squalor have been finally overcome. And if socialism could achieve those things, who would not be a socialist?

However, according to figures recently published in the *New Scientist*, the record of 'actually existing socialism' is far from encouraging. In France and West Germany, heavy industry emits into the atmosphere each year 66 tonnes of sulphur per thousand inhabitants. In East Germany, despite a lower industrial output, the figure is 251 tonnes per thousand. And in fact all the 'socialist' economies are far worse polluters than their West European counterparts. So much for the benign results of socialist planning.

Strangely enough, the incriminating figures are reproduced in the exhibition catalogue. Despite having been written by members of the socialist establishment, the catalogue contains an article by F. B. Singleton, in which the author hesitantly experiments with the truth. The organisers manage to disguise the figures, displaying them on the wall in the form of gross rather than per capita yields of sulphur. Nevertheless, however inadvertently, the truth is revealed. Socialist planning is not the friend of the earth, but its enemy.

The dreamy follower of Morris will retort: 'Those are not genuinely socialist economies, but only "socialist" in inverted commas'. To which Michel Foucault once gave the perfect reply: 'Those inverted commas should not be around the reality of eastern Europe but around the illusion in your head'.

Morris imagined that he could retrieve the purity of the medieval craftsman by undoing the work of capitalism, and like many socialists, he confused the inherent evils of industrial production with the accidental facts of ownership. Had he been closer to the spirit of Sir Thomas More, he would have recognised that the craft of the middle ages bears the stamp of human dignity not because it was part of a socialist plan, but because it was the outcome of religious devotion. And if there is a lesson to be learnt from the ICA's half-baked propaganda, it is that Morris's socialism, which rushed into the space vacated by religion, can never fill the spiritual vacuum that surrounds it.

27 March 1984

The Genesis of Anti-Semitism

The campaign to portray British society in general, and the Conservative Party in particular, as 'racist' is gathering momentum. If I were convinced that those most active in prosecuting it had any genuine attachment to British customs and institutions, or any genuine allegiance to the Crown, I should feel more sympathy. But when the very same people urge us, from the platforms placed at their disposal by such bodies as the GLC, to destroy the traditional school curriculum and to censor textbooks in the interest of 'multi-cultural' education, then I doubt their motives. For what is the purpose of such a change, if not to perpetuate the conditions which have traditionally led to racial conflict? What is 'multi-cultural education', if not a means to ensure that our minorities continue to identify themselves as such, and so remain detached from the political condition which surrounds them, enduring victims of an enduring disadvantage?

No doubt everyone is now thoroughly bored by this artificially induced hysteria. But one important aspect of it has been so far overlooked. At the risk of boring you further, I mention it here, since it seems to me to touch on the basic question of loyalty: the question of who is attacking whom, and why. I refer to the failure of the anti-racist lobby to concern itself with the principal form of European racism: hatred of the Jews.

In the aftermath of the Second World War it was quite normal for left-wing writers and politicians to denounce anti-semitism and to identify it as one of the 'reactionary' social movements over which socialism was beginning to triumph. The Soviet propaganda machine gave its muted support to these denunciations and was able effectively to conceal for two more decades the real fate of the Soviet and East European Jews under communism.

Circumstances, however, soon began to govern sentiment. In particular, the state of Israel emerged as the greatest single obstacle to Soviet policy in the Middle East and the natural instrument of American influence. The propaganda machine turned its annihilating rhetoric against Zionism, and Jews within the Soviet empire were now persecuted more openly as agents of the 'Zionist state'. Revulsion towards anti-semitic feeling was an obstacle to the new campaign against Zionism, and quietly 'anti-semitism' was dropped from the agenda. Its place was taken by 'racism', a concept in any case more adapted to Soviet strategic requirements in the Third World.

I would not wish for one moment to suggest that left-wing rhetoric is controlled from Moscow. But all rhetoric depends upon repetition for its survival, and it is therefore unsurprising to find so little mention of anti-semitism among those who advocate 'struggle' against fascism, racism, monetarism and the police state of Mrs Thatcher. That force which led to the greatest racial crime in history, and beside which the timid protest of the National Front seems like a mere carnival of the depressed, is passed over altogether, as though it had never really occurred.

'So much the better', you may say. 'So much the greater proof that we have emerged from that particular darkness.' However, I do not believe that we have. Even in England, it seems to me, the legitimising of 'anti-Zionism' has cast a shadow of anti-semitic feeling, so that belligerent or questionable actions by the state of Israel are condemned as expressions of this or that quintessentially 'Jewish' characteristic. I shall give an example. On 23 March the *TLS* published a most extraordinary poem – if so desultory a piece of prose could be called a poem – by Peter Reading, purporting to be an eye-witness account of an incident in the Lebanese civil war. A boy spatters a 'fat juicy jeep of Israelis' with machine-gun fire; a front-seat occupant oozes blood, the boy's fire is returned, and then:

> as from a colander, into the pavement streamed out the juices
> of the assailant, a slight soldier/homunculus. Well,
> nobody looks for a *motive* from these Old Testament shitters –
> thick hate is still in the genes. I learned the boy was aged 12.

Bad writing always hides more of its meaning than it reveals. Nevertheless the meaning of those last two lines seems clear: the Israelis (for who else could be referred to?) are 'Old Testament shitters' and thick hatred – presumably their hatred – is 'still in the genes'. Moreover, since clearly the duty of such vermin is to be fired on and patiently accept their extinction, they had no motive to retaliate.

To associate the Jewish religion first with excrement (in deference, perhaps, to Freud's theory of money love) and then with a hatred that is genetically determined – what is this, if not anti-semitism, in its pure, unreconstructed form? It is surely testimony to the changed climate of taste that such a poem should have found its way so innocently into the *TLS*. And even if the influence of these lines, worthy of the pen of E. J. Thribb, is likely to be minimal, I cannot escape the impression that the sentiment conveyed by them is echoed by many who lack Peter Reading's ability to discover its appropriate literary expression.

3 April 1984

The Fate of the Liturgy

When parliament in 1974 entrusted the Anglican liturgy to the Church of England, it hastened the process of disestablishment, whereby the national church has become one contending sect among many, distinguished only by the residual and largely unused privileges of its bishops. The most important consequence was that, for the first time in its history, the Church of England was free to ignore completely the wishes of its congregation, whose representatives in parliament could do no more than utter words of impotent dismay at the ensuing sacrilege.

The Book of Common Prayer – that priceless repository of Anglican emotion, whose inspired language joins together eternal destiny with an enduring, but temporal, political allegiance – this book, which had dispensed its sacred consolations through four centuries of social change, suddenly disappeared from the churches, to be replaced by 'Alternative Services' written in the fickle idiom of human liberation. C. H. Sisson (*PN Review* No. 2) summed the matter up in the following words:

> It was one of the great conquests of the sixteenth and seventeenth centuries that the Church commanded a language at once profound and familiar. Now, after immense deliberations, it injects trashy and unmeaningful speech even into the liturgy. There is no such thing as passing on profound truths in superficial speech.

Sisson was merely one among many distinguished writers, Christian and non-Christian, who joined the movement of protest against the new liturgies and who influenced parliament to discuss the matter again in The Prayer Book (Protection) Bill of 1981. This movement was not comprised only of disenchanted intellectuals, lamenting (to use the words of the Book which they defended) that 'there was never any thing by the wit of man so well devised, or so surely established, which in continuance of time hath not been corrupted'. Opinion polls, both here and in America, showed a majority of Anglican churchgoers to be in favour of the old service; spokesmen for the main political parties, university teachers and almost the entire national press agreed with them.

One section of the community alone seemed unpersuaded: the clergy of the Church of England. Only clergymen and their immediate associates were prepared to deny what was evident to most of their congregation: namely, that the language of the 'Alternative Services' (which rapidly became alternative only in name) is more profane than common and more suited to idle conversation than to prayer. It is a language which lacks both the sacred quality of liturgical utterance and the dignity of an experience consciously fought for and consciously shared.

It is to be supposed that the ordinary worshipper in the Church of England attends services not from some merely private enthusiasm, however evangelical, but from a desire to worship God in a way that also renews the validity of his earthly ties. Modern Europeans are historical creatures, weighed down by an indefeasible obligation to the unborn and the dead. They worship God easily only through forms and liturgies which enable them (in the words of a great Czech philosopher) to 'confess to history': in other words, to accept the bond which unites them with those who have vanished and with those who have yet to be. We should not be surprised, therefore, if the 'Alternative Services' have failed in their professed aim of filling the churches.

The Church of England derives its claim to liturgical authority from precisely those historical ties which attach its congregation to the Book of Common Prayer. After decades of vacillation there are signs that the Church is once more aware of this all-important truth, and prepared to be more generous towards those who live by it.

Six weeks ago the Archbishop of Canterbury published an article in the *Daily Telegraph* in which he upheld the indisputable claim of the Book of Common Prayer, arguing that 'no one ought to leave theological college without demonstrating a knowledge of the Prayer Book, and having experienced it in living worship'. The Archbishop's view was more recently echoed in a leader in the *Church Times* (29 March).

However, theological colleges, having largely rejected earthly authorities, including those essential to the continuance of a national church, are unlikely, without further prompting, to respond to such calls. There is a growing body of evidence that those who prepare men for the Anglican priesthood remain wedded to the 'alternative' services and to the view that the Book of Common Prayer is antiquated, merely because it is – like all religion – mysterious. Such a view is the enemy of liturgical utterance. It fails to see the true purpose of liturgy, which is to provide the language through which the sacred may be apprehended. If you doubt the value of such a purpose, then remember that it is only in such a language that a dying person can be consoled.

Tomorrow, however, a new Prayer Book (Protection) Bill will be given a second reading in the House of Lords. There is a faint hope that, on this occasion, parliament may respond to the pleas of Anglican believers and establish a select committee empowered to examine the fate of Cranmer's liturgy. And, when all is said and done, the fate of Cranmer's liturgy is also the fate of the Anglican Church.

10 April 1984

A Hominist Homily

There is no force more dynamic, more progressive, more avid for improvements than the force of human folly. Lest he should forget this, a teacher must repeatedly acquaint himself with books that he would rather eat than read. The other day, therefore, I shut myself away with a pile of feminist literature, and for some time my mind was numbed by what must be the most boring form of collective paranoia since Mussolini. Overcome at last, I fell into a deep stupor and began to dream.

I seemed to be in a London club, in a room heavy with tobacco smoke; all round me were smart City gentlemen. They had been drinking, and their voices rang out in a cheerful, boorish cacophony. One voice, however, thinner, higher, but more strident than the rest, made itself heard above the chorus. It belonged to a young man who wore a necklace in place of a tie and who was trying to win attention. Undeterred by the indifference of his neighbours, he raised his voice ever more loudly, until, taking advantage of a lull, he jumped from his chair, waved his arms and commanded the room in the name of justice to be silent. With a murmur of acquiescence, his astonished companions sank back in their chairs.

'Men', he cried, 'I address you as members of the largest oppressed class in the history of the world, victims of centuries of exploitation. The time has come to rise up against your oppressor. The time has come to rid yourself of your mistress, woman.' A few hands were raised in protest, but were at once turned towards the nearest glass of port.

'Look at yourselves: look at the devastation wrought in you by matriarchal society. Your work, your talents, your energies – all these are removed from you. For the sake of her and her children, your days must be sacrificed to humiliating toil. To provide her with home, comforts, pleasures, you must renounce all hope for a life of your own. By day you belong to your work; by night you belong to her, returning always in defeat from your little experiments in freedom to the prison that she has built from the product of your labour.

'Under matriarchal order, men are oppressed in their very psychology, subject to a jealousy more terrible than any force of arms. They must bend their projects, their actions and their thoughts in the direction imposed on them by woman. In every act they are subject to woman's morality, which scorns all tiny liberties and commands obedience to the law of home. Between the home where she commands you and the work towards which she compels you, only a few little crevices of freedom remain, and these too are threatened. Your lunches, your breaks, your business trips, all these are closely surveyed. In all your meetings and conversations you are exposed to her interruptions, her egoism and her domineering abuse. She has even pursued you to the door of your club, and now beats upon it, claiming rights of membership!' A mild protest arose, and the speaker leaned forward with an intenser stare. Strangely, however, the more intensely he stared at them, the less interest did his audience seem to show in what he said.

'Do not be deceived,' he continued. 'Do not think that our enslavement is merely external, a matter only of unjust institutions and unjust laws, which compel us to assume the burden of her maintenance. No, there is another slavery, an inward slavery, prepared for us in the most intimate encounter with our enemy, who withholds her favours until we offer the 'commitment' which she demands.

'This is the most sinister dominion of all. We can obtain sexual solace only at the cost of liberty. Pleasure, for us, is also the supreme sacrifice. We are the means to satisfy her sexual craving – a craving so voracious as to demand a life of sexual servitude. For woman, man is nothing but a sex object, whose own modest needs are ruthlessly exterminated in obedience to her vaster imperatives.

'What is to be done? The answer, I believe, is clear. We must found a true hominist movement. Men must organise themselves as a class, to effect a change in the basic structure of human society. We must abolish the means whereby the matriarchal order ceaselessly reproduces itself. We must abolish motherhood. Let their babies be produced in test-tubes and brought up in battery farms. Let them work as we do, and suffer as we do the weight of others' dependence. Let every burden be shared.

'There must also be a cultural revolution, an overthrow of the illusions which govern us. We must fight the ideology of the family, the ideology of commitment and marriage, the ideology of female privilege and male subordination, the ideology which assigns all work to us, all leisure to our enemy. . . .'

The audience was beginning to wilt. One gentleman had already slumped forward, his head resting on the table. Just as the speaker was beginning to announce the overthrow of the capitalist system and the final emancipation of mankind, however, the dozing gentleman suddenly started awake, and boomed out: 'Do you know – he reminds me of my mistress!'

At these words, I too awoke, and returned to the page which had defeated me. Its tone and language, I discovered, had been borrowed by my dream.

17 April 1984

C. H. Sisson: An Appreciation

C. H. Sisson was born in 1914 and celebrates his seventieth birthday on Sunday. His preference for plain initials over Christian names unites him with another generation of writers – T. S. Eliot, C. S. Lewis, W. H. Auden, F. R. Leavis – for whom the art of writing was no part of the cult of personality.

Like them, Sisson believes literature to be one of the few serious occupations of mankind. Like them, he sees the decline of literary culture as a social and political disaster of incalculable proportions. Unlike them, however, Sisson has achieved eminence late in life, long after the transformations which afflicted him have become established features of our social world. His warnings, therefore, are more like regrets than prophecies, and his melancholy verses have yet to be accepted for what they are; the distillation of a common loneliness.

Sisson was born in Bristol and brought up among working-class people, an experience which gave him a life-long distaste for the sentimental socialism of Auden, Spender and Day-Lewis. 'I could not help noticing', he writes, 'that it was not from a world I inhabited – which actually contained working people – that these three Saint Georges came riding to the relief of the poor. They came, it seemed, from what they represented as the closed middle class of "majors, vicars, lawyers, doctors, advertisers, maiden aunts" (their maiden aunts, not mine) whom they made a special point of denouncing. . . . When they spoke of the workers it was as if they were speaking of people in some far-off fairyland, or alternatively of a remote race of South Sea Islanders, or of a favourite breed of beetles.'

Under the influence of these upper-class intellects the Union of Bristol University anticipated that of Oxford and voted that it would not fight for king and country. Sisson was by then reading English and philosophy at Bristol, and was outraged by the combined foolishness and arrogance which had led to this self-destructive declaration. Later, on a visit to Nazi Germany, he had the dubious consolation of seeing that a fight for king and country would soon be necessary.

In the meantime he found a fuller and more lasting consolation in books, and in particular in T. E. Hulme – a writer who denounced not only the humanitarianism, but also the humanism of socialist intellectuals. Sisson began to acquire the two passions which were later to find in his writings such vivid and compelling expression: that for the Anglican

Church, and that for the 'hidden' constitution of Britain, of which the Anglican Church has been so memorable an emblem.

It was many years, however, before these passions bore literary fruit. In the meantime – after a brief spell in Germany and France (where he acquired a warm but critical admiration for the nationalist philosopher Charles Maurras) – Sisson joined the Civil Service. Except for three years in the army, he remained in the Civil Service for 40 years.

Sisson's army years were spent as an 'OR' – a status he retained throughout his short military career. His commanders were impressed by his knowledge of French and German, and therefore sent him to the Indian North-west frontier, under the impression that this was the place where such accomplishments could be of most service to the Crown. The experience is directly recorded only in a few poems and in a slight but amusing satire: *An Asiatic Romance*, published in 1953. Its effect upon Sisson was, however, as profound as anything that he underwent. He was stirred to the depths by the experience of political power deprived of the limiting influence of a civic culture.

For Sisson, wartime India, under the failing dominion of the British Raj, was the antithesis of Britain. In India power, violence and suffering were not made tolerable by the common understanding and moderating influence of civil institutions. Instead they were openly flaunted and ruthlessly anatomised, as though by the hand of a cruel surgeon. Sisson returned to England and to Whitehall with a deeper sense of the meaning of government and a deeper conviction that the art of government is more easily lost than acquired.

Until retirement in 1974 he stayed at his desk, rising to the rank of under-secretary, but largely unknown to the outside world. His outlook was too serious and too committed to allow him the luxury of a literary persona. Like Eliot in his bank, Wallace Stevens in his insurance office, Philip Larkin in his library, Sisson devoted himself to literature not for the sake of glory, but for the love of words and for the sake of truth. He belongs to that class of poets for whom the deficiencies of modern experience are to be remedied not by escape, but by application and by an honest but ironical confrontation with the real social world.

Sisson's first book of poems, *The London Zoo*, appeared only in 1961. His literary production hitherto had been mainly in the form of essays, in the *New English Weekly* and elsewhere. Both the tone and the content of these essays – now collected as *The Avoidance of Literature* – owe much to Eliot. In them he rehearses his attachment to the history, religion and literature of his native land, and in particular to the seventeenth-century divines who did so much to provide the language in which the idea of a national religion could be given cogent expression. For Sisson the great figures of the early Anglican Church – Donne, Herbert, Vaughan, Hooker – remain the teachers of modern Britain.

In *A letter to John Donne*, he exhorts the former Rector of Sevenoaks to

Come down and speak to the men of ability
On the Sevenoaks platform and tell them
That at your Saint Nicholas the faith
Is not exclusive in the fools it chooses,
That the vain, the ambitious and the highly sexed
Are the natural prey of the incarnate Christ.

And in a series of essays printed privately at Sevenoaks in 1967 he describes the 'historical church', the *Ecclesia Anglia*, 'with its tail of protestant sects fading imperceptibly into the great mass of what might be called the *prejudice of disbelief*', as the 'centre of political England'.

Not surprisingly, Sisson was one of the most prominent of the many writers who lent support to the recent movement in defence of the traditional Anglican liturgy – a liturgy saturated with that sense of historical community by which Sisson, along with so many of his countrymen, has tried to live. No doubt the failure of this movement has come as no surprise to Sisson, who writes always as though words are effective against the Philistine and the humanist only when used wrongly – and he would rather lose a battle then use words wrongly in the course of it.

The unfashionable nature of his opinions, and the frequently sour manner of their expression, caused his existence as an essayist to go for many years unnoticed. Two books, however, appeared in his early middle age and established his reputation as a writer of wide-ranging intelligence and great imaginative power. The first, *The Spirit of British Administration* (1959), remains the classic exposition of the nature and function of the Civil Service in a nation governed by what Enoch Powell has called 'prescriptive monarchy'. The second, the novel *Christopher Homm* (1965), is perhaps Sisson's masterpiece – the story of a working-class life, beginning with the lonely death of its protagonist and proceeding with excruciating exactitude towards his birth. This 'negative narration' is a striking technical achievement. It also has a powerful emotional effect, endowing Homm's arbitrary sufferings with the ineluctable logic of predestination. Maybe there is a certain cheating in this effect: the joylessness of Homm's life is as much a literary artefact as an honest observation. But Sisson cheats with such style as to disarm his critics.

Those two books marked the true beginning of Sisson's literary career.

Since then, thanks to the industry and support of Michael Schmidt, his devoted publisher, Sisson's reputation, as poet, critic and translator, has become secure. This week his *Collected Poems* appears, hard on the heels of the *Anglican Essays*, in which Sisson mourned so eloquently the vanished learning of his church.

Sisson is a shy and private man who lives with his wife in the small town of Langport, no longer troubled by the rigours of civil administration. His poetry now is faintly pastoral, his essays terse, sad and unreconciled. He continues to speak for the Anglican Church and for the idea of monarchy, but in an oblique and complex language, aware of the treachery of words. As early as 1939 he affirmed that 'bad writing is writing which expresses the politically manoeuvrable sentiments and is therefore part of the system of force which is government'. Sisson the writer has never been part of that system of force: his work, even at its most political, looks above the political process, focusing upon the enduring institutions which it is our duty to remember, and on the way of life which they contain.

In a powerful study of Walter Bagehot (1972) Sisson attacked in dismissive and often devastating terms the spirit of Victorian liberalism, the spirit that must have everything explained and which pours scorn on the incomprehension and simple veneration by which the mass of people live. 'The final point in the statement must rest', he affirmed, 'on a certain incomprehension, and incomprehension is the beginning of theology.'

Bagehot, to Sisson, was the representative figure of modern politics, the politics of economic man, for whom everything human must be measured in terms of the profit and the loss, and for whom mystery and piety are politically significant only because 'ignorant people' respond to them:

> Bagehot was a founding father of the apologetics of 'fact'. Clever, sceptical men of affairs, the class whose activity consisted in deceiving the others, saw, according to him, nothing else, and what the others saw was nothing. Facts were what Bagehot could use, to clear a way for himself in society, and to make money. They are likewise the weapon of the contemporary civil servant, to turn away wrath and to make a game so complicated that no one else can play it.

In such words, Sisson condemns both his own former profession and the illusions it presently serves. Over them he holds the banner of a spiritual inheritance, a solemn, sensitive Toryism, whose value is the greater because it cannot be made intelligible to such as Bagehot. By a strange irony of circumstance, Bagehot's tomb at Langport stands by

Sisson's garden, and the mortal remains of the Victorian egoist now nourish the vegetables of his modest detractor, who eats them frugally, but with relish.

19 April 1984

The Honeyford Case

The British political process is often praised as an example of the 'spirit of compromise'. Those who esteem this virtue are apt to forget another on which it depends: the refusal to compromise over the truth. Someone who turns from the facts has a motive to silence the opponent who draws attention to them. Thus begins the censoriousness and bigotry which have extinguished the spirit of compromise over half of Europe, and which may yet extinguish it here.

In the winter issue of the *Salisbury Review* an article appeared challenging the fashionable pieties concerning 'multi-cultural education'. Its author was Ray Honeyford, whose experience and education make it impossible for him to believe the nonsense put out by the Commission for Racial Equality (a government quango which survives by discovering racial conflicts where no one had previously noticed them).

Mr Honeyford is headmaster of a multi-racial school in Bradford. He must confront each day the fate of white working-class children, who constitute the 'ethnic minority' in a growing number of inner-city schools and whose educational opportunities are increasingly threatened.

He must take note of the large-scale absenteeism among Asian children, whose parents frequently send them to the Indian sub-continent during term time, in blatant disregard of the laws of England. He must encounter Asian parents who are determined to impose the values and attitudes of the Indian sub-continent on their children, and in particular to subject their daughters to restrictions which are incompatible with the practices of British education and which the left would condemn as sexist were they not imposed by people with brown skin.

He is brought into contact with the extensive propaganda against our schools and curriculum produced by people who despise our traditions of understatement, civilised discourse and respect for truth. He must deal with teachers who perceive the professional advantage of supporting multi-cultural education and of making race into the kind of 'high profile' issue that the sowers of discord would like it to be. He is asked to 'respond positively' to suggestions that he censor textbooks, that he give equal weight to Shakespeare and to the works of Linton Kwesi Johnson (author of the immortal *Inglan is a Bitch!*) and that he show no preference for standard English over creole or pidgin.

Mr Honeyford, with the natural instinct of the rational animal, recorded some of these experiences, drew attention to the problems presented by multi-cultural education, criticised the fatuity of fashionable solutions and presented, in British fashion, a sceptical conclusion. All of which is part of the normal operation of the spirit of compromise.

Mr Honeyford's article came, however, to the attention of the local National Union of Teachers, which saw an opportunity to display that concern for truth and evidence which has ever been the virtue of the teaching profession. It passed the following resolution, and broadcast it to the world in a 'Press Statement':

> We strongly condemn the views expressed by Ray Honeyford in an article in *The Salisbury Review*, winter 1984. We feel that these views contravene the local authority policies on race relations and multi-cultural education. In the light of this, we urge the local authority to take immediate action and remove Mr Honeyford from his present post.

Mr Honeyford's article discusses critically the local authority's policies; therefore he *contravened* them; therefore he should be sacked. This totalitarian argument is clearly of wide application.

More sinister, however, is the accompanying justification. By quoting fragmented sentences out of context, by treating foregone conclusions as though they defined the principles of debate, by misrepresenting evidence and invoking a spurious consensus, the NUT statement seeks to persuade its readers that Mr Honeyford is a man of bigoted 'racist' views, making 'offensive remarks about ethnic minorities', advocating a kind of educational 'apartheid' and wishing to 'poison people's minds against a fair and decent attitude to the question of multi-ethnic education'.

The attack was followed by another, in an article written for the *Bradford Telegraph and Argus*. The author (a member of the NUT) insinuates that Mr Honeyford *must* be a racist, since he has made no attempt to dissociate himself from another gentleman, who is. It is true that Mr Honeyford did neglect to dissociate himself from this other gentleman. He also neglected to dissociate himself from Adolf Hitler,

John Birch, Pol Pot and Ghengis Khan. Perhaps this was a culpable oversight. But does the author of the *Argus* article display, in his argument, a genuine concern for the truth and a genuinely educated intelligence? It is small comfort to learn that the only evidence that he ever received an education is that he too is a head teacher in Bradford.

Mr Honeyford's crime was to tell the truth as he saw it. In particular, he told the truth about Pakistani politics – something that the left will allow when justifying Soviet policy, but not when praising British institutions. For this truth he must be silenced. The ruthless bigotry of those who wish to silence him is matched by their contempt for education. For such people, the dismissal of a headmaster of proven ability is a small price to pay for his replacement by one who spouts the same ignorant rubbish as themselves.

24 April 1984

The Palumbo Case

The generation to which I belong experienced, during its formative years, one of the greatest catastrophes that the world has ever known in peace time: the rise of modern architecture.

Theoretically, of course, modern architecture has been in existence for some time. The Bauhaus, Mies, Fry, Le Corbusier and others had concealed, here and there in the landscape of Europe, meticulously crafted boxes to which pilgrimages were made, and before which mouths were opened to take in air or to let out gibberish. The Leninist ideas of the Russian Constructivists and the Bauhaus were taught in schools of architecture, and Le Corbusier's exhortations to tear down Paris and Algiers in the interests of hygiene were being studied by a younger generation of like-minded maniacs. On the whole, however, until the late 1950s nothing much had been done about it, and the occupants of our inner cities slept in relative tranquillity.

Secretly, however, architects and planners were preparing our doom. By a deft combination of aesthetic propaganda and hard economics, this anti-social fraction was able to win the support of influential people and to deceive the public for long enough to put its designs into operation. So effective was its publicity that when, at last, its members emerged into the open, seized control of our cities and shook them free of human significance, the public merely gazed on their work in mute astonishment.

The architects and planners were rewarded with honours and dignities, and the British public was told, in no uncertain terms, that anyone who complained at their enlightened refurbishing of the human condition merely revealed his ignorance. It was insinuated that the protestor had not read Loos or Giedion, had not studied with the appropriate reverence the surviving photographs of Mies van der Rohe's pavilion at Barcelona, had not understood the unanswerable logic of Le Corbusier, had not recognised that a facade is an act of hypocrisy and ornament a crime.

Slowly, however, a spirit of resistance was born. Long before the criminal destruction of Newcastle, the public had begun to suspect, behind the rhetoric of modernism, the real nature of the 'invisible hand' which guided it. People began to look askance at architects and planners, and to watch their movements more carefully.

At first there was little that could be directly done to impede them. The culprits had gained fortunes and titles, and were able to get their way in most matters that could be settled by the offer of a trip to Bermuda or a case of Lafite. Nevertheless, the British public experienced one of its periodic awakenings. It began to remember that it is governed not by men but by laws, and that the laws exist in order to curtail the power of those who have too much of it.

By the late 1970s the climate had changed. Planning applications were regularly resisted; old buildings, street plans and traditional scales were respected; facades, ornaments and soft materials were again acknowledged as the true vehicles of human significance. It was possible to repudiate the aesthetic of the modern movement without being drowned in ridicule. It was possible to praise Belcher, and Lutyens, and the other great masters of the twilight years.

It was even possible to utter (although in whispers) the most important truths of all: that architects and planners may not be necessary; that their universal interference in the building process has not necessarily been for the benefit of mankind. It was possible at last to breathe freely, in the knowledge that the 'masters' of the modern movement were all safely in their graves and that the lesson of their destructive egomania had been learnt.

At least so we thought, until a most extraordinary recent occurrence. Next to the Mansion House, in a charming corner of old London where Poultry and Walbrook merge with Queen Victoria Street, stands a beautiful cluster of Victorian buildings (some designed by Belcher) which enhance the medieval street plan with gay corners and skylines and exuberant detailing. Today a public inquiry opens into a plan put forward by Peter Palumbo (who has been steadily acquiring the necessary freeholds and leaseholds over a period of 23 years) to clear the area, abolish the medieval street plan, expose the drab flank of the Mansion House and construct a nightmarish square of windswept concrete dominated by a huge tower block, designed by none other than Mies van der Rohe, whose dead hand has ruled so successfully over the darkening of New York.

The danger is compounded by the fact that Mr Palumbo's motive is not profit but enthusiasm – the very same enthusiasm for the new, the exciting, the progressive, which speaks in such megalomaniac accents from the pages of Le Corbusier, and which we supposed had been interred with the bones of the modernists. In today's inquiry, therefore, battle is joined – let us hope for the last time – between the new spirit of conservation and renewal, and the old spirit of progress and destruction.

1 May 1984

The Abuse of Charity

'Love thy neighbour', said Christ; and 'Who is my neighbour?' came the prompt reply. Because there is no simple answer, Christ responded with a famous parable. The Samaritan extends his help to a stranger; but he acts under the impulse of compassion, and without a rational plan. Maybe he should have looked around first, lest there were some more needy victim? Maybe, by refusing their help, the priest and the Levite conserved it for someone more deserving? Maybe it would have been better to leave the victim to die, so as to draw attention to the plight of the oppressed peasants who had been driven to kill him? Maybe the assailants were terrorists, engaged in a 'war of liberation', and their victim a pampered member of the ruling class?

Political calculation, when it intrudes into the charitable motive, also destroys it. The clear obligations of the heart become clouded by the monstrous ambitions of the brain. The help we can understand and offer seems unreal; while the help which lies beyond our understanding, and for the sake of which we must take up arms in a never-ending struggle, seems uniquely worthy of our energies.

English law excludes political activity from its definition of charity. But, as the example shows, every act of charity may be given a political interpretation. Hence every charitable foundation may be 'politicised' by those who see no distinction between the relief of suffering and the 'struggle' for a better world. A most instructive example is provided by War on Want, a charity ostensibly devoted to the relief of poverty. Many who give money for this admirable purpose may be surprised at the organisation's own interpretation of its calling.

At War on Want's annual general meeting in 1983 the main speaker was a member of the central committee of Swapo and the theme throughout was that of 'struggle by peasants' and workers' organisations to overcome inequality and oppression' – and so on. It is not difficult, now, to interpret those expressions, or to understand what might be involved in War on Want's support for 'groups organising for change' and groups 'disseminating alternative news'. Nor is it hard to understand the real meaning of the general secretary's closing remarks, in which he emphasised the need to develop links with both the peace and labour movements, which he saw as War on Want's 'natural allies'.

As a matter of fact War on Want is extremely suspicious of the charitable motive, which, by relieving present suffering, perpetuates the *status quo*. It prefers the broader view and in particular the 'struggle' for radical social and political change. It often says as much. In 1981 it launched a campaign against unemployment that was justified by the then general secretary in the following terms:

> We realize that the unemployed do not want the old fashioned kind of charity handouts, paternalism and charities doing the job governments should do.

Old-fashioned paternalists who, like the Good Samaritan, step in and do the government's business only impede the process of political transformation to which the energies of War on Want are now largely directed.

War on Want gives active support to the 'people of Namibia' in their struggle against 'South African oppression' and to the 'refugees' who over the last few years have gathered in neighbouring Angola, very often with automatic rifles on their shoulders. And those seeking to help this cause are invited by War on Want to contact organisations that work for the violent overthrow of the present political order in Southern Africa.

The organisation was particularly active in Grenada, before the US invasion, and provided £250 000 for 'development' projects. A statement issued by the vice-chairman, regretting the overthrow of this revolutionary paradise, implied that the 'development' projects promoted by War on Want benefited enormously from the benign supervision provided by a single-party Marxist state. In a recent newsletter War on Want has declared that it does not provide emergency relief, 'but', it asks rhetorically, 'should we refuse to give urgent support when organizations such as Swapo or the Revolutionary Democratic Front in El Salvador ask us to do so?'

Someone who believes that the people of El Salvador will be happier under the rule of the 'Revolutionary Democratic Front' – as happy, say, as the people of Cuba – may wish to support this cause. But is it charitable? The answer to that question is provided by another: what if the belief is wrong? What if the people of El Salvador would be *less* happy after the Revolutionary Democratic Front has seized power?

The worth of the Samaritan's action was unquestionable. He sought not to change the world, but to relieve the suffering of one individual within it. He did not calculate the profit and the loss, nor did he need to: for what he did was good in itself and required no further justification. Can the same be said of the actions of War on Want? And if not, should it enjoy the privileges accorded to a charity?

8 May 1984

The Art of Motorcycle Maintenance

People need things, almost as much as things need people. The critical moment of their mutual support is the moment of breakdown. Suddenly, the object upon which everything depended – the car, the boiler, the drain or the dinner suit – is unusable, and you contemplate its betrayal in helpless unbelief. It is some time before you overcome your self-pity enough to recognise that its need is greater than yours. But where do you turn for the person who will assist it? This question, the most irksome faced by civilised man, is constantly posed by my pathetically dependent motorbike.

Time was when everything usable was also repairable: chairs, sofas, carts, hats, accordions, carpets – all were in a state of flux, as new defects revealed themselves and new patches were affixed to cover them. Objects entered the world of human users only to pass at once from Being to Becoming.

Repair was not so much a habit as an honoured custom. People respected the past of damaged things, restored them as though healing a child and looked on their handiwork with satisfaction. In the act of repair the object was made anew, to occupy the social position of the broken one. Worn shoes went to the anvil, holed socks and unravelled sleeves to the darning last – that peculiar mushroom-shaped object which stood always ready on the mantelpiece.

The custom of repair was not confined to the home. Every town, every village, had its cobbler, its carpenter, its wheelwright and its smith. In each community people supported repairers, who in turn supported things. And our surnames testify to the honour in which their occupations were held. But to where have they repaired, these people who guaranteed the friendliness of objects? With great difficulty you may still find a cobbler – but for the price of his work you could probably buy a new pair of shoes. For the cost of 15 digital watches you may sometimes find a person who will fix the mainspring of your grandfather's timepiece.

The truth is that repair, like every serious social activity, has its ethos, and when that ethos is lost, no amount of slap-dash labour can make up for it. The person who repairs must love the broken object, and must love also the process of repair and all that pertains to it. The modern motor vehicle is the subject not of repair, but of 'after-sale service', a euphemism implying that only the firm who made it can restore it, according to specialised procedures of its own and with a view to ensuring that it will never again be 'as good as new'.

Which returns me to my theme. Here and there you may still find places where the ethos of repair lingers, and where you will not be brushed contemptuously aside merely because your vehicle is of a model, a year or a character which falls outside some manufacturer's prescription. On Ladbroke Grove one such place still survives, a peculiar testimony to declining values, amid the planning blight of Kensal Town. Only the name – Hamrax Motors Ltd, in yellow plastic lettering – seems to unite this little Victorian terrace with its surrounding world.

Above the ruined classical mask of the shop, however, is affixed a more ancient label – an enamel plaque in royal blue, bearing the title 'Imperial Motors' – and beneath it, in the window, is a most extraordinary revelation of ancient customs. Where you would expect the chrome extravagance of the latest bum-tickler from Japan, or the polished props of the fetishist's day-dream, you find only inexplicable twists of wire, dusty fuses, disordered piles of sprockets, tappets, axle-nuts and cotter-pins. Beyond, in the deep interior, stand shelf upon shelf of smudged cardboard boxes, each labelled with some hieroglyph and each overflowing with small metallic parts.

In the cramped counter of this shop men congregate from every corner of England: steel-studded ton-up boys from Watford, gaberdine-clad Sunbeam buffs from the depths of Devon; solitary rallyists who have bumped themselves from Wales on farmyard bikes of their own devising. With infinite patience, the eccentric need of each is catered for: a chain link for an ancient single-cylinder Matchless will be searched out with as much concern as a complete gearbox for last year's Kawasaki. Indeed, the more recondite and intricate the job, the more the staff will welcome it, and problems of repair awaken interest proportionate, not to their profit, but to their rarity.

Hamrax Motors consists of three terraced houses knocked together, and every corner of the dark interior is given over to the storage of motorcycle parts, which are stacked on shelves and hung on the walls like votive offerings. To reach the workshop you must go out of the shop and down a flight of stone steps beneath an arch. This touching architectural detail, which once gave drama to the street below, typifies the shadow-filled grandeur of the Victorian slums. Alas, the rage for hygiene and social justice has left nothing standing, save only the patched fabric of Hamrax itself, sustained by the life-giving ethos of repair and by the sense that an Englishman's bike is his charger.

15 May 1984

The North London Polytechnic

The students at North London Polytechnic have discovered a member of the National Front in their midst. The discovery has been greeted with boundless enthusiasm by the local Socialist Workers' Student Society, the dominant faction in the Students' Union.

To come across a lone, defenceless member of the class enemy, a 'self-confessed Nazi', whose views are abhorrent to all decent people – what better occasion for a show of righteous intimidation? These bravoes have therefore issued a call to arms against 'the Nazi Harrington' and have (to use the fashionable euphemism) 'picketed' his lectures, in order to exclude him from the teaching to which he is entitled.

As a second-class citizen, Mr Harrington cannot appeal to the National Council for Civil Liberties. He has therefore, in the treacherous manner of the petit bourgeoisie, taken his case to law and sought an injunction. This cowardly assault on the right of students to organise against racism has led the Socialist Workers Student Society to denounce the law and all its works and to incite students to defy it.

A mild reminder from the director, Dr MacDowell, that large-scale disruptive action may lead to the closure of the polytechnic called forth the following retort: 'It is pure hypocrisy for MacDowell to talk of freedom of speech and freedom of agitation for Nazi Harrington and in the same instance threaten, by the closure of the polytechnic, the freedom of education of 7,000 students and their right to organize against Nazi's' (sic).

Clearly the fight for an education does not always leave much time to acquire one. The sentence is typical of a flood of illiterate and inflammatory leaflets from the Socialist Workers' Student Society, inciting the students of North London Polytechnic to crime. The interesting thing is that these professed opponents of discrimination and brutality have used every available measure of intimidation in order to ruin the career of a fellow student, while the 'Nazi agitator', instead of summoning his stormtroopers to the rescue, has merely petitioned the courts. One does not have to be a National Front sympathiser to wonder who, in this encounter, is the 'fascist'.

How is it that the Socialist Workers Party has been able, on this and many previous occasions, to disrupt the educational activities at North London Polytechnic? The answer lies with two institutions: the National Union of Students and the polytechnic's governors.

The NUS is a kind of government quango, through which taxpayers support 'permanent revolution' on the campus. It is not representative of student opinion, but nevertheless controls student funds and diverts them in whatever direction its student officers see fit.

The Students' Union at North London Polytechnic, which disposes of £200 000 per annum, uses the officially funded magazine *Fuse* as a platform for agitation and propaganda; the current issue even carries a full-page announcement inciting students to intimidate Mr Harrington, and gives the times of the lectures he is due to attend so that he may be 'picketed' off the campus. This is wholly typical of the way in which the Students' Union is able to abuse the control which the government has granted to it.

The behaviour of the Students' Union would matter less if the governors of the polytechnic had preferred academic principle to political expediency. However, they have shown no desire in the present dispute either to discipline the culprits or to protect Mr Harrington, or to prevent his having to have recourse to the courts.

This neglect of duty is by no means new. In March 1983 left-wing activists occupied part of the polytechnic, invited a representative of Swapo to address them, and set up a 'Palestine Liberation Workshop', a 'radical social work' seminar and a 'rave up' with women from Greenham Common. Those responsible were never disciplined. In October 1983 similar activists picketed a distinguished visitor whose views they found uncongenial. Again they were not disciplined.

The most disturbing recent case, however, concerns the award of degrees by the sociology department. HM Inspectors recently presented an unusually critical report on the sloppy and possibly biased teaching in this department and criticised the practice of circulating examination topics in advance – a practice which clearly threatens the element of unseen assessment, traditionally regarded as integral to a degree.

The Council for National Academic Awards subsequently advised the directorate that the practice must stop. At once a coachload of students descended on the council's head office and 'persuaded' the chief officer to withdraw his advice. The students returned to the polytechnic in triumph, waving in their hands the chief officer's letter of recantation. 'This', said their newssheet, 'is a powerful example of what united student activity can achieve'.

Those who would deny education to some, and make degrees easier for others, by 'direct action' have no place in an institution of higher education. Only by removing them can the governors show their concern for academic values and for the mass of students and staff who adhere to them.

21 May 1984

Representation and Election

Writing in the *Guardian* on 16 May, Peter Jenkins eloquently presented what might be called, 'the Tory case against Mrs Thatcher'. He argued that the present government has repeatedly acted in ways that either ignore constitutional conventions or threaten to destroy them. Toryism, he implied, is about balance – the 'checks and balances' of the constitution, and also the balance of social power. Throughout its history the Tory party has been concerned to limit the power of each dominant faction by bestowing an equal and opposite power on its rivals. Thus was established the tradition of Tory democracy, from which the present government has allegedly strayed.

Mr Jenkins gives as his principal example of this straying from tradition the move to abolish the metropolitan authorities. He sees the GLC, for example, as a part of the unwritten constitution of the kingdom, and the elections by which its high officers are appointed as essential to the process whereby the interests of the governed are represented before those who govern them.

The metropolitan authorities are, however, recent additions to the fabric of British government, and their growth has been persistently opposed by Tories of the old school. Lord Salisbury, for example, regarded the growth of the LCC (the predecessor of the GLC which he himself set up in a moment of folly) as a threat both to the autonomy of parliament and to the representation of the people.

The LCC seemed to Lord Salisbury to exemplify just the same concentration of irresponsible power as resided once in the cartels of manufacturers and now in the leadership of the TUC. The Tory attempt to curtail the powers of local government received a profound setback under the un-Tory government of Mr Heath, whose reorganisation of county boundaries in accordance with inscrutable bureaucratic imperatives created devastating opportunities for the 'rational' oppression of the British people. The GLC has been no exception to the process. All that has changed under Mr Livingstone is that the inability of parliament to represent the interests of the British citizen before those who pretend to speak for him has become a matter of public scandal.

To understand 'traditional Toryism' we must also understand the distinction between representation and election. In another, equally lucid piece of journalism, which appeared in *The Sunday Times* on 13 May, Andrew Stephen delivered a delicate analysis of the 'People's Republic of

Islington' (that 'bastion of democracy', as Mr Jenkins ironically described it). Mr Stephen showed that this largely working-class community had voted to subject itself to the whimsical government of middle-class radicals, whose claim to represent its interests is about as plausible as the claim of Mao Tse Tung to represent the interests of the Chinese peasantry. The radical barons of Islington represent the interests of their own class, and of whatever minority might temporarily seize hold of their fashion-ridden consciences. But they are unrepresentative of the community, not despite but partly because of the fact that they gained power by election. Had they been appointed they would have been answerable to those who appointed them. As it is, they are answerable in the short term to no one, and risk no more, in the long term, than a return to the irritated indolence whence they came.

To say as much is not to belittle democracy but to point to the reality of 'elected dictatorship'. Election can lead to representation only in certain conditions, and, at the local level, these conditions do not obtain. First, most decent citizens – who mind their own business, pay their rates and make limited demands on their neighbours – do not have time or energy to waste in local politics. Councillors are therefore chosen from the ranks of those with a special interest in controlling local funds and with the freedom and mobility to devote themselves to the electoral process. Their government is as likely to be representative of local interest as is the government of *Animal Farm*, following elections in which only the pigs can stand.

Second, elections are intelligible only when issues are clear. Hence prospective councillors posture as members of political parties, thereby importing into the local election the recognisable colours of national politics. It is as though two candidates for the chairmanship of a football club should stand one as Labour, the other as Conservative. The true Tory will vote Conservative; but his vote will bear no relation to his interests as a footballer.

Third, the two major contributors to local funds – central government and local business – are disenfranchised. Their money is purloined and redistributed without regard to anything other than the votes of those who receive it, so endorsing that persecution of the industrious (in truth, the world's most persecuted minority) which, in the eyes of the resentful, constitutes 'social justice'.

It is arguable that, in its highest form, representation can exist only in a court of law. But the historical constitution of parliament has endowed it with some of the character of a court of law, which imposes a strong condition of answerability on all those whom it appoints to high office. If powers of taxation are to be rightly used, they ought first to be restored to parliament. And it is this which parliament – in true Tory fashion – is presently trying to achieve.

29 May 1984

The Power of the Press

Macaulay described journalists as the 'fourth estate'. He was referring to the enormous power wielded by those who direct the flow of information. Most governments in the modern world, being unsure of their legitimacy, appropriate that power, so as to control the press 'in the name of the people'. But some governments, ours included, still permit journalists to gather information, and to publish it, without official approval. It is an inevitable consequence of free association that power accumulates in private hands; the only question, in this as in every case, is how to ensure that it is used responsibly.

The difficulty should not be underestimated. Journalists have the power to publish information damaging to individuals and to the national interest; they also have power to justify themselves, to beg questions in their own favour, to set up kangaroo courts in which they figure as prosecutor, solicitor, counsel, jury and judge.

Thus, by a scandalous deception, two investigative journalists from *The Sunday Times* recently obtained confidential information about the bank account of Monteagle Marketing Ltd. This information was then used to discredit Mark Thatcher over the so-called 'Oman affair'. Had such techniques been used by Mr Thatcher against *The Sunday Times*, the British public would naturally be reminded every Sunday of his fault and the inflated language of the Sunday editorial would be put through all the tricks of rhetoric so as to blacken his name. As it was, *The Sunday Times* decided to display its virtuous conscience to the nation. It would have been wiser, it admitted, not to have used a 'made-up' name in obtaining the confidential information. But 'this was a minor and probably unnecessary journalistic ruse; the journalists felt that they had to conceal their identities – a normal practice of investigative reporting'. The journalists did not use a false identity; they merely concealed the true one.

We, the journalists, have accused ourselves; we have defended ourselves; we have passed judgment; and we are right.

The Oman affair was a comparably mild example of the way in which politically motivated journalists can manufacture scandals and flatter themselves that, in doing so, they are discharging an indispensable public function. Fortunately there are still journalists courageous enough to prick the preposterous humbug of their colleagues, as John O'Sullivan did on this occasion (*Daily Telegraph*, 19 March). 'What could be more ordinary', he asked, 'than a father agreeing to be a co-signatory for his son's business bank account?' And yet this ordinary fact, precisely because it is confidential, can be 'exposed' and painted with all the colours of a sinister intrigue. It is however in everybody's interest that such ordinary facts be regarded as unpublishable, and most of all by those who have the power to publish them, the unscrupulousness to obtain them and the effrontery to posture, in consequence, as the 'conscience' of the nation.

The task of such people is simplified by *The Investigative Researcher's Handbook*, recently published by Stuart Christie, who advocates the use of false identities, false bank accounts, forged documents and doctored credit cards. He also finds a convenient justification, for those troubled by lingering scruples, in the need to 'expose and isolate those organisations and individuals whose will to power breeds and thrives on social and economic injustice'. In other words, investigative journalism is justified by the 'revolutionary morality' of Lenin, according to which the end always justifies the means, provided only that the end is socialism.

It is in the same spirit that Duncan Campbell has pursued his researches into the defences of the United Kingdom, tirelessly exposing information about American 'military installations'. Naturally, anyone who seriously believes that the presence of American bases in Britain presents a danger to the nation will wish to make publicity for his cause: such is Mr Campbell's right and duty. But some publicity is more dangerous than the threat which it purports to disclose. It needs little knowledge, either of the habits of terrorists or of the problems of strategy, to recognise that the constant broadcasting of classified information about military plant and installations could do irreparable damage to the national security, whether or not the information has been legally obtained

However, the politically motivated journalist who lacks either convincing arguments or the power to express them will always rest his case in information. And the more confidential the information, the more harm that is done by publishing it, the better it is for his cause. Information is the source of the journalist's power and the bond which secures him to his public. To expose what is confidential, while insinuating that some sinister force is attempting to hide it, always brings a massive personal bonus to the one who spills the beans. Not only does he confirm thereby his power to damage others; he also reinforces his favourite moral posture, as the heroic champion of the truth against the 'vested interests' that would suppress it. No matter that the victim is powerless to retaliate or is exposed to danger, no matter that the security of the nation is jeopardised. The end justifies the means, and the end is power – the power of those favoured by the journalists, and of the journalist himself as their glorious champion.

5 June 1984

The European Parliament

That most people are not interested in the elections to the European Parliament, have only the vaguest idea of that parliament's powers and duties and would not be able to tell a Euro-MP from a speak-your-weight machine has been lamented as yet another sign of the political ignorance of the British public. In fact, it is the sign of a strong and flourishing political culture, which refuses to take this body of pampered mediocrities as seriously as it takes itself. No doubt the Italians, having lost hope for a stable administration, have every reason to believe that they would be better governed from Strasbourg than from Rome. But their case is not ours. The worst thing that could happen to us, after centuries of stable government, is to be ruled from abroad by a parliament of Social Democrats, Euro-communists and hysterical radicals, moulded by cranky republican theories.

Unfortunately, however, the British public's contempt for the European Parliament is not shared by the opinionated classes. Always active, always vociferous, always in search of an opportunity to try out their harebrained schemes for human improvement, nothing seems to them more likely to bring lasting benefits to mankind than a parliament entirely composed of people like themselves. This is the real source of the popularity of Euro-politics among the radical middle classes.

In the House of Commons such people encounter two important obstacles to their schemes. The first is the British constitution, in which unified sovereignty is wonderfully combined with diversified power. The second is the duty of representation, which obliges members to give up their egomaniac ambitions and attend to the pension of Mr Higgins, or the passport of Mr Patel. Constitution and representation take the fun out of politics, and neutralise some of its power.

Euro-politics, however, is free from those constraints. To the British public the European Parliament is a joke. But to its members it is fun – well paid, irresponsible fun – and with marvellous opportunities for social and political scheming. Only one thing is lacking, and that is power. Without power the European Parliament is a harmless institution, in which second-rate politicians are paid comfortable salaries to stay out of mischief and count themselves kings. But the radical contingent wants power and will be satisfied with nothing less.

The Italian radical Altiero Spinelli has therefore devised a scheme which will enable him and his kind to enjoy in Strasbourg the power that they could never wield in Rome. This is the treaty to establish the European Union, soon to be voted upon, which would render our loss of sovereignty permanent and irreversible. Some states – Italy included – never had much sovereignty to lose. But for the British citizen this treaty will, if signed, finally destroy his political culture, by destroying the centuries-old artefact of allegiance to the Crown.

The treaty sets up a new political entity – the Union of Europe – with 'autonomous powers' to achieve monetary, economic, political and fiscal union. It will be a sovereign body, entitled to redistribute the resources and the reserves of the member states in obedience to the whims of a 'Commission' and its president. Once the union is established, member states will lose autonomy in almost every matter from taxation to social welfare. The union's laws will take precedence over national laws, and it will take positive initiatives to break down national barriers.

Its aims go far beyond the economic requirements of a 'common market'. Indeed, they include measures of a profoundly political kind, calculated not to further free exchange, but to stifle it. Thus Article 56 assigns extensive duties to regulate the social policy of member states. It aims to create 'Union-wide collective agreements' between trade unions and management, 'worker participation' in industry and 'equality between men and women'. And if free trade gets in the way, so much the worse for free trade.

Of course none of this is very well worked out. The half-baked quality of the treaty can be seen by comparing Articles 46 and 47. The first proposes a 'homogenous judicial area', in order 'to fight international forms of crime, including terrorism'. The second insists that 'the Union must (note 'must', not 'will try to') attain within a period of two years . . . the abolition of personal checks at frontiers'. In other words, we must open our frontiers to the terrorist populations of Paris and Rome. This invocation to drop our weapons and fight with symbols is typical of the whole spirit of the treaty. The Chamber of Mediocrities at Strasbourg would rather create ineffective powers against terrorism than leave effective powers in the hands of sovereign bodies other than itself. Indeed, it is impatient with all forms of national sovereignty and rides rough-shod over every true historical allegiance in pursuit of its dangerous purposes.

If it is allowed to fulfil its ambition, Euro-politics will be the death of Europe. And every vote cast in an election to the European Parliament fuels its illusion of legitimacy. The British response is therefore the right one. For you can be sure that, whoever you vote for, he will believe in the power of the institution to which he aspires. And that is the belief which threatens our independence.

12 June 1984

In Praise of Hayek

'We are ready to accept almost any explanation of the present crisis of our civilisation except one: that the present state of the world may be the result of genuine error on our part, and that the pursuit of some of our most cherished ideals has apparently produced results utterly different from those which we expected.' So wrote Friedrich von Hayek in 1944, reflecting on the common structure, common belligerence and common cruelty of the totalitarian systems which had plunged the world into war.

Hayek argued that the uncontrolled destruction of the world which began in 1939 was the result of a nearly universal attempt to control human destiny. By uttering such a thought at a time when intellectuals were calling not for less but for more social control, Hayek established his reputation as a shocker. He shocked, too, with his demonstration that the similarities between 'fascism' and communism are far more significant than the differences, and with his belief that socialism contains the seeds of totalitarian government precisely in its ideals and not, as its apologists say, in its imperfect application.

Hayek's distinctive contribution to political thought rests, I believe, in two complementary arguments, one directed at the theory of socialism and the other at its strategy. Neither argument has been effectively answered by socialists, who, taking comfort in the fact that they, unlike their libertarian and conservative critics, have a rational plan for the improvement of society, have consistently refused to see that they are criticised precisely for their belief that social problems might be solved by a rational plan.

Hayek inherited his first argument from the men who had taught him at the University of Vienna – Ludwig von Mises and Eugen von Böhm-Bawerk. Mises claimed that the socialist attempt to achieve a rational allocation of resources inevitably brings about the destruction of the price mechanism, and therefore of the knowledge required for economic decisions. Hayek went further, arguing that the information contained in the price mechanism cannot be collected by any central agency, not because it is too complex, but because it resists translation into a plan.

Economic knowledge is given to us only in use, displayed and preserved in countless daily transactions. Unhampered markets transmit this knowledge, which is otherwise irretrievably dispersed. For, being at once practical and social, economic knowledge is the property only of society as a whole, and is no more capable of existing as a plan than is the knowledge how to play a good game of football.

Hayek's development of this argument is remarkable in two ways. First, he defends the market economy not as a realisation of human freedom (though it *is* that), but as the true source of necessary information. The incompetence of socialism is 'epistemological'. Socialism deprives us of the very knowledge which its projects require. By being 'rational', it ceases to be reasonable. Second, Hayek extends the argument far beyond the economic sphere, to produce a theory of 'spontaneous order', recreating in modern form Burke's defence of 'prejudice' against the enlightened rationalism of the French revolutionaries. Thus, just as the rational plan is incompetent to deal with the minute problems of economic distribution, so too, Hayek argues, is statutory legislation incompetent to resolve the constantly evolving conflicts between individuals.

Of course a modern state needs central legislation, just as it needs an economic policy. But, Hayek argues, the purpose of centralised devices is to recreate, in unpropitious conditions, the 'spontaneous order' of peaceful co-existence, and the knowledge of ourselves and each other which that order contains. The purpose, in other words, is to redress the balance against Reason in favour of reasonableness.

Hayek's second major argument concerns not the aims of socialism, but its methods, and in particular its attempt to beg all questions by the manipulation of language. In defending the market economy Hayek uses terms which do not feature in socialist polemics. The socialist speaks of 'capitalism' and redescribes the world in terms of a universal opposition between capitalism and socialism – as though all human life were determined by the 'ownership of the means of production', and as though political institutions had no reality except as the extension of economic control. Such language reinforces the foregone conclusion and prevents discussion of the real choices which lie before us.

In a similar way, Hayek argues, the socialist has reinterpreted the major problems of moral and political thinking by the use of devices which, whether or not dishonest in intention, are systematically mendacious in their effect. Instead of freedom, socialism offers 'economic freedom'; instead of democracy 'people's democracy'; instead of justice 'social justice'; and instead of 'peace', the 'peace with socialism' of Leninist propaganda. At every point of disagreement the socialist expropriates the question. The first task of his opponent is therefore the redemption of language and its restoration to its rightful place as the vehicle of truth.

Hayek's arguments are at every point contestable. But his devotion to that task, and the insight with which he has placed it before us, have justified his reputation as one of the great political thinkers of our times.

16 June 1984

On the Eating of Fish

Increasingly, Englishmen spend the summer not at the seaside, but in the country. For pastoral sentiment forms the rhetoric of urban life, and the person whose daily horizon consists of walls and chimneys imagines a countryside beyond them, into which he will soon be released, free from man-made squalor and man-made anxiety.

Pastoral sentiments are to be resisted, with the same fervour as pacifism, vegetarianism and wholemeal bread. For they encourage us to forget the truth, which is that nature too is man-made. Some say (though they are a scholarly minority) that it was made by Theocritus and Virgil. Others blame nature on the Dutch landscape painters, others still on the Augustan poets. Personally, I hold the farmers responsible. It is they who manage this expensive tapestry. In particular, they support the animals, which provide the main visual delight in any country scene. With their discreet munching and rustling, animals transform the inert cloth of green into a cloak of living movement.

The cows, sheep, hens and horses owe their comfortable existence to man. So too do wilder and more colourful things. Pheasants, partridges, ducks and hares all take their lives from the men who kill them, and who take trouble so that they might survive. Vegetarians and other animal-haters detest this symbiotic harmony. But they should remember that the hunter threatens only the individual creature in his sights, while they threaten the species.

Food has become a moral issue. We are told repeatedly that everything we eat is bad for us. Such speculations are impious and selfish. Life, too, is bad for us, and if we wish to live well, we should live for others. Eat, therefore, that others may live. Eat animals – as many animals as you possibly can – so as to fulfil your duty to the great chain of being.

But this brings me to a problem that has yet to be properly solved: the problem of fish. Those Englishmen who still spend their holidays by the seaside do not take pleasure in the life beneath the waves. Indeed, their enjoyment would be greater if the sea were dead. Realising this, they eat not fish and chips but fried chicken, hoping that the vast quantities of fish meal on which the battery hens are fed will make a greater inroad into the remaining maritime fauna. Killing fish would of course be a help to fish, if only we could increase their chances of survival. But we cannot, so that this turning away from fish and chips towards fried chicken offers a threat not only to our last remaining national tradition, but also to the life of the sea.

Or so I used to think. I therefore drew the conclusion that eating fish is wrong. And I had the support of British fishmongers everywhere, whose stalls bear witness to a distinct lack of enthusiasm for anything that emerges from the water. Bland white tablets divorced from their anatomical meaning, headless flakes of muscle, yellow fishcakes, oily brown kippers looking like a pair of dustman's gloves – such sights testify to a profound loathing for the life of the deep and a desire to return all scaly, slimy things to the place whence they came.

But the problem is not so easily solved. There is another reason for eating, besides the fact that it gives support to nature's lower orders. Wine cannot stand alone; it needs food as its moral foundation. Fish is the only possible accompaniment to white burgundy, and fish must therefore be eaten if white burgundy is to be drunk. Not any fish, however: not the denatured artefact of the English fishstall, but fish in all its natural horrendousness, with grinning jaws, bulging eyes and the full carnival of colours that plays such an inexplicable role in the fashions of the deep.

Overeating these creatures does not ensure their survival. But the human species justifies its existence by its inventive powers. We may soon discover ways of helping the John Dory, the grey mullet, the hake and the scallop, as we have helped the partridge and the hare. We will have the motive, however, only if we continue to eat fish. Perhaps, therefore, eating fish is as much a duty as eating animals. For those who appreciate white burgundy, it may also be a pleasure.

That last remark is slightly contentious. I conclude, therefore, with a recipe for a dish which provides the perfect accompaniment to a fine old Meursault. Take two heads of hake. (The fishmonger will have thrown the vile things into the waste-bucket.) Turn them into a stock, using fennel, onion, celery, lemon juice and Chablis. In the strained stock you must then simmer (for no more than five minutes) six scallops and 2 lb of monkfish. Since monkfish generates a lot of water, leave it to drain into the stock. Then reduce the liquid, thicken it with a white roux, add six capers, some green peppercorns, salt, fresh basil and double cream. Cut the fish into mouth-sized pieces, cover with the sauce (which must be as thick as treacle) and bake for the least possible time in a pie, made with short pastry into which you have incorporated a quantity of flaked almonds. Fortunately, children hate this dish; it will therefore be enough for the whole family.

26 June 1984

On the Teaching of Teachers

Complaints against the teaching profession are frequently unjust, blaming the teacher for the unteachable child. The majority of children will be increasingly unteachable, however, until the day that television is outlawed. Only then will children again need hobbies, books and conversation – the three indispensable stimuli to learning. Meanwhile our only hope is that television will be entirely taken over by left-wing propaganda, thereby becoming so boring that the intelligent child will cease to take an interest in it.

The educational benefit of this outcome will depend on the supply of good teachers. And that will depend on how teachers are taught. If there is a single major cause of educational decline apart from television, it lies here – in the deficient education of the teacher. Some blame the teacher training colleges, many of which were founded or expanded in the late 1950s in response to the population explosion. But this too would be unjust. Teachers acquire their education also at polytechnics and universities. Why then do so many of them seem incapable of grasping the first educational idea?

The answer lies, I believe, in the tendency to teach 'education' as an academic subject rather than a skill, a practice displayed in the BEd degree and in the Graduate Certificate of Education. Only in one thing are the teacher training colleges to blame, which is in their frequently repeated complaint that university graduates were less qualified to teach in schools than their own alumni. This complaint reflected the knowledge that only those who could not get a place at university would go to a training college, and the burning envy which such knowledge inevitably nurtures.

Coming as it did when envy, or egalitarianism as it is more politely known, was a real political power, the complaint was immediately effective. It was decreed that the colleges could award degrees in 'education' and also that no university graduate should be allowed to teach in a state school without having first spent a year at some accredited institution, studying for the 'graduate certificate'.

The latter decision had two important consequences. First, it placed an obstacle before the good graduate. The more he loved his subject, the more impatient was he likely to be with the pseudo-academic nonsense that he was now required to ingest if he was to become a teacher. And the more he loved his subject, the better his degree and hence the better his chances for a job outside teaching. Consequently, the single most important qualification that a teacher could have – love of a subject, and the resulting ability to make it interesting to others – ceased to be a qualification for teaching.

The second important consequence was the provision of a period of diseducation in which, under the fraudulent guise of academic study, potential teachers could be indoctrinated in the new approach to the classroom. They were to study ludicrously fragmented subjects such as the psychology of education, the sociology of education, the philosophy of education – all of which can be used to convey the political attitudes judged appropriate to the new kind of schoolteacher. In particular, all proved useful in promoting the prevailing egalitarian superstitions: the hatred of grades and examinations; the idea that 'social class' is both an evil in itself and perpetuated by traditional modes of education; the idea that education should be 'relevant' to the social context of those upon whom it is inflicted.

All those shibboleths were given a new authority and handed out to teachers as a necessary part of their initiation into the art of teaching, further undoing for many of them the only certainties that really matter: the certainty that the subject which they really know is for that reason worth teaching, and the certainty that there is a real distinction between those who are good at it and those who are not.

Once established, the practice of diseducating teachers could not be easily overthrown. Institutions such as the University of London Institute of Education began to grow, providing lucrative prebends to academics who had been unable to make their mark in any central area of their disciplines, and generating a body of self-styled experts whose influence in the world of education increased proportionately as the influence of genuine and dedicated teachers declined. Schools and colleges were soon intimidated by this factitious expertise. And ministers began to appoint 'educationists' to committees of inquiry, in order to answer the charge that those who 'really know' about education have not been consulted in this or that matter of policy.

The truth is that those who really know about education are to be found in classrooms, labouring against the odds to inculcate that passionate concern for irrelevant information which is the true sign of an educated mind. Increasingly, such people are being driven from the state schools into the 'private sector', where they may yet find refuge from the persecutory ambitions of those who resent their influence.

But not for long. The force that drove them from the place which was rightfully theirs will also destroy those 'centres of privilege' where they have taken refuge. And it will be given the seal of approval from expert 'educationists', whose 'hidden curriculum' has aimed at just such an outcome.

3 July 1984

The New Class

In an interview, the late Michel Foucault once remarked that 'anything can be deduced from the general phenomenon of the dominance of the bourgeois class'. It would be truer to say that, for Foucault, the dominance of the bourgeois class could be deduced from anything. All around him – in laws, institutions, human relations, in language itself – he saw the unmistakable marks of bourgeois dominion. The very same power which oppresses the inmates of the 'bourgeois' prison rules also in the madhouse and the clinic. Everywhere languish the 'victims' of bourgeois society, who have paid with their souls for the upkeep of a 'normality' which they cannot share.

Foucault's insights were not hard-won. For it is a tautology that human relations are also human powers, and to attribute these powers to the bourgeoise is to utter no more than a ruling cliché, whose survival value is due not to its truth, but to its comforting mendacity. For who, in the last analysis, belongs to this bourgeois class, the power structures of which everywhere surround us? The only plausible answer is 'everyone', including Foucault.

In the interests of science, therefore, I offer a narrower definition. The bourgeois, I propose, is a city dweller, who does not engage directly in production but occupies some administrative position. He earns a salary rather than a wage and depends, however indirectly, on the covert taxation which sustains the modern city. By virtue of his skill he is both socially and geographically mobile.

Now we are quite familiar with this character. He is frequently rootless, liberated, individualistic and impatient with customs and traditions which block his access to power. Indeed – and here we may agree with Foucault – power is, for such a creature, a more precious commodity than it is for the average worker or farmer.

Living as he frequently does in a state of spiritual insecurity, the bourgeois is anxious to remake the world in his own image. He often wishes for a 'politicised' reality, set on the path of 'progress'. For only in such a mobile, uprooted, forward-looking world would he cease to be in conflict with the 'normality' that surrounds him.

The revolutionary supposes that it is the upholder of established things who is the representative of bourgeois values and bourgeois power. On the contrary, it is the revolutionary who is the true bourgeois, and it is with the triumph of revolution that power is finally (and 'irreversibly') transferred from the worker and the farmer to the urban middle class. Only then, as Engels said, does the government of people give way to the administration of things. (In truly revolutionary government people *become* things.) The nature of bourgeois power can therefore be most clearly seen by a study of the new style of city administration.

City administration is increasingly carried on by professionals, with a career in meddling and with little inclination for productive labour. They are happy to benefit from others' taxes, provided only that they can also use those taxes to initiate change. Little in the surrounding order pleases them, and traditional values – which testify to attitudes resistant to their reforming purposes – excite their heartfelt contempt.

An example is the Bourgeois Republic of Haringey, which has begun to devote its extensive powers of taxation to the establishment of a new social order, unrecognisable to anyone who would identify himself as merely British. The Women's Committee has been particularly active in imposing the bourgeois ideology of liberation on Haringey's lower orders. Its measures range from the introduction of contraceptive machines into women's lavatories to the recommendation of new sex laws, including the repeal of the offence of living off immoral earnings and the introduction of a wholly new crime, whereby the bourgeois power can intrude into the privacy of every home to ensure that 'emotional coercion' (more politely known, perhaps, as marriage) should not override the demands of sexual liberation.

Most interesting, however, is the foreign policy of the Bourgeois Republic. This requires everything from the establishing of support groups to the sending of delegations. One delegation has gone to Grenada, in support of the dispossessed revolutionaries, and another to Cyprus, to give credence to an ignorant condemnation of the new Turkish Cypriot state. The local Turkish Cypriot community has since been excluded from its customary place at Haringey's Multicultural Bookfair and will have no say in the running of the Cypriot Community Centre. Such is the effect of the new administration, which, wishing to replace the British spirit of community with something more universal, more rootless, more impeccably bourgeois, merely aligns itself with primitive parochialisms that prevail in foreign parts.

10 July 1984

The Triumph of Nothingness

The *Listener* has recently carried a series entitled 'The Return of Grand Theory', introducing the reader to such thinkers as Gadamer, Foucault, Habermas and Althusser. Interestingly, half the articles either begin or end by protesting that the thinker in question is *not* an exponent of grand theory, or indeed of any theory at all, while judging him, all the same, to be of supreme intellectual importance.

Reading these articles came as a depressing reminder of the ease with which intellectual achievements may be discarded. Anglo-American philosophers are constantly reproached for not considering the works of Gadamer et al, when the truth is that we *have* considered them, and judged them to be largely worthless. It sounds arrogant to say it, and would that Russell were alive, that it might be said more rudely. But, so that it shall be on the public record, I shall say it now.

Most of the thinkers urged upon us as 'correctives' to our Anglo-Saxon parochialism are, in my view, charlatans of the first order, who prefer paradox and posturing to the hard-won insights of philosophical argument. Their reputation is derived from two extraneous circumstances: first, their gobbledegook, which offers to the second-rate academic an impenetrable cloak of false expertise; second, their conclusions, which are almost invariably 'subversive of the established order', in a way that dignifies the gestures of armchair rebellion whereby the academic reminds himself that he was once alive. In short, they provide to the intellectually balding a dashing wig of long hair.

Consider Althusser, the most influential and the most difficult-seeming of the grand theorists. A philosopher in a British university would probably fail an examinee who wrote like this:

> This is not just its situation *in principle* (the one it occupies in the hierarchy of instances in relation to the determinant instance: in

society, the economy) nor just its situation *in fact* (whether, in the phase under consideration, it is dominant or subordinate) but *the relation of this situation in fact to this situation in principle*, that is, the very relation which makes of this situation in fact a *variation of the – 'invariant' – structure, in dominance, of the totality*.

A British academic would try to teach his students to see that such a passage not only says nothing, but is also *designed* to say nothing. From blocks of abstractions it erects an impassable barrier, behind which its nothingness may be concealed. Althusser's *For Marx* is composed entirely of such boxes of fortified emptiness, and it is not surprising that his disciples can agree only about the meaning of the title: Althusser is very definitely for Marx, not against him. The depressing thing is that, had he been against Marx, he would have been greeted with the derision that he deserves. Only the assurance of his impeccable political credentials enabled him to succeed; but that alone was sufficient.

The style of the charlatan is a style without hesitation. Seldom in Althusser's text will you find words like 'perhaps' or 'possibly', nowhere will you find any serious engagement with points of view other than those approved by the author. Althusser defers to only one other human being, but his deference is total and idolatrous. That human being is Marx, and Althusser impresses on his reader that *Capital* has the status of a sacred text, which can be understood only by those who already believe it. 'It is not possible to read *Capital* properly,' he writes, 'without the help of Marxist philosophy, which must itself be read, and simultaneously, in *Capital* itself.' In other words, those who are against me do not understand me, and those who understand me know that I am right. The sentiment, like the language, is one that a British philosopher would regard himself duty-bound to subvert.

I do not say that Althusser's text is entirely without theory. But as he says, 'this theory is the materialist dialectic, which is none other than dialectical materialism'. The neophyte, contemplating such utterances, is likely to be overcome by a certain awe. They have the same vertiginous effect as Stalin's pleonasm: 'the theories of Marx are true because they are correct'. Indeed, the more tautological an utterance, the more does it induce that state of readiness which is the prelude to unquestioning faith.

Althusser shows how gobbledegook may be regarded as wisdom, so long as it has a left-wing tone of voice. Indeed, gobbledegook like Althusser's, which shrouds left-wing dogma in an impenetrable darkness, will at once be given a place of supreme academic authority. Enclosed by Althusser's dark, the dogmatist is protected from every opposition, consoled in the belief that he cannot be threatened by that which he has learned not to see. If we use Althusser's language, then the possibility that Marxism might be mistaken cannot even be stated! Thank God that some British academics still regard it as their duty to frame their arguments in a language of which their opponents might equally avail themselves; and try also to open their students' eyes to the reality of disagreement. But for how long will their efforts be successful if the 'grand theorists' dominate the syllabus? I wonder.

17 July 1984

On the Meaning of Holidays

Holidays were once holy days, in which people attended to matters more serious than work. Some were put aside for penitence, others for rest. If people travelled during holy days it was on a pilgrimage, to some place made sacred by history and prayer. Festivals were not tourist attractions but local celebrations, like the Sienese Palio, designed to display, in heightened form, the spirit of a place to those whose place it was. Through these obligatory days of rest man conquers time, dividing the week and the year and imposing an order that is fitted to his purposes. He also divides the world into significant places and reinforces the local attachments whereby life is renewed. A place is holy because people make it holy, with customs, ceremonies and monuments that mark it out from the surrounding land.

In a holy place the pilgrim confronts God in concrete and intelligible form, and eternal truth becomes a story, inseparable from a space and a time. Hence people worship God through the intermediary of saints and prophets. For our experience of the holy is an experience of *this* world, or rather of the presence in this world of meanings which transcend it.

Monks and nuns sacrifice themselves for the upkeep of holy places. Because of their devotion, the landscape is marked by prayer; and a landscape from which they have been banished is peculiarly sorrowful, with no meaning other than the senseless reproduction of the human species. Hence people like the English, who live in unsanctified places where only architecture bears occasional witness to things more serious than work, have a peculiar need to travel in the summer. Such is their mental confusion, however, that they suppose themselves to be seeking only the sun. Their skin changes from light to dark and their hair from dark to light, and to many eyes this seems like the meaning of the exercise. To look for religious purposes in the movements of a tribe whose holidays are dictated not by their churches but by their banks is surely fanciful. And besides, the most serious among them, who wander from church to church and monastery to monastery, do so, they say, only for the sake of culture.

Their behaviour, however, contradicts their own self-understanding. On entering an Italian gallery most Englishmen wander insensibly past the pictures towards the windows, from which they can observe the pantiled rooftops, the cool dense alleyways, the crumbling campaniles, of a place in which others are content to live without vacations. They are rejuvenated by the sound of bells, which mark the hours and which call the faithful constantly to prayer. The experience which they remember is not the momentary surprise upon confronting a fresco that they already know from a thousand reproductions, but the smell of stale incense, the glimpse of priestly cloth in a sacristy, the clean vestibule of a *pensione* kept by nuns. Such an experience contains, in embryo, the meaning of pilgrimage. For a second you confront the reality of prayer, in a place 'where prayer has been valid'. The art which draws the English pilgrim to the Italian town is indeed not the cause of its beauty but the effect of it.

This hidden source of rejuvenation is not merely Christian. Sacrifice which is truly local is also truly universal. A piece of transitory English flesh may therefore be as deeply stirred by the temple gong or the muezzin, as by the angelus bell or the lonely trumpeter on the tower at Kraków. These sounds all remind us of home: of the home that others have created, and which we too must create if we are to live peacefully.

Summer holidays depend upon those who do not take them. If every Spanish or Italian town ceased to live, as Paris ceases to live in August; if nothing remained of the daily worship of the people; if every place suddenly lost its holy character and became a market, a discotheque, a leisure park, peopled by strangers hungry for distraction – if these things happened, then we should experience no rejuvenation in our travels. The element of pilgrimage would vanish, and the wearisome pursuit of culture and experience would be no more than that.

Those who cannot travel must provide their own spiritual refreshment. But it will gain from their confinement. Whoever doubts this should take his next holiday in Poland, whose people have no choice but to remain where they are and to find in the grim contours of their obligatory poverty whatever simple graces are available. Everywhere in Poland the traveller encounters the reality of prayer. Only this can explain the most incredible event in recent history: that a whole people should rise against its oppressors, with hardly a single violent action. In order to prepare ourselves for Comrade Scargill's final triumph, we should do well to consider the Polish example and study how to sanctify again the landscape of England. The least that we should do, I believe, is restore to the religious orders the land which our most oppressive monarch once stole from them.

24 July 1984

The Open University and the Closed Mind

Like many people whose radio is constantly tuned to Radio 3, I often listen to the Open University, usually while washing up. Having heard the last recital and the news, and quietly dreaming at the kitchen sink, I am suddenly disturbed by a flourish of trumpets, followed by bright, cheery voices inviting me to learn. For whatever reason, the subject tends to be sociology, which sounds, if I remember rightly, something like this:

Announcer: Hello. This is Unit Four of the foundation course in sociology, and our topic tonight is the exploitation of the worker in capitalist society. We begin with a brief discussion between our two course lecturers, Dave Spart and Chris Toad, who will be putting alternative points of view. Dave will begin.

Dave: Hello. Yes. Some people think that the exploitation of the worker in capitalist society is an economic phenomenon, due to the fact that the capitalist class *as a class* controls the means of production and so compels the workers *as a class* to work for less value than they produce. That's the view that I'd like to put before you.

Chris: And I'd like to put forward the opposite view, that the exploitation of the worker in capitalist society is not primarily economic, but political, caused by the fact that the bourgeoisie *as a class* controls the power structures from which the workers *as a class* are excluded.

Announcer: You will find these two positions spelt out on page fifteen of your commentary, where you will see that, while Dave's view is that of Marx, Chris's comes closer to Gramsci. Which of them is right? This will be your topic for the coming week. Dave, once again I'll ask you to speak first.

Dave: Given that the capitalist controls the means of production, what need does he have to control the political process as well? Why not allow a kind of illusion of influence to the workers, by giving them votes, if that serves to maintain capitalist relations of production? Basically, bourgeois democracy is just a functional mechanism. What matters is the economic base. The real social relations between people are forged at the economic level, and that's where the exploitation occurs. You see this in the relations between men and women; also in the relations between whites and blacks.

Chris: But sometimes the superstructure takes over. I mean, the functional mechanism of bourgeois democracy can become an instrument in the hands of the capitalist class, as in Britain today. By controlling the choice of parties, candidates, issues and outcomes, the capitalist class can *create* the situation where the worker has no choice but to accept exploitative social relations . . .

I confess to finding such dialogue fascinating. By creating little disagreements, framed in a common language, and by incorporating into the language everything that is truly questionable, an aura of rational argument can be sustained almost indefinitely, even though not a single serious question is asked, nor a single serious thesis provided. Dave and Chris assume, as their common ground, all the major Marxist claims: that there are social classes, that 'capitalists' form such a class, as do 'workers', that the first exploit the second, that they do so as a class, and so on. But why is it illuminating to describe a society as capitalist, and why should we think of ourselves primarily as members of a capitalist society rather than as citizens of a liberal democracy? To the listener who asked those questions, Dave and Chris would have nothing polite to say.

That of course is what is meant by bias and, in my limited experience, the Open University sociology course is certainly biased. But why all the fuss? What is the harm in a few young dons yapping away at each other in Marxese, while others listen to their radios, taking careful notes?

It should be remembered that the Open University is not a normal university. Most of its students are older people, some retired, who for one reason or another have missed out on education. Their minds are neither impressionable nor truly open, and often little besides self-esteem depends on whether they obtain a degree. Moreover, if they wish to know what they are in for they have only to turn on their radios and give it a try. It is possible that someone could listen to Dave and Chris and feel a genuine relief at discovering exactly what he had always missed, and exactly what he should most enjoy studying.

Anyone who is foolish enough to embark on an Open University sociology course without first listening to it, or who, having embarked on it, decides that he cannot tolerate the bias, is probably heading for a failure. And the bright student, who learns to write a perfect examination answer in Marxese, gains a precious reward from his studies: he learns a language which isolates him totally from his fellows and encourages both himself and them to renounce all attempt at dialogue. In that way many fruitless quarrels are avoided and many consoling illusions preserved.

There, it seems to me, lies the strength of the Open University, which, unlike such closed shops as Oxford and Cambridge, makes it clear from the start what a student will sound like when he graduates. And if people wish to sound like Dave and Chris, good luck to them.

31 July 1984

On Roads and Railways

Modern conservatism began as a response to the dangerous overestimation of human capacities. Emerging as a political force in the early nineteenth century, it prided itself on its realism and on its ability to take a long-term view of human destiny, sacrificing short-term benefits for the sake of the larger continuities on which political survival depends.

By and large the Tory party has retained its commitment to the long-term view, despite the difficulties involved in conveying that commitment to an increasingly hedonistic electorate. At the same time, the party has fallen under the influence of an ideology which it once rightly resisted, as the distillation of all that is most destructive in the short-term view of things – the ideology of business. And when the Tory party seems most seriously to neglect its duty to the nation, it is often because business has prevailed. A case in point is that of transport.

We are familiar with the noise, the dirt, the danger and the general heightening of frenzy that are engendered by the motor car. Most of us would be happy to see motor vehicles excluded from towns and the roads handed over to pedestrians, cyclists and – for the chronically indolent – the occasional sedan chair. But no such ban could be contemplated without a serious government policy – a policy of determined reaction against the motor car.

We are equally familiar with the ruin caused by roads – the ruin of towns, villages, wildlife and countryside. The creative capacity of roads is even worse, however, than their capacity to destroy. Roads enable people to live in one place, work in another, rear children in a third, take their leisure in a fourth and remain obscurely attached to a fifth which they sometimes visit. Roads scatter the population, destroying home and community and placing a veil before our purposes, which can be fulfilled only after a frenzied burst of motion to some other place.

Roads are therefore a major cause of man's estrangement. Under their influence he lives subject to the illusion that he can be better satisfied in some other place, and in some other company, than those to which fate has assigned him. Left to themselves, roads begin to govern the lives of those whom they were intended to serve. That which was designed as a means becomes an end in itself, and human life no better than a means to its upkeep. The citizen of Los Angeles, who rejoices in the greatest available freedom of movement, must perforce spend much of his day in a motor car if he is to work, eat and converse as nature requires. The town in which he lives has the dimensions of a county, and a trip to the theatre or an invitation to dinner may cost him half the night in travelling.

We are familiar, too, with the consequences of our dependence on fossil fuels, whereby we purchase present prosperity at the cost of future enslavement. Conservative politicians frequently warn us of the danger presented to the West by the Gulf war, and of the possibility that the Soviet Union may one day be able to control the flow of oil from the Middle East. But the danger is the result of our own stupidity in choosing the easiest form of energy.

A true conservative policy would involve the following measures: a cessation of all motorway construction; a high fuel tax; a restriction of motor traffic in towns; the installation of cycle lanes; an expansion of the railways and a restoration of the branch lines. The last move would in turn require the railway unions to be brought to heel, so that manpower could be reduced, automation extended and the right to strike curtailed. But no conservative politician should entertain any principled objection to such proposals.

Instead we find the government – responding to the call of 'business' – making further plans for our destruction. The Department of Transport seeks to drive a motorway alongside the River Aire, demolishing large parts of the beautiful village of Saltaire, planned by Titus Salt in order that the modern worker should enjoy the same fruitful attachment to place and community that gave life and meaning to his ancestors. The department seeks also to convert 70 miles of London's roads into trunk roads and to change Marylebone station into a coach terminal.

That last plan is in many ways the most significant. For it involves a direct sacrifice of the railway – one of the greatest achievements of Victorian England – to the roads, emblems of our short-sightedness. Marylebone station, placed in one of the most peaceful corners of Victorian London, perfectly illustrates the power of the railway to penetrate into the heart of a city without damaging its life or character. If the Government has its way, this monument to patriotic sentiment will become a diesel-breathing hell-hole, coughing out its stream of monsters onto the motorway which desecrates the nearby graveyard of St Mary's Paddington Green.

The great Mrs Siddons, who frowns so tragically from her violated tombstone at the follies of modern England, will then be shaken to the core. When at last she crumbles to dust and her sad eyes no longer speak for the nation whose spirit she enriched, let her be replaced by another muse – the muse of comedy. For at irremediable folly we must, however painfully, study how to laugh.

7 August 1984

W. Curtis Green, Architect

The news that the Dorchester Hotel has changed hands provides the occasion to celebrate its architect – or rather, the architect who did his best to redeem what was, in 1929, the most hideous building yet to have been constructed in London. W. Curtis Green inherited the shell of the Dorchester from Sir Owen Williams, an appalling vandal who littered the land with concrete follies and ended his career as the architect of Britain's first motorway. Green, by contrast, was one of the last exponents of Edwardian Baroque, the happiest of twentieth century styles, without which London would be infinitely more dreary than it is.

Everything good about the Dorchester is due to Green, who added delicate corners and soft edges to the concrete monster that Williams had left to him and finished the building with a sumptuous club-like interior. According to *Building* magazine of May 1931:

> Here is a Grand Babylon hotel that verily matches the keen imagination and gusto of Arnold Bennett . . . here qualities and vulgarities have been weighed skilfully on the balance of the expensive palate. There is elegance which no more than borders on strict refinement, there are luxury and opulence that are not too thinly veiled, there is a sense of well-being: the sense of being 'right there' . . .

And much more in the same vein. But the simple word for this interior – in which styles and details from many eras are warmly and boldly synthesised – is 'classical'. Green's work is an imaginative appropriation of a tradition to which he adds his own distinctive personality, uniting form and detail in a coherent public language.

His thoroughness and exuberance are displayed at their most accomplished in the showroom built for Wolseley Motors at 160 Piccadilly, now occupied by Barclays Bank. Every feature of this building repays study: the gilded wrought-iron grilles that grace the windows, the bronze doors with their luxuriant Florentine knocker, the internal columns covered with coat upon coat of Japanese lacquer in a subdued vermilion, the Japonaiserie panelling, set in meticulously modelled classical surrounds – most of all, the grand affirmative facade, which provides one of the boldest corners in London, its massive Roman forms handled with a Ruskinian reverence for detail.

My own favourite among Curtis Green's buildings, however, is a work of his apprenticeship: the power station which he built in 1901 for the

Chiswick line of the London United Electric Tramways, now a neglected adjunct to Stamford Brook bus terminal. This masterpiece of industrial design illustrates a vital architectural principle – that, in the last analysis, the only thing which matters is the facade, since this is the only aspect of a building with which *all* of us, and not just the occupants, have to live.

Green created, in the two visible facades of the Chiswick Power Station, an exuberant memorial to the classical tradition. Into a pre-Renaissance lattice he inserted grand Roman arches, embellished with Baroque voussoirs and keystones. A concave attic story taken from Hawkesmoore's orangery surmounts a Palladian cornice, which in turn overshadows niches in the idiom of Belcher, while above the door a humorous bas-relief parodies the Night and Day of Michelangelo. (Green's deities are Electricity and Motion, the latter gently toying a tram with her outstretched provocative foot.)

The whole facade has a gallant, festive appearance, not without a tinge of gentle irony. The interior of the building, however, is nothing but a vast hall, now empty of its machinery and containing only a delicate cast-iron balcony, surmounted by a marble switchboard which has been pillaged of its instruments. Modernist fanatics will therefore condemn the facade as 'dishonest'. For it gives no indication of the cavernous interior, being concerned only to conceal the realities of industrial production behind a comfortable civic veneer.

As Wilde observed, however, in matters of the greatest importance it is style, and not sincerity, that counts. Architecture, like dress, is an exercise in manners, and good manners involve the habit of skilful insincerity – the habit of saying 'good morning' to those whose mornings you would rather blight, and of passing the butter to those whom you would rather starve. If we were scrupulously honest, we should also be intolerably rude. And where modern architects have been allowed to exercise the vice of honesty, people have been understandably appalled and alienated.

To design a facade requires peculiar accomplishments, the first of which is drawing. Green filled book after book with sketches and watercolours, learning to build while learning to see what others had built before him. In a lecture to the Athenaeum Club in 1956 he regretted the manner in which the great tradition of English building had been cast aside by impetuous charlatans, for whom sketching and study had ceased to be the necessary preliminaries to architecture. It was to these charlatans, however, that the new commissions were going, and Green died before he could be recognised as the model of what an architect should be, and of what the modern architect is not: modest, respectful and well-mannered.

14 August 1984

In Search of a Loyal Opposition

The miners' strike illustrates the most important problem confronting the government: the lack of political opposition. A battle which should be conducted in parliament is conducted on the streets, not by politicians but by a deluded rabble fired by demagoguery. It therefore takes on a prolonged, violent and unstable character – the character not of discussion but of force.

With a little care the dispute could have been confined to parliament, a place whose recognised function is to confine malcontents within four walls and there to provide them with the impression (sometimes illusory, sometimes not) that by interpreting the world they also change it. It would have been necessary, however, for a political party to define the issue and to rally the discontented miners to its cause. It would have been necessary for the flames which have been fanned by Mr Scargill to have been ignited and quenched in parliament. The Labour Party did not do this – that is, it did not do it in advance of Scargill, who therefore seemed to be leading the parliamentary party.

Had the issue been defined in parliament it might have been defined more wisely. It would not have been left to a known agitator, whose unconcealed contempt for British institutions has caused widespread alarm, to present the miners' case. In particular, the matter could have been defined by someone other than the immediate protagonist. Nor would that have been difficult. There are plenty of arguments for running the coal industry at a loss which are in no way tainted by the ruthless sentimentality of Scargill.

Miners are tough characters, used to high wages that they could not hope to match in any other work for which their skills have fitted them. Their communities are isolated, self-absorbed and with a Gothic sense of prevailing hardship. Miners spend hours together in close confinement, in conditions of discomfort and jeopardy, calculated to induce a firm spirit of solidarity. Such people do not relinquish privileges without a fight, and must be handled with the utmost prudence by any politician who seeks to deflect them from their purposes.

The Labour Party might also have made the miners into an illustrative case of socialist principles. It is difficult to contemplate their condition without recognising their claim to be well rewarded for their vile labour. It is easy to be persuaded that their immobile working-class communities should be subsidised by the state until such a time as the single source of livelihood may be renewed or replaced. Rehearsing those sentiments, the Labour Party might even have come to the right conclusion: that it is about time that coal-mining were abolished forever – a conclusion which, since the adoption of D. H. Lawrence by the compilers of the A-level syllabus, has become part of our national culture.

None of that has happened, for the reason that the Labour Party is politically and intellectually bankrupt. It has lost faith in democratic socialism and found no philosophy with which to replace it. In so far as the miners' case is expressed in socialist terms, it is expressed through the extra-parliamentary channels typified by Scargill, and by the few Labour Members who are dim enough to believe that his language carries conviction.

All this places the Tory Party in a difficult situation. Tories believe in the political process – the process of controlled opposition and public debate – and recognise that the time will come (and ought to come) when they must relinquish power. In the present circumstances, therefore, their main duty is to create and educate the opposition that will one day defeat them.

It is in this duty, however, that the Government is principally failing: or at least, so it seems to me. If the Labour Party ever again comes to power, it will be by default. It is in the long-term national interest that the Tory Party should be defeated (when defeated) by another party equally loyal and equally representative of popular sentiment, that rises to power by its own merits. Only the Tory Party, however, has the power to create this new opposition and to make it into a real threat. The Tory Party, therefore, should now be doing for the SDP what the SDP has failed to do for itself: it should be schooling the SDP as a loyal and powerful opposition, able to focus in its parliamentary presence the prevailing sentiments of discontent.

The Tories must first adopt, on behalf of the SDP, an unequivocal leader – Dr Owen, say – and address their more belligerent remarks to him, rather than to Mr Kinnock. They must choose some major issues on which the SDP could take a principled stand in opposition to them. They must (but ever so discreetly) provide the SDP with a language and a philosophy other than the discredited ideology of socialism, or the baffling compromises of the Liberal Party. Most of all, they must persuade the nation that they are really frightened of the SDP, and of the loyal masses of socially mobile, patriotic, easy-going moderates who threaten at any moment to sweep it to power.

But will they do all that? I doubt it.

4 September 1984

On Rights and Duties

In a recent letter to *The Times*, Dr David Jessop raised what is perhaps the most important question for the critic of the post-war political consensus: the question of social responsibility. It is well to emphasise individual freedom, but what is the value of freedom if the sense of duty is destroyed?

The Welfare State emerged as the consensual answer to the 'Social Question' of Victorian England. And like every political solution guided by conscience, it proved not to be final. The creature of the Welfare State proved to be devoid of the very moral responsibility which had originally created him. Either he was a beneficiary of the system – in which case he began to claim as a right what had been once offered as a charity. Or he was a provider of the system's resources – in which case he was encouraged to regard the poor as beyond his personal concern, the pampered recipients of wealth which was his by right and unjustly extorted.

Both parties to the new arrangement therefore suffered a diminution in the sense of responsibility: the first for his own welfare, the second for the welfare of others. At the same time the resources appropriated by the state were increasingly diverted from their intended purpose, being used to create and maintain an army of bureaucrats answerable neither to those who provided the funds, nor to those who stood in need of them.

Once the charitable gesture had been prised loose from the individual and handed over to the state, it ceased to bear the mark of human freedom. It could then be neither genuinely given nor gratefully received. No person could be praised for offering it and no person blamed for withholding it: indeed, no *person* could be discerned anywhere, who might be held answerable either for his own misfortunes, or for the misfortunes of his neighbour. Human kindness gave way to mechanical 'redistribution', operated by officials concerned most of all to entrench their newly granted privileges.

The Welfare State tends, therefore, to destroy both the charitable motive and the gratitude that is owed to it, by persuading everyone, both rich and poor, that hardship, even my hardship, is not my concern. The 'compassionate' state is in fact a state dedicated to the abolition of compassion. It conforms to the dangerous tendency of socialist politics: the tendency towards a public realm devoid of personal liability. In this public realm, if I follow the rules, I need never be called to count either for my own life, or for the life of my neighbour. It is, incidentally, one of the strongest arguments for monarchy that it identifies the state with a human person, and so reminds us of the layer of responsibility with which every official uniform is lined.

There is surely no easy answer to Dr Jessop's question: no simple formula for reintroducing into the secular politics of a modern industrial state this element on which its moral health depends. Certainly it is not enough to liberate the 'wealth creators' from their fiscal shackles, or to 'privatise' our national resources. Such moves may be economic good sense, but they will not replace impersonal privilege by individual duty. Moreover, the emphasis on wealth and its creation reinforces the ruling illusion that the problem is merely technical, to be solved by more resources and by yet another application of the impersonal intelligence of the bureaucrat.

The vacuum at the heart of the impersonal state cannot be filled by the state itself. There is no ideology, no political goal, no scheme for redemption, no 'irreversible shift' or 'final solution' that will return to the political order the personal conscience which has been expelled from it. All 'direct action' by the state is tainted by the impersonality that it seeks to overcome. The vacuum can be filled, therefore, only by the sacrifice involved in placing my personal answerability before any of the easy benefits that conflict with it. It is not the system that must be changed, but I myself. Responsibility is either mine or no one's. To shift the burden is to succumb precisely to the fault that is complained of. Resistance to impersonality is therefore primarily a personal concern.

But how are responsible beings created? The answer is widely known, but seldom uttered. Responsibility stems from the habit of viewing our own actions from a point of view outside ourselves. Such a habit is engendered by authoritative institutions, whose edicts and expectations we learn to internalise as we mature. Everything depends on those institutions and on their preparedness to wage war against the natural egoism of the child. At least one of these institutions, moreover – the school – is now (rightly or wrongly) in the hands of the state. Does this not provide to the state an opportunity for *indirect* action that might, in the long term, tip the moral balance? It is just possible that it does. I therefore refer Dr Jessop's question to Sir Keith Joseph.

11 September 1984

The Belgrano Affair

Mr Tam Dalyell's obsession with the Belgrano is boring as only the obsessions of public people can be. But if a bore goes on long enough he has to be confronted.

Suppose then that it is all true. Suppose that the Belgrano, having advanced so far towards the Falklands, had turned round and begun to head for port without entering the 250-mile limit within which no enemy ship could assume itself to be safe. And suppose 'peace initiatives' were at that moment being made, with whatever credibility might, in the circumstances, attach to them. Would we then have acted rightly in sinking the ship?

The answer, I believe, is yes. First we must remind ourselves of the overriding moral premise, which is that the war was not our doing. It was started by Argentina, through an aggressive action which limited our sovereignty and presented us with a *fait accompli*. Part of our territory was seized by force, in defiance of all procedures recognised either by international law or by the tenuous morality of nations. We had no choice but to respond. The responsibility for every death in that war lies with Argentina, and with those Argentines who initiated, applauded or supported the original aggression. The Belgrano sailors were sent to their deaths not by our torpedo, but by the state to which their allegiance was owed. Moreover, they knew this, accepted it and died as men should, honourably and blamelessly in their country's cause.

That said, however, there is the problem of our own military conduct. There is a distinction, even for the offended party, between a war conducted justly and one conducted in defiance of the limiting scruples that ensure the morality of every defensive act. Had we infringed that morality, which must govern our actions even in the limit of danger, then part of the blame for the loss of life must lie with us. But I believe we did not infringe it.

In setting the 250-mile limit around the Falklands our high command said that enemy ships within that limit would be attacked. But it did not say that enemy ships outside it would *not* be attacked. To say the latter would be to refuse the realities of war, in which the first objective must be to neutralise those enemy forces which pose a genuine threat to our forces.

Our troops had no foothold on land: they were fighting 10 000 miles from home, in icy and dangerous waters, with no more secure a base than that which could be provided by a navy yet to be tried in the exacting conditions of modern weaponry. Our high command had one overriding duty, which was to protect the fleet, the loss of which would have meant the certain deaths of thousands. Danger could come from the air, and this forced the fleet to steer east of the Falklands. Danger could also come from the sea, and in this case could be neutralised by no evasive action. Our commanders therefore had a duty to hunt out the Argentine navy and inflict upon it a blow that would effectively destroy its power. There is only one decisive way of achieving that end, which is to sink an important ship at sea. The Belgrano offered itself, and it was sunk. Moreover, the Argentine navy thereafter presented no serious danger

It is irrelevant that the Belgrano was heading homewards – or relevant only in one particular: namely, that this evasive action would show that the Argentines too had perceived the logic of our strategic thinking and recognised that, by all unwritten rules, the Belgrano had to be sunk.

It is also irrelevant that peace initiatives had been made, however bona fide. The essential premise of any meaningful negotiation is a balance of power. The Argentines, having secured control over the disputed territory, could be brought to make concessions only by a threat of force, and the threat had to be credible. In order that serious negotiations could begin, therefore, a decisive military blow was by then absolutely necessary. Whoever doubts this should recall the peculiar *braggadocio* with which all Argentine pronouncements following the seizure of the Falklands were embellished. The language was the swaggering bravado of the bully, who can negotiate only after his bluff has been called. The sinking of the Belgrano could not possibly have closed an avenue to peace that already existed: it might have opened an avenue yet to be explored.

It was fortunate for our troops that the aggressor in this war was a 'right-wing' junta. Had the Falklands been 'liberated' by a left-wing dictatorship, our high command would have fought a far harder and perhaps ultimately hopeless battle against a state decreed constitutionally incapable of wrongdoing by many of the makers of British public opinion. It was also fortunate for the Argentines that they were governed by such a regime. For our victory unseated the junta, as it could have unseated no leftist dictatorship. The Falklands war is therefore now painted by the British left not as a triumph of civilisation over moral chaos (which it was), but as a catastrophe.

Let us not lament the Belgrano. Let us praise instead the bravery of the men who tracked her in those dangerous waters, and who unhesitatingly obeyed orders that might at any moment have sent them to a horrible death.

18 September 1984

The President's Palace

The intellectual case against modern architecture is acknowledged to be strong. The question is, what to do about it? How should we build, and what should we destroy? A few architects and critics are beginning to address themselves to the first of those questions. A few anti-architects are therefore needed, to address themselves to the second. Modern buildings of peculiar and symbolic loathsomeness must be singled out for demolition, and the same publicity and resources devoted to their destruction as once were spent in erecting them.

When a building exists, however, a thousand otherwise innocent people begin to acquire an interest in its survival. You could not now destroy Le Corbusier's *Unité d'habitation* in Marseilles without a storm of political and academic outrage. Not only will people be homeless (for there are people, it seems, who would rather live in Le Corbusier's building than under the stars): many more will be unable to complete their doctoral dissertations, or will be forced to rewrite 20-year-old lectures on the theory of modern design. So how do we begin?

I believe that we must think ahead, and plan the demolition of some buildings at the moment of their conception, so as to deprive the enemy of his long-standing strategy of *fait accompli*. It needs just one acclaimed modern building to be demolished on the morrow of its completion for the public to perceive that the problem can be solved. It will immediately become apparent that it wants only courage to set our civilisation again on the path of righteousness.

And in fact the opportunity lies presently before us, devised by a figure who has already several times tipped the balance in favour of reactionary ideas: President Mitterrand. Being monarch in all but name, the French president must establish his republican virtue by some symbolic anti-monarchical gesture. The tradition has therefore been established whereby each president, before leaving office, desecrates some part of royal Paris. For Paris is undeniably the greatest architectural representation of the glory of the crown.

President de Gaulle, in authorising the construction of *La Défense*, effectively curtailed the triumphal vista which leads from the Louvre in the general direction of America. Pompidou was bolder, and placed his monument to vulgarity in the Marais, intimate stage of the *grand siècle*, and the heart of Europe. Mitterrand wishes to go further still and to vandalise the Louvre itself, by placing a 60 foot high glass pyramid in the

Cour Napoléon – the open court which dominates the Tuileries. By this means he will effectively destroy at the root the imperial flourish which de Gaulle merely clipped at its extremity. The architect is to be I. M. Pei, better known for the extension to the Washington Art Gallery than for the soulless towers in Bleeker Street which oppress the sky above Greenwich Village.

The president's monarchical powers are displayed in the haste with which the project was begun. The commissioners for historic monuments (successors to an office held first by Prosper Mérimée) were peremptorily summoned in January, and the plans unveiled before them in the course of an hour or two. Mr Pei spoke with the help of a translator, a few slides were shown and a few bland official observations were made.

The commissioners were flabbergasted at what they saw: a Babylonian fantasy, involving an underground culture-palace linking the wings of the Louvre, dominated by the glass pyramid and embellished with all the vulgarities that come naturally to those who believe in 'consumer sovereignty' over art. Asked to vote then and there, the majority of the commissioners declared themselves against the scheme. It made no difference, however. Work began at once, and the presidential office launched a campaign of propaganda designed to persuade the ordinary Parisian of the inestimable benefits to himself, to his city, to France and to mankind as a whole, that must inevitably ensue from the new *machine à culture*. We may therefore expect the Louvre to be desecrated by 1987, in time for the next presidential election.

But here is our chance. Let the Gaullists enter an electoral promise to undo Mr Pei's work, at whatever cost. Let them begin now their plans for the demolition, sign up the contractors for scrap, the restorers, the gardeners; let them undertake to leave everything exactly as it was. Not only would they be sure, then, to win the election; they would also have struck the first decisive blow against the madness of our times, by showing that what has been done can, if we wish, be undone.

And if it can happen in architecture, it can happen also in politics. When the public realises this, socialism, enlightenment, progress, equality, every shibboleth that has threatened French culture since the Revolution will fall from its throne.

25 September 1984

The War of Religion

Set against the background of world events, the Pope's denunciation of 'liberation theology' may seem unimportant – as unimportant as the Bishop of Durham's carefully stage-managed apostasies, or Dean Cupitt's tub-thumping repudiation of his faith. In fact, however, the Pope's gesture is one of the most significant developments in the Christian Church since the second Vatican Council.

For the first time in recent years a Christian leader has recognised what has been obvious to unbelievers for decades: that Marxism is a religion, and that it is as incompatible with Christian thought and practice as is the religion of Khomeini or the worship of the sun. Moreover, Marxism is a *primitive* religion, unable to distance itself from the busy nothingness of this world, unable to introduce either clarity or serenity into the minds of those converted to it and unable to offer the supreme consoling vision of a transcendental God. It is a religion of turmoil, hatred and blind superstition, clothing the world in violence and feeding upon human sacrifice.

Where the Marxist sees 'liberation', the Christian sees only murder, terror and self-justifying sin. Poverty, hunger, even death itself – all these features of the human condition which true religion fortifies us to accept are, for the Marxist, occasions of demonic outrage. His god History roams the world in search of abstract justice, and where History alights the blood of the innocent must flow. His church is the most bigoted that the world has known, and his inquisition the most murderous and implacable, tolerating no government except Marxist theocracy and extinguishing opposition at whatever cost.

Like every primitive religion, Marxism is haunted by imaginary devils. 'Capitalism', 'imperialism', 'deviationism', 'revisionism', 'infantile leftism', 'fascism': everywhere in the path of the Marxist lie dark and inscrutable enemies, and without the benefit of constant incantation he must surely be waylaid by them and deprived of his soul. Those in the grip of this superstition must therefore constantly fortify themselves with the most astonishing invective. The 'word magic' of the Marxist is an attempt to 'appropriate nature', to summon the forces of History against the enemy. When he calls you a 'bourgeois fascist, McCarthyite cold-warrior' he gives vent to a superstitious fear of your disagreement, and like every person in the grip of superstitious terror, he is dangerous. It was just such a terror that once prompted Khrushchev to leap on to the rostrum of the

United Nations and cry 'We will bury you!' This was neither a prediction nor a decision. It was a spell.

The normal practice of the Roman Catholic Church on encountering a primitive religion has been to incorporate it: to elevate its rites into sacraments, its gods into saints and its joys and terrors into moral sentiments. But certain special features of Marxism make it resistant to this process. First there is the theory, which effectively reverses the dogmas of Christian theology. Marxism offers immutable laws of History in place of the Will of God, earthly communism in place of heavenly salvation, 'primitive accumulation' in place of original sin. Second there is the practice, which replaces common morality with the exalted fervour of a revolutionary elite, to whom all is permitted.

There is a further feature, however, which is yet more destructive of Christian values. Every religion, however primitive, embodies in its ritual an apprehension of the sacred. Without that apprehension no society can easily survive. Marxism sets its face against the sacred and laughs it to scorn as the great human delusion. But when nothing is sacred, Nothing is sacred. The Marxist – who is but a mediocre creature like ourselves – begins to believe in the sanctity of Nothingness. An exultant nihilism comes to dominate his sentiments. He cannot thereafter desist from tearing down institutions, laws, customs and values, and a day passed without an act of desecration is a day lost to Giant Despair.

This sacrilegious frenzy is familiar to us largely from the writings of bishops and theologians. During the 1960s and 1970s the disaffected priesthood overwhelmed the media with its insulting imbecilities. And not one of those who professed to speak for the Christian churches perceived the danger of Marxism: not one of them saw that Marxism is precisely a perversion of the religious instinct, a channelling of religious emotion away from its true end, towards the vain task of earthly redemption. And nobody saw, therefore, that where Marxism triumphs, bigotry, hatred and superstition must inevitably triumph in its wake.

Of course, there are important insights in the writings of Marx, as in the writings of Nietzsche, say, or Jean-Paul Sartre. A theologian who wishes to be of his time, and not just in it, must be open to influence from such secular visionaries. But the real question remains: whence comes my faith and my authority? The Church's answer must always be the same: not from this world, but from another.

Let us be thankful that a Christian leader has at least affirmed the self-evident truth, that poverty, inequality and 'exploitation' are legacies of original sin, whereas the Marxist determination to abolish them involves a new sin of our own.

2 October 1984

King Arthur's Crime

For the High Court to proceed against Arthur Scargill for contempt is one of the most glaring of the many absurdities in the present conflict. Mr Scargill is above the law, and it is ridiculous to suppose that the law should be applied to him – as ridiculous as to suppose that the law should be applied to the Queen.

If the High Court were to take seriously the nonsensical suggestion that Scargill is a subject of the Crown, then it should be serving a writ not for contempt, but for sedition. This common law offence covers three crimes – seditious libel, seditious utterance and conspiracy to act in furtherance of a seditious intention – and it is arguable that, had a mere subject behaved like Scargill, he would be guilty of all of them. The seditious intention – which is a necessary ingredient in each offence – was defined by Mr Justice Stephen as

> an intention to bring into hatred or contempt, or to excite disaffection against, the person of the Sovereign, or the government and Constitution of the United Kingdom as by law established, or either House of Parliament or the administration of justice, or to excite Her Majesty's subjects to attempt, otherwise than by lawful means, the alteration of any matter in Church or State by law established, or to raise discontent or disaffection among Her Majesty's subjects or to promote feelings of ill-will or hostility between different classes of her subjects.

For the crime to occur, there must also be a disturbance, appropriately caused by the seditious utterance or conspiracy. People have been found guilty of sedition as recently as 1972, and a person who behaved exactly like Scargill, while lacking the legal immunity accorded to heroes, could well be found guilty as well.

It is undeniable that Scargill has sought to bring the government and the judiciary into contempt, that he has excited Her Majesty's subjects to attempt, otherwise than by lawful means, the alteration of matters established by law and that he has sought to raise discontent among Her Majesty's subjects and to promote feelings of ill-will and hostility between different classes. He expressly declares himself to be engaged in class warfare, speaks with excoriating contempt of all who are opposed to him, and supports bands of violent followers in actions which are both unlawful in themselves and calculated to set men against their workmates and against the police. The overall intention has been to set the working class as a whole against those who (in Scargill's benighted opinion) do not belong to it.

The violence of the picket line is not merely the spontaneous expression of local sentiment, but also the result of a concerted and resourceful organisation which deploys its thugs in the way that the Nazi Party deployed its shock troops – so as to intimidate and coerce all who dare to defy the leader's ruling. Precisely who or what is the power behind this organisation is a matter of dispute. But the evidence is sufficient, if not to implicate Scargill, at least to provide a case for him to answer.

On any natural understanding of the events of the last few months, Mr Scargill has harboured a seditious purpose; and on any natural interpretation, his purpose has been achieved. The nation *is* divided, the miners also divided, and enmity and hatred have been let loose in quantities to which our constitution is unaccumstomed and for which our police are unprepared. Nor is there any hope of any early relief, now that the bigots of the Labour Party have joined their voices to the raucous chorus of destruction.

But Scargill is above the law. His contempt for the judiciary is natural in a man who believes that justice resides not in the patient exercise of the common law of England, but in the violent overthrow of the power that sustains it. Too many people share that belief, and too much instinctive disorder has been unleashed on behalf of it, for Scargill to be treated now as a subject of the Crown. He has the hero's disdain towards things by law established.

The only solution is to transport him to a place where his idea of justice is enacted, where the 'dictatorship of the proletariat' has extinguished forever the power of the ruling class, where he will not be bothered by the whims of an independent judiciary, and where all trade unionists will automatically obey the instructions that are issued by their leadership.

Such places exist, and Mr Scargill has been loud in praise of them. It would surely be no injustice to compel him to reside in one of them. Not only would he then be able to take up a citizenship and an allegiance more suited to his ardent temperament, he would also be relieved forever of the intolerable sights of exploitation that greet him every day in the dark world of capitalist oppression. And in order that his departure should be arranged with every appearance of legitimacy, the proposal should be put to a national referendum in which everyone could vote, even the miners, who, thanks to Scargill, have not so far voted on the matter than concerns them.

10 October 1984

The Eleventh Hour

Anyone who studies the history of arms control negotiations with the Soviet Union is likely to be struck by a sense of unreality. From the first days it has been Soviet policy to make agreements unverifiable and to break them with impunity; to vilify the West for the deployment of every new weapon, while serenely deploying the same weapon itself; to sign international conventions which tie our hands, while proceeding to ignore those conventions when interest requires; and to encourage vociferous and independent 'peace movements' in the West, while ruthlessly liquidating them at home.

Observing this, and observing too the frank and often repeated pronouncements of the Soviet leadership (typified by Andropov's Lenin Day Speech in 1982, in which he reaffirmed 'the triumph of the magnificent cause: the victory of communism throughout the world'), I am reminded of Max Frisch's play *The Fire Raisers*. During a period when house after house is being destroyed by arson, two men insinuate themselves into a suburban household, refer in jocular and enthusiastic tones to its combustible potential and politely ask for a place to store their fuses, incendiary devices and drums of petrol. Not wishing to confront them or in any way to break the routine of complacency whereby they live, the householders meekly comply with their desires, telling themselves whatever comforting untruths can be hastily improvised in answer to each new development.

The effect of Frisch's play is most disturbing. By the end you can hardly keep yourself from leaping on to the stage and tearing at the cocoon of falsehood. At the same time you know that, however loudly you shout, you will not be understood, and that it is you, in the end, who will be led away as a lunatic.

Even so, it is necessary to tell the truth, if only for conscience's sake, if only in order to dissociate oneself from the criminal complacency of one's surrounding world. Consider then, the Soviet deployment of chemical weapons – weapons which first brought home the character of modern warfare. Repeated attempts to prevent the deployment of these weapons, culminating in the American unilateral renunciation of their first use in 1969, have made no impact whatever on the Soviet Union, which has continued to manufacture, to deploy and even to use these weapons, in ways and quantities which have only one plausible explanation: that the Soviet Union intends to use them in Europe when the opportunity occurs.

The facts are set out by Manfred Hamm in an alarming pamphlet*. And the facts speak for themselves. Every motorised division in the Soviet Army includes a chemical warfare battalion of at least 60 vehicles. Every artillery gun is equipped with chemical shells. Every soldier is trained in the exercise of chemical warfare and equipped with protective masks and clothing. Stockpiles of chemical weapons, according to unclassified estimates, are as high as 700 000 tons – including agents which attack the nerves, the skin, the blood and the respiratory system of their victims. Warsaw Pact exercises furnish conclusive proof of the readiness to use these weapons for offensive purposes, in a sudden massive onslaught.

Training for chemical warfare is conducted throughout the Soviet Union and begins long before the conscript enters military service. From secondary school on, every Soviet citizen is required to attend classes in civil defence, and to participate in military drills. Intensive training endures throughout his life and contains important elements of preparation for chemical warfare.

The threat is not only against our troops on the ground. A chemical cloud can force a fleet of ships to disperse, so as to lose its vital protective shield; chemical bombardment can make landing craft ineffective; and chemical-carrying rockets can neutralise our bases and nuclear installations. Soviet preparedness to use these weapons has been displayed in Cambodia and Afghanistan; moreover, lacking any legal opposition or independent public opinion, the Soviet Union is under no internal pressure to renounce them.

When it was suggested that the neutron bomb be introduced into our European forces, a massively orchestrated campaign, led by the Soviet Union, effectively prevented deployment. The Soviet Union meanwhile introduced similar weapons, so gaining the advantage If it were not suggested that we should arm ourselves with an effective chemical deterrent, there would be the same outcry and the same cynical noises from the Soviet leadership.

As Mr Hamm demonstrates, chemical weapons have been used only where there has been no fear of retaliation. Without the power to retaliate we leave ourselves vulnerable to a mode of attack which could destroy us within days or hours. Yet Nato is virtually without chemical weapons of its own. If I now say 'Wake up, it is the eleventh hour!' I shall be accused of scare-mongering. Well, I *am* scare-mongering; and you *ought* to be scared.

16 October 1984

*Manfred Hamm, *Chemical Warfare, The Growing Threat to Europe*, Institute for European Defence and Strategic Studies.

The New Racism

Readers of this column will be familiar with the case of Mr Honeyford, the Bradford headmaster who dared to tell the truth about multi-ethnic education in our innner cities and who has been consequently silenced by the bigots who control public education in Bradford. Not content with this result, the radical middle classes, led by a Ms Jenny Woodward, are now pressing for Mr Honeyford's dismissal. Ms Woodward has induced 200 parents – all Muslims – to ask for the withdrawal of their children from Mr Honeyford's school, saying, 'We made a point of asking that the children be kept together. Of course it is unrealistic. We don't want them transferred at all. The answer is for the authority to remove Mr Honeyford' (*Times Educational Supplement,* 12 October).

Ms Woodward is quite wrong. The answer is for the authority to do as it was asked and remove the children. If the parents are genuinely disturbed by the influence of Mr Honeyford, it is their right as British citizens, and their duty as parents, to send their children elsewhere. If they are not genuinely disturbed, then they deserve to take the consequence of their irresponsible behaviour. For those who promote conflict must be prepared also to suffer it.

But how is it that such a situation could have arisen? The answer is to be found in the magic word 'racism'. For several years now influential 'educationists' have been encouraging us to see in every institution of our society the marks of an ill-defined but supposedly all-pervasive evil. With characteristic contempt for truth and evidence, the radical 'educationalists' have invited us to interpret the misfortunes of black children and the comparative achievements of their white contemporaries as the result of 'institutionalised' habits of racial discrimination. When figures showed that Asian children tend to do better in our schools than white children, the radicals hurriedly redefined all Asians as black, so as to maintain the statistical evidence in their favour. It could then still be said that 'non-whites as a class' are systematic under-achievers: a sure proof that they are victimised.

To the unprejudiced observer the performance of Asian children gives the lie to the myth of 'institutionalised racism'. To the race relations lobby the myth is an emotional necessity and cannot be refuted by anything so neutral as a fact. As one of the few members of the teaching profession to tell the truth, Mr Honeyford has incurred the wrath of those who live by denying it: he must therefore be branded as a 'racist'.

An important influence behind this paranoid way of thinking has been the London University Institute of Education, and in particular the director of its 'Race Relations Programme', Professor Chris Mullard. Mullard is a sociologist, who has devoted his life's work to defining 'racism' and to accusing others of practising it.

His message, although presented in obscure sociological jargon, is simple: racism in our society is a 'structural' fault, and its existence is proved merely by the disparity of achievement between 'black' and 'white'. Hence nothing that you or I can do will exonerate our 'white' society. The well-meaning attempts at racial integration, the refusal to judge pupils by anything except their achievements, the adoption of a core curriculum – even the attempt to reject this curriculum in favour of some ludicrous 'multi-cultural' alternative – all testify to the 'racist' consciousness expressed in the 'structures' of 'white' society.

How has this wicked idea of 'racial guilt' come to seem respectable? Professor Mullard tries to justify it by means of the quaint liturgy of Marxist sociology. 'Capitalism,' he argues, 'requires stratification on racist lines . . . and requires racism as a justification for certain forms of *political* practice.' In the face of such language it is very hard to gain acceptance for the truth. But let us repeat it in any case. Liberal democracy (which is what the Marxist really means by 'capitalism') has repeatedly endeavoured to make individuals equal before the law, to introduce a politics of freedom and toleration and to render every institution open to talent: in short, to remove every *institutional* obstacle to individual success.

For Professor Mullard it is precisely British institutions that must be overthrown, even though they are the true barrier to the 'racism' which he professes to condemn and from which he claims, as a black, to have suffered. But then one may reasonably wonder who is the true 'racist' – the teacher who truthfully confronts the problems of multi-ethnic education in a modern city, or the comfortable professor of 'education' who declaims: 'All the time I spent writing *Black Britain*, I found not solace, comfort or tolerance, but a disturbing desire to break, smash and riot, to bellow: "Whitey! One day you'll have to pay!" ' (Chris Mullard, *Black Britain*, preface).

30 October 1984

In Memory of Iran

Who remembers Iran? Who remembers, that is, the shameful stampede of western journalists and intellectuals to the cause of the Iranian revolution? Who remembers the hysterical propaganda campaign waged against the Shah, the lurid press reports of corruption, police oppression, palace decadence, constitutional crisis? Who remembers the thousands of Iranian students in western universities enthusiastically absorbing the fashionable Marxist nonsense purveyed to them by armchair radicals, so as one day to lead the campaign of riot and mendacity which preceded the Shah's downfall?

Who remembers the behaviour of those students who held as hostage the envoys of the very same power which had provided their 'education'? Who remembers Edward Kennedy's accusation that the Shah had presided over 'one of the most oppressive regimes in history' and had stolen 'umpteen billions of dollars from Iran'?

And who remembers the occasional truth that our journalists enabled us to glimpse, concerning the Shah's real achievements: his successes in combating the illiteracy, backwardness and powerlessness of his country, his enlightened economic policy, the reforms which might have saved his people from the tyranny of evil mullahs, had he been given the chance to accomplish them? Who remembers the freedom and security in which journalists could roam Iran, gathering the gossip that would fuel their fanciful stories of a reign of terror?

True, the Shah was an autocrat. But autocracy and tyranny are not the same. An autocrat may preside, as the Shah sought to preside, over a representative parliament, over an independent judiciary, even over a free press and an autonomous university. The Shah, like Kemal Atatürk, whose vision he shared, regarded his autocracy as the means to the creation and protection of such institutions. Why did no one among the western political scientists trouble to point this out, or to rehearse the theory which tells us to esteem not just the democratic process, but also the representative and limiting institutions which may still flourish in its absence? Why did no one enjoin us to compare the political system of Iran with that of Iraq or Syria?

Why did our political scientists rush to embrace the Iranian revolution, despite the evidence that revolution in these circumstances must be the prelude to massive social disorder and a regime of terror? Why did the western intelligentsia go on repeating the myth that the Shah was to blame for this revolution, when both Khomeini and the Marxists had been planning it for 30 years and had found, despite their many attempts to put it into operation, only spasmodic popular support?

The answer to all those questions is simple. The Shah was an ally of the West, whose achievement in establishing limited monarchy in a vital strategic region had helped to guarantee our security, to bring stability to the Middle East and to deter Soviet expansion. The Shah made the fatal mistake of supposing that the makers of western opinion would love him for creating conditions which guaranteed their freedom. On the contrary, they hated him. The Shah had reckoned without the great death wish which haunts our civilisation and which causes its vociferous members to propagate any falsehood, however absurd, provided only that it damages our chances of survival.

For a while, of course, those vociferous elements will remain silent on the embarassing topic of Iran, believing that the collapse of Iranian institutions, the establishment of religious terror, the Soviet expansion into Afghanistan and the end of stability in the region are all due to some other cause than the Iranian revolution. Those who lent their support to this tragedy simply turned their back on it and went elsewhere, to prepare a similar outcome for the people of Turkey, Nicaragua, El Salvador, Chile, South Africa – or wherever else our vital interests may be damaged.

Of course, if is difficult now for a western correspondent to enter Iran, and if he did so it would not be fun. He could not, like the ghouls who send their despatches from Beirut, adopt a public posture of the front-line hero. He would have to witness, quietly and in terror of his life, things which beggar description: the spontaneous 'justice' of the revolutionary guards, the appalling scenes of violence, torture and demonic frenzy, the public humiliation of women, the daily sacrifice of lives too young to be conscious of the meaning for which they are condemned to destruction.

He would also have to confront the truth which has been staring him in the face for years, and which he could still recognise had the habit of confessing to his errors been preserved: the truth that limited monarchy is the *right* form of government for Iran, which can be saved only by the restoration of the Shah's legitimate successor. But such a result would be in the interests not only of the Iranian people, but also of the West. Hence few western journalists are likely to entertain it.

6 November 1984

On Sentimentality

F. R. Leavis tried to do for my generation what Wordsworth did for Matthew Arnold's: he tried to teach us how to feel. Such was the difficulty of the task, and such the imperfection of his own thought and character, that Leavis could never have succeeded, even with better chances than those he had.

But he succeeded in a lesser enterprise: Leavis taught us to distinguish the true from the false among our feelings, and the real from the unreal among their objects. He alerted us to the great disease of modern life and literature: the disease of sentimentality. Because his lesson was so important, I shall repeat it. To understand sentimentality is to understand what is rotten in the state of England and in the voices which currently cry out most loudly in our ears.

Real love focuses on another individual; it is saddened by his pain and gladdened by his pleasure. The unreal love of the sentimentalist reaches no further than the self, and calculates only pains and pleasures of its own. It says, 'Look at me feeling this, and see how noble, tragic and grand I am!' It may seem to grieve at the other's sorrow, but it does not really grieve. For secretly the sentimentalist welcomes the sorrow which prompts his tears. He sees in it another excuse for the noble gesture, another occasion to contemplate the image which truly moves him: the image of his great-hearted self.

Sentimentality is therefore ruthless: it is hungry for suffering, since suffering is the occasion of its greatest triumph. The sentimental lover seeks the downfall of his beloved, in order to delight in the spectacle of his own tragic emotion. And it is not only love that is liable to this corruption. There is sentimental fear, sentimental pity and sentimental anger.

The anger of Mr Dalyell over the sunken Belgrano, of Mr Scargill over the closing coal mines, of the Greenham Common women over the deployment of Cruise – all these exhibit, in my view, a corrupt and self-regarding posture. In all of them the image looms largest of the noble self, the champion of justice, moved by the righteous indignation of a passionate heart. And sentimental anger is dangerous: there is no more sentimental emotion than that of the terrorist, for whom nothing is sacred save only his own magnificent and implacable rage.

There are tactical difficulties for the sentimentalist, however. If he is to enjoy his intoxicating recompense, he must hide his motives. He depends on rhetoric, which is the art of shining a spotlight on the self and so casting all that opposes it into a comforting obscurity. The sentimentalist sees, in the end, only the dim outlines of external things. Whatever threatens his dear illusions is excluded from his perception. While the real lover attempts to understand and forgive his beloved's failings, the sentimental lover refuses to perceive them. While the truly indignant man seeks to understand the cause of his anger and is often compelled to relent by the reality that opposes him, the sentimental champion knows only that his cause is virtuous and his opponent wrong. Sentimentality is therefore cut off from reality and devoted to the task of misperceiving it. Hence sentimental poetry is marked by vagueness, unreality and a lack of observation – universal hallmarks of bad writing.

Leavis argued that what is bad in literature is bad also in life, for literature is life observed. Sentimentality is as much a moral as an aesthetic failing. Oscar Wilde described sentimentality as the other side of cynicism. The sentimentalist does not really believe that anything has meaning besides the wonderful drama of his own existence. He alternately scorns the world for its nothingness, and makes of it an object of blind adoration. In either case, things and people have no intrinsic value for him: at best they are excuses for the exultation on which he feeds.

Hence we should fear the presence in British public life of the sentimentalist lobby. While Benn, Scargill and Livingstone transform difficult politics into simple drama, mass movements of sentimentality – the peace movement, Third Worldism, feminism – sweep through the ranks of the middle classes, recruiting them to causes which have nothing to recommend them save the spurious clarity of a collective aim. Political problems are complex and political solutions rare: to the sentimentalist, however, such problems have the simplicity of every human drama, and their solution is dictated by a warm current of emotion on the crest of which he rides in triumph. When politics is dominated by sentimentality, the self takes the centre of the stage, judgment is clouded and all is vague, rushing and apocalyptic.

The sentimentalist is someone with a non-negotiable purpose, and his attitude to the reality which threatens him is to deny that it exists. No one should be surprised, therefore, at his refusal to compromise or to take his opponent's point of view. When the sentimentalist occupies a political platform it becomes a stage, and politics – the boring art of conciliation – gives way to a dramatic conflict which must be played to the end.

13 November 1984

The Crusade against Monetarism

Defoe observed that the streets of London contained many 'stout fellows, who would fight to the death against Popery, without knowing whether it be a man or a horse'. In our day, the synod of the Church of England is full of similar fellows, prepared to fight with equal gusto against monetarism. With compassionating zeal, they tell of the starving, the oppressed, the jobless and the shoeless, and identify 'monetarism' as the all-pervading cause.

Everywhere we see the effects of this Satanic power: declining industry, rising crime rates, social disintegration and abject poverty. Monetarism also forbids the provision of massive 'foreign aid' to countries governed by socialist planning. Hence it is the true cause of the Ethiopian famine. Having decided that man's problems are 'social' rather than spiritual, the radical clergy can no longer blame the sinner for his sin. The hatred expended on the picket line is not the doing of wicked individuals, but the blameless effect of an abstract cause. It is almost blasphemy to suggest that the decline in religion might be more dangerous than unemployment, or that the lack of spiritual guidance is more likely to generate crime than the failure of the government to embark on spendthrift policies. Spiritual guidance is precisely what the radical clergy cannot provide. Had it been otherwise, they would have drawn our attention seven or more years ago to the true calamity of Ethiopia, raising their voices in protest at the destruction of the world's oldest Christian society by atheist fanatics committed to a war against the soul of man.

But let us return to monetarism. The Bishop of Durham should be firmly told that this is neither a man nor a horse, but a theory. Quite reasonable people have been known to subscribe to it and to support the course of action which it recommends. Some of these people are Christians, aware of their responsibilities and aware too that it is not by government policy that the soul is lost or saved.

The basis of monetarism is the Quantity Theory of Money, a long-established but disputed theory based on the acceptance of the Fisher equation. Suppose M is the stock of money, V the velocity at which it circulates through the economy, P the average price level of goods and services and Y a volume measure of those goods and services. MV is then the total money value of goods bought, and PY the money value of goods sold. These values must be the same: in other words, $MV = PY$.

The theory receives its empirical application by assuming that Y is constant (or growing at a given rate), that the economy is at full employment (in the economist's sense) and will remain there, and that V is a constant. All those assumptions are dubious. Milton Friedman has argued, however, that the monetarist theory, suitably qualified, is applicable to modern market economies. Hence the rise and fall of the price level (P) will be determined by the rise and fall of the money supply (M). By controlling the money supply, therefore, we control also the rate of inflation.

The theory may be false: perhaps the Bishop of Durham has been granted a revelation that tells him so. Nevertheless, a politician who sincerely believes it to be true may feel that he has a Christian obligation to act on it. For a government which issues currency gives an assurance of its value, and cannot – without breach of trust – willingly devalue it. If the Quantity Theory is true, a government which increases the money supply does exactly what it appears to be doing: it devalues the currency. Hence it violates the Christian obligation to honour promises.

Moreover, it plays a devious trick on its citizens. It encourages them to sell their principal asset (their labour) for a wage, and then reduces the value of this wage, thus imposing a secret tax on labour. The canon law which forbids usury ought surely to apply to this pernicious form of it, in which no capital asset is offered in exchange for an unjust percentage.

A government has a greater obligation to cure inflation than to provide employment. For inflation is the government's *doing*: it is the government which issues the promissory notes that induce our dependence, and which chooses to multiply them in breach of trust. Unemployment is not the government's doing, even if it is the occasional consequence of its policy. If I starve my invalid wife, her death is my doing; but when a starving Ethiopian dies as a result of my inaction, his death is *not* my doing, even if I am in some measure to blame for it.

Traditional Christianity devoted enormous intellectual labour to the study of such distinctions, knowing that we must understand them if we are to live responsibly. The new class of bishop seems happy to ignore them, for its morality is utilitarian, calculating and secular. However, a churchman whose morality is based not on the apprehension of sacred things, but on the calculation of consequences, loses every claim to spiritual authority, and his moral pronouncements are no more to be taken seriously than are those of the politicians against whom he inveighs.

27 November 1984

A Martyr to Unhappiness

Edward McKenzie, a tramp who lived in a barrel on a rubbish tip, was befriended by Mr Robert Lenkiewicz, who called him, in recognition of his singular habits, Diogenes. Mr McKenzie died six weeks ago at the age of 72. His friend, who is a painter, conceived the plan of embalming him, coating him in acrylic and displaying him naked in his library, where he would perform the function of "a large paperweight".

Mr Lenkiewicz's proposal has met with strong opposition from Plymouth council, which holds itself bound to dispose of bodies according to the statutory requirements of public welfare and which has therefore threatened Mr Lenkiewicz with legal action under the Public Health Act, 1984. I assume that Mr McKenzie left no instructions in the matter. How, then, should his remains be treated, and to whom (if anyone) does the duty of disposal belong?

A human corpse is the relic of a human person and heir to the rights and privileges of the living body. To understand the predicament of Mr McKenzie's corpse, therefore, we should understand the life to which it testifies. In retrospect a human life is like a petition, which we honour at last by conferring dignities and titles on its harmless remainder. For what, then, was Mr McKenzie covertly petitioning in his barrel, and who has the duty to honour him?

It is a measure of the freedom enjoyed by the British citizen that he may still live as a tramp. Over vast areas of the globe a person who decided to live in a barrel would be instantly suspect, accused of 'parasitism' and placed behind barbed wire. For a long time after the invention of the welfare state, good British citizens wondered whether beggars, buskers, tramps and drop-outs were still permissible. Should they not be taken into 'care'? Should not the state take these people from their misery, or rather, from our misery on confronting them? 'Yes', said the bourgeois conscience, and for a long time 'yes' was the received idea.

Fortunately our tramps and beggars have been saved by a singular literary tradition, which has constantly reminded us of the value of solitude and of the natural right of every individual to be unhappy in his own particular way. Our writers have fought splendidly against the middle class conscience, aware that its compassion is also an annihilating zeal. Beckett – perhaps the greatest defender of the validity of tramping – saw the danger over a quarter of a century ago:

> Let me tell you this, when social workers offer you, free gratis and for nothing, something to hinder you from swooning, which with them is an obsession, it is useless to recoil, they will pursue you to the ends of the earth, the vomitory in their hands. The Salvation Army is no better. Against the charitable gesture there is no defence that I know of . . .
>
> Molloy

It seems, however, that Mr McKenzie had found such a defence. Safe in his barrel, in surroundings that no health inspector would willingly penetrate, he saw the welfare state and its work of abject conformity steadily recede from him. There, in that haven of solitude, Mr McKenzie was free at last to fulfil the most basic human need: the need for a personal unhappiness. And there he discovered companionship – the precious state to which sorrow disposes us, and which has no real place in the great project of universal welfare.

Mr McKenzie's companion is surely, therefore, his true executor, and what better discharge of unspoken obligations than to preserve his corpse in defiance of the requirements of public policy? As a varnished paperweight Mr McKenzie would be honoured and vindicated; as the occupant of a council grave he will testify only to the final triumph of the system against which he so heroically defended himself.

Against the literary tradition that upholds the rights of Mr McKenzie, however, there stands another that denies them: the tradition of utilitarianism, which has effectively neutralised the official conscience throughout the English-speaking world. Mr McKenzie's corpse, the utilitarian will tell us, should be disposed of according to the general requirements of human welfare, after the interests of all have been duly weighed.

That way of thinking – which abolishes not only Mr McKenzie's rights but also those of everyone who stands in the path of welfare – is the natural enemy of human dignity. If we take it seriously, then nothing is sacred. In the interests of public health and welfare the dead should be seized by the authorities at the very moment of their death and recycled in the form of sausages and pies.

The inventor of the public morality of utilitarianism was granted a privilege that his successors would deny to Mr McKenzie. In a cupboard in University College, London, sits the corpse of Jeremy Bentham, embalmed, varnished and surmounted by a waxen head. On special occasions he is wheeled out to contribute once again to the vain calculation of the profit and the loss.

Contemplating those soft, complaisant features, one cannot help thinking how much better Bentham would have looked, and how much less damage he would have done to human life and institutions, had he spent his life on a rubbish dump, sheltered by nothing more sturdy than a barrel.

18 December 1984

Honour and Arrogance

It is an established convention that the prime minister seek recommendations from the leaders of the other main political parties before advising the Queen as to who might fittingly be named in a list of honours. The present Labour leader has adopted a policy of making no recommendations; in the circumstances, this is to be expected. It more surprising to find the same policy pursued by the leader of the SDP. For the SDP's appeal rests in its claim to combine broadly socialist – or at least interventionist – policies with an underlying respect for the principles and procedures of the British constitution.

Of course, a constitution is a living, changing thing, with vital, and also decaying parts. The Labour Party believes the House of Lords to be already decayed and fit for amputation. No doubt it believes the same of the honours system. However, if Labour has a serious principle from which such conclusions follow, it is that the entire constitution, in so far as it limits the power of a future socialist government, is a nuisance and had better be done away with. Not so the SDP, which respects the idea of constitutional government and owes its success to the public belief that it would not, as Labour promises to do, make 'irreversible' changes in its own favour. If it rejects the idea of political honours, therefore, it is for some other reason than hostility to the principle of constitution.

As things stand, political honours serve two very important purposes. First, because they include peerages, they enable the prime minister to ensure that the Upper House contains members valued by the opposing parties and competent to speak for them. If Dr Owen believes – as he seems to believe – in the persistence of the House of Lords, ought he not to ensure that his party is properly represented in it?

Second, and more important, political honours serve the function of debunking politics. Honours issue from the Crown and are granted for services to the Crown and to the people, represented in the person and office of the monarch. All of us are grateful when our favourite actor, conductor or footballer is honoured. For the Crown is the symbolic representative of a community, and by concurring in our private enthusiasms it gives them public authority and objective force.

Politicians may also be honoured, and when this happens, the status of the individual is raised, while that of politics is lowered. We come to see that honour is higher than power, and that power does not suffice (although it may help) to secure it. Through the system of honours, therefore, the public is enabled to perceive two vital distinctions: that between authority and power, and that between the sovereign state and the powers which strive for influence within it. Honours clarify the logic of politics and emphasise precisely what is most precious in our constitution, which is that political power is at every point checked and diminished by the authority which stems from another source. By knighting a politician, the Queen reminds him that it is she, not he, who rules the country. And in accepting the honour, the politician shows his loyalty not only to the sovereign but also to the constitution which denigrates his power.

Moreover, the honouring of politicians, while it lowers the status of their calling, also reconciles the public to them, by showing that politics is, after all, as honourable as football. Politicians should be grateful for this. However, such is the arrogance of their profession that they frequently affect to despise these innocent tokens of public esteem, believing themselves to enjoy an eminence that can only be diminished by symbols as ceremonial and ineffective as a knighthood or a CBE.

Politicians who reject the honours system should therefore be looked upon with the gravest suspicion. They may, like Mr Benn, affect an unworldly contempt for dignities and titles, a righteous refusal of all personal reward for their services to a higher cause. But you can be fairly sure that their real motive is quite different from that which they would like you to ascribe to them. Their real motive is power, and the desire to ensure that power becomes the single source of worldly influence and the final title to respect. By appropriating all honour to themselves and their calling, politicians hope to extinguish the major limitation of their power: the Crown itself, which is the true representative of the British people.

Since Dr Owen believes in limited politics and lacks the Labour Party's philistine contempt for custom, he ought to show his acceptance of our way of life and institutions in the most painless manner available to him.

He should endorse the system of honours by making his own suggestions for future beneficiaries. No doubt he was as pleased as the majority of British subjects at the peerages conferred on Len Murray and Frank Chapple. No doubt he too was delighted that Naomi Mitchison, tireless champion of the true Fabian persuasion, should have been honoured, alongside the greatest Wagner conductor since Furtwängler. But to feel this delight, while not supporting the institution from which it flows, is to neglect a vital public duty, obedience to which may yet prove neccessary to the SDP's survival.

8 January 1985

Two Cheers for the CIA

During hard times our grandparents would be visited by nonconformist clergy offering soup and prayer. Ought they to have refused the soup, because of the prayer that had to be swallowed along with it? Only a fanatic would say so.

During the 1960s, a period of severe cultural depression, the CIA would offer relief to those who – because they spoke out against the prevailing nonsense – were threatened with extinction. Because of this charitable gesture, the truth about Soviet disinformation continued to be uttered and western resolve survived. The CIA asked for nothing in return: no prayers had to be repeated, no doctrine believed, no declaration made. And yet, when it was revealed that the CIA had actually spent money on this noble and non-violent purpose, the entire educational establishment threw up its hands in horror and called judgement upon the traitors who had sold their consciences for pieces of silver. No one suggested that the truth of an argument is affected by the source which pays the author. Nevertheless, so great was the outcry, that the Congress of Cultural Freedom in Paris was dissolved and our own excellent monthly *Encounter* suffered a shock from which it has only recently recovered.

Of course, the sixties were years of strange fanaticisms, in which symbols of authority were arbitrarily cast down. But the superstitions of that decade survive, and among them the extraordinary myth that the

CIA is the western equivalent of the KGB. Indeed, while the CIA is repeatedly portrayed as a sinister and ungovernable force, moving mysteriously from sin to sin, the KGB has benefited from a thousand small excuses, becoming at last almost as harmless in the liberal imagination as the CIA is in reality.

This process of 'moral inversion' (as the philosopher Polanyi called it) has the strange result that, in the minds of people not otherwise disposed to madness, the legitimate protection of our interests seems like an unpardonable crime. It is true that the CIA has been accused of dreadful things, even of assassinations, and this must inevitably affect our attitude. Unlike the KGB, however, it can be called to account, charged with illegalities and cut down to size. Moreover, it does not have, as its principal domestic concern, the liquidation of all opposition to its purposes. On the contrary, opposition flourishes so abundantly that the CIA is now utterly intimidated, refusing to engage even in its most honourable occupation – the support of those publications and institutions which tell the truth about the modern world. The CIA itself is very much to blame for this posture of timidity, for its operations depend on a climate of opinion favourable to the presentation of uncomfortable truths. It ought therefore to support those who express such truths. If the establishment cries out in horror, this is because the establishment requires truth to be comfortable.

The KGB is of course unhampered by similar scruples, and provides generous support to those who share its subversive purposes. Such is the effect of moral inversion that this is rarely commented upon, and even more rarely condemned. As a matter of fact, however, a financial connection with the KGB, like a connection with Gaddafi, ought to be vigorously denounced. For it is a connection with an enemy, and in so far as it reveals a similarity of purpose must inevitably cast suspicion on those involved in it.

The ethics of financial connection are complex. Consider the British Youth Council, which provides a forum for youth activities and representation at international gatherings. This is financed largely by the government, and receives a special grant from the Foreign Office. At the same time, as a good left-wing organisation, it has been far more anxious to establish contacts with Moscow than with our allies, and is particularly assiduous, during its trips to the Eastern bloc, to avoid contact with the unofficial youth movements. For these, being genuine associations, are subject to vigorous persecution by the Party

Some might say that, because the BYC receives money from the Foreign Office, it must be a government agency and therefore an anti-communist force. The charge is unjust, however. The BYC retains its freedom and uses the Foreign Office money as it pleases. Indeed, it is against Foreign Office advice that it plans to participate this year in the twelfth World Festival of Youth and Students in Moscow.

This jamboree, dedicated to 'anti-imperialist solidarity, peace, and friendship', is a splendid KGB publicity stunt, designed to unite the youth of the world around the communist banner and to add the servile voices of western leftists to the chorus of anti-American propaganda. By attending the conference the BYC shows its independence and integrity. Only a fanatic would accuse it of being tainted by the Foreign Office connection.

You do not have to be a fanatic, however, to accuse the Foreign Office of being tainted by *its* connection with the BYC. For it is reasonable to object to the use of government money in support of a KGB propaganda exercise. Better by far to give the money to *Encounter*.

15 January 1985

Temples of Anxiety

Since Enlightenment, western man has been prey to the pernicious superstition (as Dean Inge called it) of 'Progress'. He has been disposed to believe that all human affairs are subject to a principle of improvement and therefore that no institutions or practices ought to endure.

It is reasonable to believe that science, in the right conditions, will continuously advance. And with the advance of science come the steady mastery of nature, the improvement of technology and the conquest of disease. But scientific advance is precarious. It depends upon institutions, such as universities, which owe their existence to the wisdom of supremely unprogressive epochs, and their durability to a spiritual capital which they are always spending and which they seldom replace. Moreover, every scientific advance is paid for by a simultaneous retreat, as we endeavour to protect ourselves from the unforeseen consequences of our presumptuous experiments.

Nevertheless, so long as it can flourish, science is inherently progressive. The superstition lies in the belief that what is true of science is true of every other human endeavour – of politics, morality, religion and art. In those activities, which depend on an intuitive sensitivity to life and happiness, we may experience a decline, precisely when progressive thinking triumphs. For then firm instinct gives way to unfounded speculation, careful discipline to unruly freedom of choice.

In the field of aesthetics the result has been catastrophic. Art, craft and decoration have all been subjected to a tyrannical pursuit of novelty. Where previous generations have been content to accept patiently transcribed solutions to recurrent problems, we blithely and ignorantly set ourselves on another course, imagining that our superior science is also a superior wisdom and that our technical accomplishment is a substitute for art.

A case in point is the telephone booth, designed by Giles Gilbert Scott, architect of Liverpool's Anglican Cathedral. The familiar red box is one of the last creations of a disciplined tradition, whose products also include the Gothic factory, the Palladian clubhouse, the Pullman railway carriage and the Bombay shirt. The ruling idea of this tradition has been stability: certain forms, materials, details and colours have authority for us. It is from them, therefore, that we should choose the facades that will mask the latest horrifying advance of science, and so integrate it into the life that it threatens.

In every English village there is one object that stands out as the prime focus of the traveller's attention and the fitting representation of the stable government beneath whose mantle he journeys. This object is the telephone booth: a cast iron structure in imperial red, classical in outline, but with an interesting suggestion of Bauhaus naughtiness in its fenestration. Raised on a slight plinth, and with the proportions appropriate to a column base, it is capped by a gentle pediment, beneath which a panel of opalescent glass, lit from behind, makes a kind of cornice, bearing the word 'telephone' in sober classical letters. The door, divided into three parts by its mullions, has a brass handle set into the cast iron frame, and above the cornice a little crown is embossed, symbol of national identity and promise of enduring government. So suitable has this form proved to the streets, countryside and villages of England that it now appears on Christmas-card snowscapes, beside the Gothic spire, the gabled cottage and the five-barred gate. Only what is genuinely loved can be subjected to such a degradation.

British Telecom has, however, threatened to replace these familiar landmarks by barbarous concoctions of steel and aluminium of the kind to be seen in New York. In a sense this is only right. For the telephone testifies to the moral reality of Progress. Human beings were never meant to separate themselves so far from those they love as to take pleasure in their disembodied voices. They were never meant to conduct their business so rapidly that letters cease to be effective. They were never meant to start up nervously at the ringing of a mere machine, or to give it precedence over every human contact.

The telephone is the vessel of anxiety. At the same time, therefore, the booths are really temples, dedicated to a ruling deity. The smell of stale cigarette ash and rusting iron has become, for us, like the smell of incense – the record of long, holy moments, in which the god Anxiety has reached down to us with a personal concern. To have confined so cruel a god within so pleasant a temple is not the meanest achievement of the classical concept of design. At the same time, the burden of Progress has been lightened. The traditional booth makes the worship of Anxiety into a familiar feature of the English landscape – as familiar as the Gothic spire or the Georgian rectory.

We must therefore insist that telephone booths be considered to be buildings within the meaning of the Town and Country Planning Acts. Like any other temple, they must be made subject to conservation orders. For although it does not matter very much how a phone booth looks in Birmingham, where modern architects have already done their work, it still matters on a village green, a hillside or a moor.

29 January 1985

Obligations of the Flesh

Surrogate motherhood should be seen in its wider context: not as an answer to the problems of sterility, but as the outcome of a revision in moral perceptions comparable to that foretold in *Brave New World*. The citizens of Huxley's earthly paradise have a horror of motherhood, and attach to the process of childbirth the shame and the sense of contamination that our ancestors attached to sexual union. At the same time, the sexual act itself is without danger to them – a hygienic exercise, no more problematic than the brushing of teeth and rather more pleasurable.

The idea that sexual union is to be understood in terms of its generative tendency is foreign to their perceptions, since it implies that the human body might harbour a destiny and a responsibility greater than any that can be imposed by the all-powerful, impersonal and all-absolving State. It is for the abstract machinery of government to decide who shall exist, to take responsibility for his manufacture and to circumscribe his life. The sexual organs have no function other than fleeting pleasure, and to associate them with the crippling liabilities of childbirth, or the compromising destiny of a warm physical love, is to commit a terrible obscenity.

Naturally we have not yet advanced so far. Nevertheless, certain elements of Huxley's vision have been realised. Contraception has effectively severed the sexual act from its generative tendency, and, as Germaine Greer has argued, pregnancy now appears like a misfortune, or even a disease. Moreover, a scientific view of the human embryo has revised our idea of motherhood. As well a test-tube as a womb; and what matters that it should be this womb rather than that? Why not a womb detached from the human body, and preserved in laboratory conditions as a producer of children?

The unborn child is no longer a human person, attached by indelible rights and obligations to the mother who bears him, but a slowly ripening deformity, which can be aborted at will, should the mother choose to cure herself. In surrogate motherhood the relation between mother and child ceases to issue from the very body of the mother and is severed from the experience of incarnation. The bond between mother and child is demystified, made clear, intelligable, scientific – and also provisional, revocable and of no more than contractual force.

We should not see this as an isolated result of scientific progress. In just the same way the sexual bond has become clear and intelligible, and also provisional, revocable and of merely contractual force, governed by the morality of adult 'consent'. We have suffered a universal demystification of the human body. It has ceased to be the sacred fount of our deepest obligations and become instead a mere organism, obedient to the biological imperatives which govern all living things. Because we know ourselves in another way, however – as free beings, bound by a moral law – we begin to doubt the moral prerogative of the body. It no longer seems possible to us that the merely *bodily* character of our acts can determine their moral value. Hence arises the extraordinary view that the homosexual act, considered in itself, is morally indistinguishable from the heterosexual act: for what is there, in its merely physical character, to justify the traditional stigma?

The liberal morality which tells us to permit the body's pleasures and to stifle the impulse of shame expresses, in effect, a peculiar metaphysical vision of the body as somehow detached from the self and outside the sphere of our true obligations. To the liberated conscience it seems absurd that the prophet of Islam, enjoining us to charitable behaviour, should add that we must conceal our private parts. What a ludicrous mixture of moral truth and childlike superstition! And yet, in this as in many things, Muhammad's instinct was sure. We are not separate from our bodies, but identical with them, and inculpated not only by our actions, but also by our pleasures and postures and by bodily exposure to our kind.

Traditional sexual morality was an instrument whereby people came to terms with their incarnation and took moral responsibility for their flesh. The two earthly loves which prompt and fulfil our existence – sexual love and the love of children – issue from the body by a process that we may see in neutral, scientific terms only at our peril. For these are forces by which we live and which govern our smaller obligations. To regard the process which generates them as subject to revision and revocation is to set the body outside the sphere of moral sentiment and to cease to take responsibility for one's flesh. It is to exchange the moral security of corporal existence for a fantasy of ultimate freedom, in which all our obligations are of our own devising and the tyrant destiny is overcome. But there cannot be such an ultimate freedom, and all that is achieved by our constant striving towards it is the slow alienation from our bodily condition and the gradual poisoning of the carnal source of love.

In such matters, St Augustine argued, the body appears to have a will of its own, and its constant disobedience, he added, is the testimony to original sin. But if original sin resides in the body, it is because we reside there too. Hence we should never lose sight of the fundamental truth, that some uses of the body are sinful, and none more so than those which enable us to escape the obligations which the body itself imposes.

5 February 1985

Opposing Marx

Western journalists and diplomats frequently tell us of encouraging 'changes' in the communist world. Each new leader is heralded as a liberal, and each new policy is regarded as a development towards more flexible government. We are even told of a 'struggle' between 'hawks' and 'doves' in the Kremlin, although it is a struggle so secret that it cannot be described.

None of this nonsense should deceive us. Only one development in the communist world could involve a decisive move in a liberal direction: the tolerance of opposition. Nothing else will enable rational discussion to fill the place now occupied by force. A 'liberal' leader who is immune from public criticism is really a tyrant, and a change of policy that cannot be publicly opposed is merely a change from madness to insanity.

Nevertheless there have been small improvements. Recently a Yugoslav philosophy journal carried a devasting critique of Marxism, and the author, Neven Sesardić of Zagreb University, has yet to be arrested. The comparative mildness of the Yugoslav regime should not blind us to the fact that, like every communist government, it is dedicated to the liquidation of opposition and the censorship of all inconvenient ideas. Yet Dr Sesardić has not been censored.

His article, which has been translated into English,* would prove inconvenient not only to the Yugoslav Communist Party, but also to many of my colleagues. A great many British students are required to study Marx, without being told that the theories associated with his name – the labour theory of value, the materialist theory of history and the quasi-Hegelian theory of man – have all been substantially refuted. Of course, there is profit in studying these ideas: sometimes the truth can be perceived only by those who stand on the dust heap of refuted theories. Nevertheless, it can hardly be appropriate to take them as premise, method and conclusion of a modern social science. Why then is it so often done?

The answer is simple: Marx is taught largely for his socialist conclusions, by people for whom truth is a secondary concern. He is rarely taught for what is most profound and brilliant in his writings – the theory of history, which every educated person ought to be able to state, defend and criticise. Marx is taught for his politicised economics and philosophy, despite the fact that in neither field did he make any genuine advance.

Consider the appalling argument which begins *Das Kapital*. If a quarter of corn exchanges against x hundredweight of iron, Marx tells us, then there exists in each of these bundles an equal quantity of something *else*, which is neither corn nor iron. This is the premise of the confused and untenable piece of rhetoric known as the 'labour theory of value' – and it is a transparent non sequitur. If I give you a shoe in return for a glove, then I have received a glove and you a shoe. That is the full truth of the matter.

Dr Sesardić decisively refutes the labour theory, using criticisms which have been familiar in western literature for half a century or more. Being aware of the real tendency of Marx's thought, Dr Sesardić is unlikely to make excuses, as the western Marxist does, for its fallacious premises. To the western Marxist, however, the theory has lost none of its charm. Its effect on the data of social analysis is like the effect of a magnet on a tray of iron filings. Elements which lay scattered and isolated suddenly coalesce in regimented lines, heaps become smooth and orderly, and the whole mass receives a pattern harmonious to the eye and exciting to the intellect. In Marx's system human action, social structure, economic performance and moral experience are all held together in a comprehensible totality, in which the passionate student can glimpse a vision of the imminent downfall of capitalism and the final emancipation of man. The fact that the theory is false is easily put out of mind by those ravished by its conclusion.

Unlike Dr Sesardić we teach in liberal institutions dedicated to free discussion. It is therefore right that we teach the theories of Marx, if only to guard against their seductiveness. No doubt, if Marx were compulsory, our radical lecturers would be less inclined to teach him and our students less inclined to learn. Nevertheless, it is strange that an article published in Yugoslavia should give vivid utterance to arguments that can be uttered here without penalty, which are largely valid and which nevertheless have been suppressed by those who could most learn from them.

Or is it so strange? If Marxism survives every refutation, is it not because no refutation is ever heard by believing Marxists? And if Marxists suppress all criticism when they are in power, is this not because, for them, criticism is strictly inadmissible?

12 February 1985

*Neven Sesardić and Domenico Settembrini, *Marxian Utopia?*, available from The Centre for Research into Communist Economies, 2 Lord North Street, London SW1.

Testimony to a Miracle

Recently there occurred a publicly attested miracle. Against everything that we can know or surmise of the inscrutable workings of communist government, four Polish secret policemen were charged, tried, convicted and sentenced for the murder of a priest. That the trial was in many ways a travesty of justice need not concern us; what is important is that it occurred. Nobody really knows *why* it occurred, although doubtless this event, like every event, could be given a full and convincing explanation by an omniscient scientist.

We are not omniscient: we can be certain only that a breach – momentous and unforeseeable – transfigured the metallic face of communism, like a sudden smile upon the face of a corpse. But its meaning is there for all to witness. The impersonal tyranny which has ruled over Poland for 40 years, heedless of the cries of millions, suddenly broke its posture and crazily, with unpractised movements, uttered a stuttering apology. Had he lived, Father Popiełuszko could not have achieved such a transformation. But his lonely death shook the world and caused the unspeakable to speak.

Hume argued that it is irrational to believe in miracles, since it is always more probably that the testimony of a witness is erroneous than that a law of nature has been momentarily set aside. But Hume's assumption is false. Miracles occur not when nature is set aside, but when it is transfigured by a meaning. Our understanding of the miraculous is like our understanding of the person. When we see someone smile, we see human flesh moving in obedience to electrical impulses in the nerves. No law of nature is suspended in this process: we smile not in spite of, but because of nature. Nevertheless, we understand a smile in quite another way: not as flesh moved mechanically, but as spirit freely revealed. A smile is always more than flesh for us, even if it is only flesh.

A miraculous event is one which wears, for us, a personal expression. We may not notice this expression, just as someone may stare at a portrait, see all the lines and colours that compose it and fail to see the face. The defect of miracles is not that they defy the law of nature, but that of necessity they cannot recur. If 'we had the experience, but missed the meaning', then for us the meaning is lost.

The Catholic Church is rightly cautious in canonising its martyrs, and normally requires an attested miracle as the sign of beatification. It seems to me that Father Popiełuszko's spirit worked such a miracle, and that the question of his saintliness depends only on the nature of his death. Some will argue that he was a martyr to his faith, killed because he would not renounce his duty to bear witness to spiritual truth. Others will argue that he had entered too deeply into the tainted world of politics, and paid the miserable and expected price.

The choice between these conflicting interpretations is serious, and events in Central America, not to speak of nearer home, have made us especially conscious of its significance. We praise the priest who dares to speak against injustice and to defend the law of God; but we condemn the priest who faithlessly devotes himself to transient worldly causes, squandering his authority in fruitless schemes to recreate the world. To which of those finely divided categories did Father Jerzy belong?

To concentrate the mind on such a question is not easy. Clarity comes a step nearer, however, when you visit the plain church in Żoliborż where Father Jerzy's portrait, naively executed in lurid tones, hangs beside the altar, and where solemn crowds gather at the gate of the tiny churchyard and step quietly past his grave. Candles stand everywhere in the surrounding streets, guttering and smoking in the bitter wind, and their paraffin smell reaches into the cold interior, where the motionless crowds stand silently in prayer.

In this place you encounter grief and yearning, but without bitterness and without despair. The crowd is no union of fiery radicals, bent on some work of destruction or revenge; it represents no faction or interest, no ideology or scheme. It is not there to furnish itself with some new political illusion or to stake a merely earthly claim. Its intensity is neither angry nor joyless, and when a young bridal couple emerge from their marriage in an adjoining chapel the people freely greet them with whispered congratulations and warm, self-deprecating smiles.

If a political meaning is present in this church it is merely the political meaning of every human act: the desire that faith, trust and friendship be permitted, and honourable agreements upheld. It is the desire that human society should flourish according to its innate need for spiritual meaning and not be bound by iron laws. It is the unceasing prayer that a personal expression, which miraculously transfigures the human flesh, should transfigure too the world of human government. And in one momentous particular, just such a transfiguration occurred.

In their ineluctable workings the laws of nature formed and then unformed a miraculous pattern. Many can bear witness to this sudden meaning, and the memory of it will accompany them to the grave. Such was Father Popiełuszko's final gift to his parishioners. Their faces are marked by grief, but are also marked, for all to see, by gratitude.

19 February 1985

The Representation of Minorities

How representative is the House of Commons? If you were to measure the proportion of club-footed, handsome, schizophrenic, witty, rabbit-toothed or unworldly members, you would doubtless find the result to be unrepresentative of the nation. But it is not the task of parliament to represent groups, especially groups so capriciously defined. Its task is to represent the people, and also the major interests that unite and divide them. The regimentation of members by the whips is justified only on the assumption that conflicting interests can best be opposed and accommodated through national parties.

Perhaps the most important defect of the arrangement is the resistance of the party system to new interests and its perpetuation of interests that have long since declined. Members enter the Commons only by ingratiating themselves with the parties. These, however, are controlled by people who have been severed by a lifetime of politics from the realities of ordinary existence. Hence new members must make a show of accepting and acting upon a mythopoeic view of modern society.

Thus, half a century after the disappearance of the traditional class system, the Commons is still enacting a battle that might have been scripted by Marx. Wicked Tory capitalists (most of them with working-class accents) face the oppressed proletariat (whose representatives seem to spring largely from Winchester and Balliol). Amusing though this conflict may occasionally be, it can hardly advance the real purpose of parliament, which is that of representing and accommodating the existing interests of the British people. The impermeability of the parties to new interests is surely one of the major reasons for thinking that the House of Lords and the judiciary are, in the last analysis, far more representative of the people than the House of Commons.

One new set of interests has been excluded from the House with grave and unwelcome consequences: that of the ethnic minorities. The Commons contains no black or yellow face; even constituencies with vast and concentrated Asian populations are represented by white Anglo-Saxons. Why is this? Why is there not a sizeable minority of Indians, another of blacks, and perhaps a Chinese or two? The fault, I believe, lies with all the principal parties, but mostly with the Tory Party, which could provide far greater scope than its rivals for the parliamentary aspirations of the new minorities.

Until now, the demand for minority representation has been directed largely at the Labour Party, as the natural party of opposition. For a long time black pressure groups have been urging that their members be selected for safe Labour seats. But the party has been reluctant to respond, suspecting that a constituency with a black candidate would no longer be safe. It is undeniable that old-fashioned Labour voters include many who would find, in these new circumstances, a definite strain on their allegiance. Nevertheless, the Labour Party ought to take the risk. If it does not, its isolation from the real sources of opposition will increase still further, and its credibility enter a final decline.

Rather than join the natural party of opposition, however, ethnic minorities would do better to join the party of government. If the minorities seem to be radicalised, this is partly *because* of their lack of parliamentary representation. It is inconceivable that our Asian population as a whole could identify with the polytechnic socialism of the Labour Party, or feel that it is in any way represented by the radical nuisances who dominate the party's extra-parliamentary adjuncts. In the temporary fervour of discontent the Asian community may sympathise with the party of opposition. But what does a pious Muslim, who believes in family values, single-sex schools, chastity, household, property and material success, have to do with the egalitarian ideology of Labour? Surely the Tory Party is his natural home, and he has as much claim as the rest of us to be represented within it.

No doubt the Tory Party has the same anxiety as Labour concerning the prejudices of its traditional constituents. I suspect, however, that the average Tory voter would stand the test as well as the average Labourite, and that the long-term benefit to the party would justify the risk. A safe Labour seat in a constituency with a large number of Asians would cease to be safe if the Tories put up an Asian candidate. And what is true of the Asians is true too of the blacks, who are just as likely, in the long run, to identify with the Tory Party. Radical propaganda to the contrary, the blacks have as great an interest in law, education, property and religious values as have the rest of the British people, and, if my local black church is any guide, their underlying sentiments are far too conservative to be catered for by the present Labour Party.

Of course it would be against the spirit of representation to select a candidate purely because of his racial origins. Nevertheless, the ethnic minorities have interests that distinguish them from the rest of the population. As things stand, these interests enter the political equation only after suffering a radical transformation at the hands of the socialist quangos. The direct representation of minority interests in parliament would be better for all of us. The feminist lobby, for example, would lose much of its unrepresentative influence were the Muslim desire for sexual segregation to be recognised in parliament. The radical reformers of the school curriculum would equally suffer a jolt if the real interest of blacks in educational achievement were expressed in the Commons by someone with a black face.

The radicals tell us that there is a racial conflict in Britain. If this is really so, there is no better place for it than the House of Commons, where it can be displayed in theatrical form, heightened, embellished and also resolved. This cathartic function of parliament did much to eliminate class conflict from the national consciousness: there is no reason to think that it could not eliminate racial conflict as well. On the other hand, if the radicals are wrong and there is no racial conflict in Britain, nothing whatsoever prevents the major parties from enriching themselves, at the next election, with the vital interests of the new minorities.

5 March 1985

De Anima

A philosophical question is one that cannot be finally answered. Some philosophers therefore say that such questions cannot be asked, since a question without an answer is not a question. This *gran rifiuto* has a certain dignity, but that is all. There can be provisional answers even where no answer is final, and since everything that matters to us is provisional, why should not philosophy matter too? Our experience bears witness to our need for philosophical answers. In morality, in religion – and now, alas, in politics – the great metaphysical questions ceaselessly obtrude, begging for an immediate and provisional reply.

One such question – considered by Professor Searle in last year's Reith lectures – is that of the soul (or 'mind' as the philistines describe it). Is the soul distinct from the body? If not, whence arises our sense of obligation, what justifies it and how should we behave? Every human life contains a tacit answer to those questions, and the advantage of religion is that its answer is loud and clear. For many people, however, a softly spoken and hesitant answer is all that is obtainable, and the voice which utters it is heard only occasionally, in the pauses of an over-busy life.

It would not be right to describe Professor Searle as a 'still, small voice'. On the contrary, there is something loud and bantering in his argument that we are categorically distinct from computers and possess capacities that no machine could have. There are two reasons for being dissatisfied with what he says. One is that he constantly seems to assume what he must prove – namely, that a machine can play with signs, but only we can *understand* them.

The other is that his argument is severed from all moral consequence. Even if we are, as he says, distinct from every artificial intellect, why should this matter to us? Is this the sign that we are free, that our lives have purpose and value, that death has lost its sting? Or is it just a weird addition to the sum of human misery: that we are not only, like the rest of nature, purposeless, but also cursed with the capacity to know how purposeless we are?

Religions have often encouraged the belief in the soul as an entity wholly separable from the body which incarnates it, a principle of freedom and value, the ultimate residence of the self. In morality and in worship, according to this view, the soul becomes aware of its separateness from the flesh and is inspired by the distant vision of its eternal home.

Almost all modern philosophers doubt that such a thing could be literally true, and many of them also agree with St Thomas Aquinas that it is by no means neccessary for a religious person to believe it. The soul is neither separate from the body nor truly separable, and the promise of eternity means not disembodied existence in an unending future, but the emancipation from time.

Aristotle suggested that anger is a boiling of the blood, but cautioned us that the word 'is' here does not signify identity. Anger is a boiling of the blood in something like the way that a house is the bricks which compose it. Similarly, the relation of the soul to the body is like that of a house to its bricks. The soul is a principle of organisation, which governs the flesh and endows it with a meaning. It is no more separable from the flesh than is the house from its bricks, even if the soul may survive the gradual replacement of every bodily part.

It is to the soul that we respond when we respond to another, not to the flesh, even though the soul is nothing but flesh. In responding we see a meaning that we can transcribe in words only with the greatest labour – that of poetry, which is also the labour of the liturgy.

We do not understand another merely by dwelling on his bodily constitution, any more than we understand architecture by studying it as it would be studied by an engineer. The appeal of religion lies partly in its ability to transcribe the meaning of the human form in intelligible symbols. Religion aims to extract the moral consequences which our bodily form implies, but which it implies too discreetly and too hesitantly to present a real obstacle to crime.

If you think of the soul in that way, you can also understand what it is to lose it. You lose your soul when you cease to find the soul of others; when you see others eclipsed by their bodies, their meaning extinguished by the physical laws which propel them. An example is provided by obscenity. In obscenity the human body invades our perceptions, overwhelming us with its reality as a physiological contraption. Seeing the body thus, unilluminated by the individual self, we see it as barren, disgusting and disposable. If we take delight in that we are already lost.

More subtle ways are available, however, whereby the sense of the soul's priority is lost. Perhaps the most important – and characteristically modern – of these is through the great scientistic illusion according to which the source of human life is hidden from us: in the unconscious, in the 'material conditions' of economic life, in our history, our instincts or our genes. Such an idea – associated with every pseudo-science of man, from Marx and Freud to sociobiology – severs us more effectively than any superstition from our purpose and fulfilment. For it fosters the master thought of crime: the attribution of my life and actions to something that is not myself, and for which I cannot answer.

19 March 1985

What do we Stand For?

A small state can survive only by allying itself, and its allies must be chosen from the few sorry products of human political endeavour. This fact has a special importance now that the world is governed by rhetoric, which has the power to titillate the conscience while leaving the intellect untouched. By exciting sentiments of outrage against our friends, the media take a direct route to the individual conscience. And the more their crusades damage our interests, the more presentable is the conscience which inspires and follows them.

It is therefore inevitable that a state like South Africa, which displays her most hideous blemish in the middle of her face, should be denounced so vociferously, while her tyrannical neighbours get off, on the whole, scot-free. For South Africa is our friend. In two world wars her people fought and died for our protection. In the global conflict which threatens to engulf us, she alone in the whole continent of Africa could be relied upon to take our side. It is therefore natural to feel guilty about South Africa, in a way that we could never feel guilty about the Soviet Union or China. Moreover, South Africa offends against the shibboleth of equality and, what is worse, she openly says so. Communism tells us loudly and clearly that it believes in the natural equality of man. In a sense it does: for it believes that all people are equally valueless, equally expendable means to a collective end.

It is probably true that blacks enjoy greater freedom, greater prosperity, greater opportunity and greater peace in South Africa than in most neighbouring countries (this seems to be implied by the constant tide of illegal black immigration). But the blemish of apartheid ensures that such virtues will never be considered. Those, like Edward Kennedy, who wash their consciences publicly in the ever-abundant stream of rhetoric, have found in South Africa too easy a means to put their hearts on display, and will never now be tired of so profitable a pastime.

There is, however, a deeper reason for the assault on South Africa, and one which shows that, despite all our abhorrence of apartheid, South Africa is our natural friend. In South Africa you can, within limits, speak out against the prevailing oppression. Your voice will be multiplied by the press, by the universities and by parliamentary discussion. Your rights will be defined in parliament and protected by the courts. The courts will even protect you against the government, and when – as frequently happens – law conflicts in principle with oppressive legislation, it is the legislation and not the law that is discarded.

As a result, it is worthwhile to abuse South Africa: you might actually *achieve* something. Your voice is echoed internally and answered by those in power. By contrast, you can shout at the Soviet Union till you are blue in the face and you will not change it in the smallest particular. If any Soviet citizen is rash enough to take up your cry, he is at once deprived of legal protection and harshly silenced.

An important question lies before us, and the future of the western alliance depends upon the answer. What do we in the West *stand for*? What is it, besides the fear of Soviet domination, that unites us? American diplomacy argues that we are united in defence of democracy, and that what we mean by 'democracy' is not the paper democracy of the Soviet empire, but the *real thing*. But if the 'real thing' means American-style elections, how can we stand beside South Africa, Chile and Egypt, and how can we set our face against Nicaragua where, according to one version of events, the Sandinistas' power has been endorsed by a democratic election?

Such questions suggest that the standard American theory of the western alliance is too parochial, too little informed by a sense of history, to be persuasive to anyone who is not American. To put the matter bluntly, democracy has no intrinsic value: it is not an end, but a means.

Democracy is valuable primarily as a means to responsible power – power answerable to those who do not possess it. Where responsible government exists, the exercise of power is tempered by the norms of personal association. To insist on democratic election as the sole and sufficient standard of political legitimacy is to forget both human nature and human history. It is to forget, for example, the election which confirmed Hitler in power and which extinguished responsible government in Germany.

If governments turn judges out of office when the courts displease them, they cease to be answerable to the powerless. Hence responsible government is possible only where there is a rule of law. It was the incipient lawlessness of Hitler's government, its contempt for forms, procedures and judicial limitations, that made it so dangerous a member of the community of nations. This defect was not remedied by the fact that the German people once voted it into office.

Responsible government also requires legal opposition, the right to express dissenting views and the unconstrained discussion of such views in parliament. Those fundamental institutions have existed in England, on and off, since the reign of Edward II, and without them democratic elections are of no significance. Finally, responsible government is representative, and it is in this feature that South Africa falls so lamentably short.

There is a tendency to confuse representation with election. But election conducted in an atmosphere of fear and demagoguery will rarely lead to representative government. Only in certain circumstances do the interests of the powerless afflict the consciences and govern the actions of those in power. It is because we endeavour to approach those conditions that the members of the western alliance stand together. And it is for the same reason that we have a common enemy.

2 April 1985

No Middle Road

'*The only choice* is: either bourgeois or socialist ideology: there is no middle road. . .'. So wrote Lenin in 1902. Two decades later Gramsci, leader of the Italian Communist Party, wrote that 'between fascism and communism there is no middle road,' a sentiment with which his rival, Mussolini, agreed. In 1942 the Czech politician, Moravec, broadcast to his homeland that 'the only thing to be decided today is whether Europe is to be national socialist or Bolshevik. There is no third solution'. And every reader of *Pravda* or *Rudé Právo* will be familiar with the editorial which begins: 'Only the Leninist path is the true path of socialist construction. There is no alternative except counter-revolution. Between revolution and counter-revolution there is no third way . . .'.

Such language comes naturally to those who have succumbed to 'the totalitarian temptation'. But Jean-François Revel had more in mind, in coining that phrase, than the Manichean desire to divide the world into exhaustive spheres of good and evil. The totalitarian mentality wishes not merely to divide, but also to rule. Moreover, because it sees itself locked in battle with an enemy who might establish himself anywhere and at any time, it must rule over everything. The mark of totalitarian government is therefore intolerance of every institution in which 'the enemy' might find a voice. Hence totalitarians in power pass rapidly from the liquidation of political opponents to the more important task of establishing control over subordinate institutions: over schools, universities and the press, over the judiciary, over industries and unions, over churches, youth organisations and societies of every description.

Jeane Kirkpatrick was right to distinguish authoritarian from totalitarian government: for dictatorial power may exist side by side with free associations, as in Franco's Spain. Of course, dictatorship colours the surrounding society, even when it does not exert total control over it. But someone who says there can be *no* distinction between totalitarian and authoritarian government – who believes that societies are *either* totalitarian *or* democratic – has himself succumbed to the totalitarian temptation. For him, too, there is no third way.

Of course there *is* a third way; and a fourth; and a fifth; and a twentieth. Drop from your eyes the distorting lens of either/or, of left/right, socialism/capitalism, bourgeois/proletarian, Jew/Aryan, black/white, good/evil – and you will see that the possibilities are multifarious, and that none of them is perfect. Open your mind to the truth and regard no one as your rooted enemy, save only the one who says 'there is no third way, no middle road, no compromise with *them*!'

Until recently that injunction was tacitly obeyed by the mass of British people, and by those who governed them; but times have changed. It is no longer possible to assume that your opponent acts in a spirit of compromise, or that he respects the truth as something independent of his own conceptions. Truth, for the totalitarian, is power, and must therefore be appropriated as his own exclusive possession, while compromise is not for him what it is for you or me – an ability to renounce, in the face of opposition, even one's most cherished purposes – but a manoeuvre, another means to the same end of total domination.

The totalitarian mentality does not function properly, however, until it has possessed itself of an ideology – a system of thought which divides the world effectively into 'good' and 'evil', into those who are with us and those who, because they are not with us, are against us. By a peculiar inversion the modern totalitarian, who sees the Nazi not as his fellow-in-delusion but as his quintessential foe, has built an ideology from 'anti-racism'. Between racism and anti-racism, he tells us, there is no middle road. If you are not with me, then you are against me, and therefore a racist.

The anti-racist movement, like the Nazi movement whose habits of vilification it imitates, is attempting to gain control of important autonomous institutions, in particular those where inconvenient truths may be uttered and where influence other than its own may flourish. To anyone who has studied the rise of totalitarian movements it will come as no surprise to find that the anti-racists wish to control local government and schools, two crucial centres through which power may be exerted not over the state but over something which for the totalitarian mind is far more important: civil society. Through schools and local administration the lives of citizens can in the end be more effectively controlled than through the distant thunder of an increasingly impotent government.

The first consequences are already upon us. The ILEA has begun its expected campaign of censorship, seeking to remove from school libraries all books, regardless of their literary or intellectual merit, which offend the anti-racists. Mr Ray Honeyford, the Bradford headmaster who wrote a seriously argued article, almost every word of which I believe to be true and whose message is that the anti-racist ideology is a tissue of lies, has now been suspended, purely because the anti-racists wanted to make an example of him.

Such instances are minor; but they contain a serious warning. They show that a totalitarian mentality is once again growing in the political subsoil. Censorship, intimidation, the ruthless silencing of representative opponents, the gradual control of subordinate institutions, the manipulation of ignorant sentiment and an ideology of 'good' and 'evil' – all these are now on the march behind a banner which says 'He who is not with us is against us: there is no third way!' Or, in the words of the GLC's latest anti-racist poster: 'If you are not part of the solution, you are part of the problem.'

And as before, the solution is to be final.

16 April 1985

A Voice from Old Vienna

A spectre is haunting the Labour Party – the spectre of Hobsbawm. All the powers of the old left are dancing to its sepulchral music. 'Thatcherite Toryism', it chants, 'is the enemy'; 'comrades' must 'mobilise' against the power which 'wages the class struggle against the workers' and their 'heroic trade union movement'. All must engage in true 'class politics', which has elsewhere raised the conflict with the bourgeoise 'to the level of armed struggle'. All must join forces with the movement that has established, in our beloved Europe, '10 new states setting out to construct socialism'.

Such is the language in which the communist professor, last active remnant of the Cambridge Apostles, sets out his programme for a 'broad socialist alliance' (*Guardian*, 8 April). It is a language of the distant past – of those strife-torn years in Central Europe when enmity walked the streets of the capitals and spoke from the mouths of deluded demagogues.

Can it really be the case that Mr Kinnock is listening to these ancestral voices? Can it really be that he is so ignorant of history – of the history that Professor Hobsbawm has devoted his life to redescribing – as not to know what communists do to their allies at the hour of victory? Can he really be so insensitive to words as not to hear the sound of the tocsin and know that it tolls for him?

Thatcherism is about to founder, Hobsbawm tells us, for the rats of the old ruling class are deserting the ship. How else is one to interpret the historic vote of Oxford University against its most distinguished alumna?

Few of those dons who packed the Senate to vote against her had ever been socialist. As everyone knows, Oxford is a bastion of Tory privilege.

If Thatcherism is really foundering, it is strange that we need so vast an alliance to ensure its destruction. But it is not only the theory that testifies to Hobsbawm's impercipience. In all my experience of British universities I have rarely encountered a Tory voter; least of all in Oxford. And since the character of the true Tory is to avoid public manifestations of immature sentiment, can one really be surprised when the lumpenintelligentsia is able to pack a meeting at the university which has done so much to provide its spurious credentials?

But this weird perception of Oxford is only one small part of the nostalgic fantasy which Hobsbawm projects on to the screen of the present. Thatcherism, he tells us, 'represents the feelings of social climbers and hardfaced people who have done well . . . out of free enterprise'. Actually no more effective instrument of social climbing has ever been devised than the salon socialism of old Vienna, unless it be the common-room socialism of Oxford.

As for those hardfaced people – should not Professor Hobsbawm look in a mirror? For has he not done rather well out of free enterprise, in a country where a professor, living securely on the back of an economy which he may devote his life to denigrating, earns £2 000 a month? In Poland – one of those ten favoured countries which are now 'constructing socialism' – a university lecturer starts with the equivalent of £25 a month, and only if he is actively 'constructing socialism' in the ranks of the party can he ever hope to live like Professor Hobsbawm. In the lands of 'real socialism', however, where the new ruling class no longer feels obliged to desert the ship of government, the society at the top smells rather less pleasant than the society of fashionable London.

But of course, despite the heroic victory of the Polish proletariat (not to be confused with the recent defeat of the true working class), we are not to take Poland – or any other 'actually existing' country – as our model for the future. In the spectre's words: 'As for the institutions of a future socialist society, who can discern their shape in the fog of argument about them?' Well, the fog is the spectre's creation – and a strategically useful one. For what if his allies discovered the truth about the destination towards which he entices them? What if they discovered the real nature of a body politic with the blood of the workers – and of every other class – so horribly spattered on its hands?

Perhaps they might see that the spectre has a case to answer. They might ask him not merely how the rich will suffer from his schemes, but how the poor will benefit. How will law and government be conducted?

How will freedom and prosperity be secured? Most of all, how does he propose to live with those who are not socialists and whom he presently dismisses as 'the enemy'?

Professor Hobsbawm once voiced some of the doubts that had caused a few comrades to stray from the path of revolutionary rectitude, and came up with the following answer: 'If the left may have to think more seriously about the new society, that does not make it any the less desirable or neccessary'. Ponder that utterance, Mr Kinnock, and you will begin to understand the meaning of this siren song. No matter that you don't know where you are going, just so long as you see that it is 'necessary', and even 'desirable', to go there.

Socialism is with us, and with us to stay. It is not for us to forbid its aspirations, or to deny power to those who share them. But it is wise to be sure that the people do really support a policy that would do so much harm to them, and that this historic alliance with the workers – including those who vote so persistently for the Thatcherite 'enemy' – is not merely another device for transferring power to the intellectual Jacobin.

Those hardfaced people who exhort us only to destroy our way of life, and offer nothing but a fog of disputation in place of it, should certainly speak out. But let us hope that they will be heard not in the Commons, but in the common room, where social climbing is conducted with minimum damage to those who pay for it with their honest labour.

30 April 1985

In Loco Parentis

A short while ago I heard a weatherhen of liberal sentiment defend the view that teachers should not strike. Teachers, she argued, have the *right* to strike, but it is a right which they should not exercise, since in doing so they damage the innocents who have been placed in their charge. The same argument goes for nurses, doctors and members of similar professions who are obliged to stay at work for the sake of those whom the state, in its wisdom, has put in their trust. I do not know which is more objectionable: the view that there is a 'right' to strike or the view that those who have direct care of the state's dependants are under some special duty not to exercise that 'right'. But it seems to me that teachers and nurses are as entitled to strike as anyone else. The fact that they do not is testimony only to the conscience engendered by their professions.

A strike is a conspiracy to frustrate the aims of a contract and thereby to coerce one of the parties. It may sometimes be justifiable to strike; but how such a thing could be a *right* I do not know. Every right creates a binding obligation to respect it. If there is an obligation to respect the 'right to strike' then no contract of employment could be sincerely made, since neither side would be committed to its terms. The contract of employment, however, is the cornerstone of a free economy, and to set it aside so easily is to threaten every right that we actually enjoy. Only in a slave economy is there a *right* to strike, but it is the mark of a slave economy that strikes are made illegal.

Teachers may nevertheless be justified in striking since no other course of action may secure a proper reward for their services. The state compels all children to go to school, even those who have no interest in attending. In such circumstances a teacher's job cannot be easy. Anybody who has stood in front of a class of children for six hours a day, five days a week, and endeavoured both to control them and to retain their interest, knows that this is demanding and disturbing work. In an ideal world the teacher would receive a salary commensurate with the other professions and a social status equal to theirs. In such a world, however, the teacher would not be a servant of the state. Nor would children be compelled, regardless of their interests, to attend his classes.

The sentimental liberal believes that teachers, like nurses, have a *special responsibility* to those in their charge. Why is this? Parents are compelled to educate their children, and for most people this means sending them to a state school. The illusion therefore arises that children are really the responsibiltiy of the state. The teacher, being the servant of the state who exercises that responsibility, seems to bear the burden of it.

Individuals do indeed have dreadful responsibilities – towards their parents, their children and those who are sick and needy – and these responsibilities are difficult to discharge. The state therefore offers a service which relieves us of a burden. Thereafter arises the superstition that the *state* has the duty which the individual found so painful. Finally, because the state is too abstract a thing to bear the brunt of our resentment, the burden is transferred from the state to its agents: to the nurse or the teacher who, in fulfilling his contract, also performs the duty which is really ours. When the servant has had enough – when he too says that he can continue to carry this burden only if properly rewarded – he is told that he has a *special responsibility* to those in his charge. By the perverse logic of the welfare state, the teacher becomes a father to children who are not his own, and the nurse's charity becomes an indefeasible duty of care.

In truth, it seems to me, neither the teacher nor the nurse has a special responsibility. If two people bring a child into the world, then it is *their* duty to look after him. If the state provides him with an education, then the parents receive a privilege. However, when teachers withdraw their labour the privilege expires, and parents must bear the full burden of a responsibility which is in any case wholly and immovably theirs. If they have to give up work in order to look after their children, that is what they ought to do. If it is a *hard* thing to do, that is because life is hard. But those who have children must expect on occasion to pay for this most comforting of human afflictions.

If it is difficult for parents to feel this duty, it is also because the state itself has weakened it. By making education compulsory, the state has imposed an obligation which most parents could not discharge unaided; and by compelling parents to part with their children for most of the day, the state fosters the illusion that they have no real responsibility for their offspring.

Teachers have suffered a drop in social standing partly because they are now seen as compulsory child minders for a state which refuses to recognise the right of parents to bring up their children, and for parents who refuse to recognise that they have not only the right, but also the duty, to do so. Teachers have suffered most of all, therefore, from our changed attitude to children. Nobody really knows any longer who has the responsibility for these strangers who encumber the world with their helplessness. Children come to us already branded by the claims of the state and we are tempted by the superstition that the state really does have the rights and duties which it so impertinently assumes towards them. We inwardly renounce the claim to our children's nurture, and, since the state offers education, most people willingly accept the bribe. After all, it needs a lot of education to realise that education is not so very important.

To rectify this situation will be a long and difficult process. But the process could begin, provided teachers would strike for a year or more, and provided the rest of us would rebel against the law which compels us to place our children in their care.

14 May 1985

In Praise of Common Law

Every now and then parliament tries to answer the problems raised by the Common Law of England. Sometimes it brings order and discipline to the squads of judicial reasoning, and for a while the draftsmen contemplate their work with satisfaction. Such a work was the Occupiers' Liability Act of 1957, which seemed to provide a principled solution to a century of cases concerning the duties owed by the occupier of land to those venturing on to his premises. But by the time of the new Occupiers' Liability Act 1984, it was apparent that the original statute owed its force to the common law and neither extended nor clarified its principles.

As the example shows, the codification of the law does nothing to impede – although it may sometimes distort – its development. Subsequent cases rapidly qualify the statute designed to solve them, and the judges continue to exercise their discreet but effective authority in determining the true application, and therefore the true nature, of the law. They obsequiously insist, like any courtier, that they merely carry out the edicts of their sovereign, and when casting aside the work of parliament they never neglect to say that is parliament's *true* intention that is guiding them. 'Where more than one construction of a statue is possible', they say, 'we would prefer the one which eliminates the mischief at which the statute had been aimed'; a principle which elegantly returns the legislative initiative to the judge, since it is only the common law that can tell us what the mischief was in the first place. The statute ceases to be an absolute command and becomes instead an instrument in the judge's hand, a remedy for wrongs which he alone is capable of defining.

It is surely a strength of our legal system that it gives such power to the courts: to those who really know the working of the law, and who know it not as a body of abstract principles but as a working practice and a form of tacit communication with the whole of society. Far from being less certain than statute, the common law is more certain, because more concrete. Its principles may not always be translated into words; but, like the precepts of the midwife or the carpenter, they are none the less definite for that, and none the less suited to the matter in hand.

An engaging illustration is provided by the law of attempt. Centuries of common law have unearthed an interesting, partly philosophical problem. If a man puts his hand in another's pocket intending to steal what it contains and finds that it contains nothing, is he guilty of a crime?

Some say that he is guilty of an attempted theft; others argue that theft, in these circumstances, is impossible and therefore so too is the attempt. Which argument prevails depends upon the details of the case, but nobody seems very clear about the principle.

The Criminal Attempts Act 1981 set out to remedy the defect, and in particular to abolish the 'pick-pocket's defence'. Section 1 says a person who does an act which is more than preparatory to an offence, with the intent to commit it, is guilty of attempt. It then adds that 'a person may be guilty of attempting to commit an offence . . . even though the facts are such that the commission of the offence were impossible'. The section further adds that, in cases where a person would not normally be regarded as having the intention to commit an offence, he shall nevertheless be regarded as having it, if he would be so regarded had the facts been as he believed them to be.

Thus a man entering his enemy's bedroom and seeing what he takes to be a person asleep beneath the bedclothes is to be regarded as intending murder, should he rush forward to stab what is in fact a pillow. By Section 1, therefore, he is guilty of attempted murder, even though the full crime was impossible. But what of the man who sticks pins in an effigy, believing that he thereby kills his victim? Here again, if the facts were as the man believed them to be, he would be regarded as having a criminal intention. And here again the full crime is impossible; is this then also attempted murder?

In *Anderton* v. *Ryan* (*The Times*, 13 May), the House of Lords had to consider the case of a woman who, asked by a police officer about the provenance of her video recorder, answered that she had bought it, later adding: 'I might as well be honest, it was a stolen one I bought.' (A nice kind of honesty.) Contrary to her belief, the recorder had not been stolen: nevertheless, she was charged with attempting to handle stolen goods. The judge at first instance acquitted her, on the grounds that in these circumstances attempt is impossible. The Court of Appeal directed him to convict, citing Section 1 of the Criminal Attempts Act. The House of Lords, reaffirming the original judgement, effectively neutralised the statute. It surely could not be the case, their lordships argued, that an innocent act could become a criminal attempt merely because of a factual error – as when a man believes that an 18-year-old girl is under age, or that sticking pins in an effigy is lethal.

The criminality of our actions is inseparable from their efficacity, and however wrong our projects may be in the eyes of God they interest the law only on account of their likely damage. Their lordships concluded, therefore, that a defendant could not be convicted for attempt when, whatever his belief, he could never have committed the offence, however far he had prosecuted his intention.

And perhaps that is a useful principle. But consider the man who sticks knives in an effigy, believing it to be his enemy. His state of mind is certainly more dangerous than that of the man who uses only pins, and is indeed comparable to that of the man who assassinates a pillow. Perhaps then he is guilty of attempt; but should we really depend upon the concept of 'impossibility' to explain the difference between him and the believer in witchcraft?

Once again we see the gap that opens whenever abstract principle is attached to minute reality. And we see the point upon which the facts of *Anderton* v. *Ryan* will one day be distinguished, or the case overruled,* as the House of Lords goes about its endlessly creative business. Meanwhile, it is instructive and agreeable to see a statute, four years after its enactment, yielding to the common law that it had sought to discipline.

28 May 1985

*Since the time of writing, the case has in fact been overruled (or at least consciously 'departed from'), in *R.* v. *Shivpuri* (*The Times*, 16 May 1986).

The End of Education

Higher education has a loud voice in the media, a strong arm in parliament and a free hand in the public purse. It is one of the most powerful vested interests in the modern state, and better able than most to give proof of its indispensability. Those who wish to clip the tree of learning, to prune its rotting branches, or merely to question the general value of a growth whose shade seems so lethal to every rival interest are, to those who live from the fruit of the tree, the rudest of rude barbarians.

Not surprisingly, therefore, the government's green paper on the future of higher education has provoked sincere and vehement outrage. And even if it is less uncouth than most of its critics, the paper is undeniably deficient in tact and understanding. It argues, reasonably enough, that education should be funded by the public only if it benefits the public. But its utilitarian idea of benefit, suggesting that there might be an economic standard of academic success, is riddled with confusions.

Economics is, of course, a primary concern of responsible government. And the country can prosper only if it produces the right kind of 'human capital'. Hence polytechnics and universities have a vital economic function. Prosperity, however, is not an end but a means: it is the *sine qua non*, which guarantees nothing. We should not value education as a means to prosperity, but prosperity as a means to education. Only then will our priorities be right. For education, unlike prosperity, is an end in itself.

This is not to say that the government is wrong to consider the economics of higher education, or to seek a suitable return for the expenditure of public money. It must be clear, however, not only about its own priorities, but also about the priorities of those whom it seeks to discipline. Academics do not value learning for its economic results, but for its own sake; they do not teach to provide a pecuniary advantage, but for its own sake; they do not do research to stimulate the economy, but for its own sake. Of course, education is also profitable. But if you fix your eye too firmly on the profit, you lose sight of the thing itself.

Education is like friendship: it brings help, comfort, strength, privilege and success. Friendship is unquestioningly profitable. However, you must never value friendship for the profit that it brings. To treat friendship as a means is to lose the capacity for friendship. Your companion is no longer your friend when you begin to weigh him in the balance of advantage. So it is with education: the profit of education persists only so long as you don't pursue it.

Furthermore, the profit comes to us by an 'invisible hand'. Economic planning is no more likely to succeed in this field than in any other. Who could have foreseen that a society whose elite was educated primarily in languages which are no longer spoken should prove capable of managing the largest, the most profitable and the most powerful colonial administration that the world has known? And who could have foreseen that a society whose educational system is dedicated to science and technology should have produced only indifferent science, faulty technology and a flourishing underground culture profoundly hostile to both?

In this area wise planning means the careful avoidance of plans. Research must take its own course, guided only by that interest in truth without which it has neither result nor motive. And education should provide not the narrow details of tomorrow's technology (which will soon be yesterday's) but the intellectual discipline which adapts itself to new and changing circumstances precisely because it is attached to none. Higher education, in short, must be pointless and irrelevant. Otherwise it has no value.

That said, it is only fair to praise the government for questioning much that passes for higher education in this country. When the tide of drivel has swollen to such proportions that the University of Bradford can offer a first degree in a subject ('peace studies') that doesn't even exist, it is surely time to ask whether there might not be better uses for the taxpayer's money.

Take an impartial look at a modern campus, at the literature which students are asked to study, the questions they are required to answer, the standards of conduct to which they are expected to conform, and ask yourself how far what you observe accords with any ideal of disinterested learning. Or attend a conference of the British Sociological Association and listen to semi-literate papers defending 'the social construction of solidarity in the face of a dual strategy of paternalism and repression', the thesis that 'women are policed through the control of their bodies' and the idea that 'flashing' is an instrument of male domination. Or pick up a copy of one of the new journals of literary theory, *Semiotica*, for instance, or *Poetics Today*, and wade through the acres of jargon produced by people who can neither write with skill nor read with understanding, and who have lost all sense of the difference between a genuine question and a will o'the wisp.

Perform any of those exercises and then ask yourself whether the expansion of higher education has really produced, on the whole, the disciplined intellect and cultured perception which the critics of the green paper suppose to be threatened by the government's parsimony. Ask yourself what has been the consequence of filling universities and polytechnics with academics who would not have been considered a generation earlier and yet who at once obtained tenure. Ask yourself whether bad education is really better than no education at all, and whether a government is really under an obligation to maintain the flood of vociferating ignorance that pours from our academic institutions. You will then perhaps commend the green paper for seeking to judge those institutions by *some* standard, even if the standard chosen is one that does not apply.

11 June 1985

On Charter 77

Ten years ago, in the heyday of western illusions, the Helsinki accords were signed and the regimes of Eastern Europe loudly undertook to guarantee the liberties of their subjects. The Czechoslovaks even ratified the International Covenant on Political and Civil Rights, which they had signed in 1968, so including the covenant in their country's law. The 35 nations who signed the accords recently met in Ottawa to examine the extent to which the human rights guaranteed at Helsinki had been upheld. Predictably, the Soviet bloc countries permitted no examination of their record and the meeting ended without a final document.

If we wish to know what is at issue in this attempt at dialogue, we should discard the uncertain language of 'human rights' and refer instead to the reality from which it derives: the reality of law. In particular we should look at the law of Czechoslovakia and at those citizens who have tried to uphold the law which supposedly applies there.

The Czechoslovak authorities neither applied nor obeyed the laws guaranteeing fundamental rights which were passed in 1976. In 1977, therefore, a group of courageous citizens signed a document, Charter 77, solemnly beseeching the government to uphold its own laws and to protect the people against those who violate them. One of the three first spokesmen of Charter 77 was the philosopher Jan Patočka – a pupil of Edmund Husserl and a writer increasingly recognised as the greatest luminary of modern Czech culture. Although an old man and in poor health, Patočka was brutally interrogated by the secret police and, as a result, died of a brain haemorrhage.

Despite this crime, his fellow signatories continued to step forward to uphold the cause of justice, truth and law. Some were arrested and imprisoned on trumped-up charges; others were harassed by searches, interrogations and day and night surveillance; all lost whatever privileges they might otherwise have enjoyed. And yet, every year, three more spokesmen step forward and dutifully expose themselves to persecution and imprisonment.

Charter 77 documents and declarations are published in *samizdat* editions, which are neither mentioned nor mentionable in the official press. Nevertheless, publicity afforded to them in the West ensures that these documents are noticed, not only by the people of Czechoslovakia (who learn what is happening in their homeland from western television and radio), but also by the regime. By degrees, this tiny institution, composed entirely of social outcasts, has become the major voice of Czechoslovak public opinion, and one which the authorities must either silence or listen to. The formidable combination of moral courage and intellectual force displayed by the Chartists has made the first course of action increasingly difficult. Even VONS, the committee established to support the unjustly prosecuted, continues to perform its magnificent task in the face of exemplary jail sentences imposed on its founders.

The steadfast refusal of the Chartists to be deflected from their moral purpose has therefore compelled the regime to listen to their utterances and to take whatever small measures might serve temporarily to shore up its sinking credibility. Laws are not exactly respected, but they are less flagrantly set aside; freedoms guaranteed by the Helsinki Act are not upheld, but they are no longer denounced as bourgeois illusions and imperialist propaganda.

Meanwhile, however, the regime continues to prosecute its undeclared war against the Czech and Slovak nations, hampered by the Chartists but not prevented by them. In 1982 Petr Hauptmann, a construction engineer working on a building site at the border crossing of Rozvadov, crossed into West Germany, hoping to settle there and to earn money so that his wife and children might follow him. He was interrogated at length by the West German authorities and, being habituated to 'socialist law', assumed this to be normal in the case of potential immigrants. Meanwhile one of his children fell seriously ill and, urged by his wife, he returned home, having been assured by the Czechoslovak consulate that he would not be imprisoned.

On return Mr Hauptmann was charged with intentionally leaving the republic – a charge which he might reasonably have expected, and the penalty for which he might reasonably have borne. He was also charged with spying, the sole evidence for this being that he had been interrogated by the intelligence service of a 'hostile' power. As a result he was jailed for ten years.

The meaning of this case should be understood by those who reflect on the Helsinki agreement. The Prague regime wishes its citizens to live in a state of war; it wishes them at all costs to understand that contacts with the 'enemy' are dangerous; and it wishes them to feel the danger as emanating not from the regime and its servants, but from the West. It seeks to negate the natural peace-loving sentiments that unite the Czech and Slovak nations with the rest of Europe, since it recognises that it has no other claim to legitimacy than the mendacious promise of protection against 'hostile' and 'imperialist' powers.

In countering that benighted paranoia, Charter 77 continues to make the only real contribution to peace that has originated in communist Czechoslovakia since 1968. By reminding us that a government can be at peace with its neighbours only if it is first at peace with its subjects, and by showing peace to be inseparable from the rule of law, it provides a lesson not only to the authorities in Prague but also to the world. Peace in Europe can be achieved only when the Communist Party acknowledges that power alone cannot be the source of its own legitimacy, and that a legitimate government must bow before the law. Those who have sacrificed so much in order to bring communism before the law are the friends not only of their homeland, but of the entire civilised world.

25 June 1985

The Lesson of Oman

Opinions differ about the real cause of the Ethiopian famine. But one thing is certain: the blame will be placed, in the end, on the West. For only western governments are responsive to blame. This feature, which ought to silence blame, serves rather to attract it. After all, you cannot blame Colonel Mengistu, who is only obeying his instructions; nor can you blame his masters in the Kremlin, who are only obeying theirs.

The situation in Ethiopia is to a small extent clarified by a glance at neighbouring Arabia. Following our insane renunciation of Aden, the Soviet Union succeeded in establishing a 'People's Republic of South Yemen' and so gained control of the base which commands the Horn of Africa. The unfortunate Yemenis were subjected to the yoke of communism, while their masters began to look further afield – westwards to Ethiopia and northwards to Oman. The destiny of Ethiopia is therefore usefully compared with that of Oman, a country which has also been plagued by drought and civil war, and yet which, thanks in part to the British Army and in part to Sultan Qaboos who was trained by it, has kept communism at bay.

The southern part of Oman – the Dhofar – borders on the new Marxist republic, and the Yemenis, under Soviet guidance, established centres for training and indoctrinating those Dhofari tribesmen who could be enticed or dragged across the border. The Soviet propaganda machine – acting partly through its acolyte, the Transnational Institute in Amsterdam – broadcast to the world the sad plight of the Omanis in their 'national liberation struggle' against a feudal sultanate. Fred Halliday, a Fellow of the Transnational Institute and now Professor at the London School of Economics, wrote a biased and simple-minded book for the British market, and the western press responded, as it always responds, with a bland affectation of neutrality, so consigning the Omanis to their fate.

The Soviet Union hoped for an easy victory. The hereditary sultanate was a recent invention, and Sultan Said bin Taimur had sturdily resisted the reforms that might have purchased the acquiescence, if not the affection, of his subjects. Ibadi Muslims believe that the Prophet's successor cannot inherit his office but must be elected by those whose dignity fits them for so sacred a task. The last elected Imam had been deposed by Sultan Said and had fled to Saudi Arabia. In such circumstances the Dhofari tribesmen, many of whom had adopted neither the Arabic language nor the sophisticated customs of Muscat, were ripe for rebellion.

When Qaboos deposed his father in 1970 his first act was to conclude a military agreement with Britain. Before the Soviet campaign had reached its climax he had activated this agreement, and the rebellion in the Dhofar was over. With characteristic magnanimity the young Sultan invited the rebels into his army and civil service, there to co-operate in his Atatürkist plan of development.

Oman possesses a commodity which is attractive to western markets: oil. It is possible that Ethiopia possesses such commodities, but until western capital is made welcome there nobody will be able to discover them. Communism therefore ensures Ethiopia's poverty, while Qaboos's enlightened autocracy opens Oman to trade. A country that until 1970 was virtually without hospitals, roads or schools, and whose population had been governed by custom, *Shari'a* and ceaselessly fragmenting tribal loyalties, is now a modern state, with welfare facilities, roads, schools, modern industry and modern communications. There is even to be a university in Muscat, although opinion is divided as to the wisdom of importing so dangerous an institution into a society that has for centuries been innocent of education.

Oman, like Yemen and Ethiopia, bears the visible mark of a mature culture. Forts and watchtowers, walled towns and villages, terraces, wells and waterways impress upon the stony landscape the marks of an ancient way of life. The religion is the religion of the desert, where man is alone with God and disposed patiently to accept his commandments. The Ibadis are on the whole tolerant and suspicious of enthusiasts. Only in the matter of the elected Imam do they claim any superior wisdom to their fellow Muslims, and even so they concede that an Imam is neither always required nor always desirable. Prosperity has come rapidly to the towns and villages, and even to the Bedouin, who now cross the desert in motorised convoys, their camels croaking from the gated backs of cattle trucks. It is not surprising, therefore, if the Omanis have, albeit with traditional reserve, attached themselves to the Sultan.

Nobody who knew the facts would enter the twentieth century if he could avoid it. For centuries Arabs have made the wise choice of remaining in the dark ages, governed by custom and holy law, secure in the recognition that true religion, true poetry and true companionship are not only the best that man can hope for, but all that he really needs. It is easy, therefore, to sympathise with Sultan Said, who recoiled from the brave new world of petrodollars and who hoped to shut it out. However, such a course is no longer open. The Arab lands must make the choice which the twentieth century forces on them: to yield to communism, or to resist it.

If they resist and prosper they will certainly be vilified. Westerners are more disposed, in the end, to accept the tyranny of communism than an autocracy which stands in its way. Autocracy, however enlightened, offends the modern conscience, while communism, however cruel, placates it. For communism encapsulates the dominant religion of the age: the religion of human equality. This religion will make life as hard for Sultan Qaboos as it has made it easy for Colonel Mengistu. But it has not yet brought famine to Oman.

20 August 1985

The Lesson of Lebanon

Those who visited Lebanon 20 years ago will recall a thriving, prosperous – if somewhat seedy – community in a region of poverty and war. To arrive there from the 'United Arab Republic' of Egypt and Syria was to pass from suspicion and tyranny to lawful government, free opinion and religious toleration. To achieve such conditions in the dismembered fragments of the Ottoman Empire has never been easy. To achieve them in a country where Christian and Muslim, Maronite, Armenian and Orthodox, Sunni, Druze and Shia lived side by side, honourably bound to the ancient customs which distinguish them, was one of the most remarkable results in modern times of true political culture.

This political culture would not have existed but for the Christians of Lebanon, who brought to government a respect for law and a spirit of willing negotiation. This spirit was shared by the Sunni Muslims, and it was from the bargain struck between these two communities that the constitution emerged, guaranteeing the rights of Christians and ensuring to them a decisive influence in government. The constitution was in some ways inequitable. But it *was* a constitution, and it permitted that most precious of political achievements and one absent from much of the region: a rule of law.

The Christians of Lebanon are long established, their title to the land being far older than that of the Muslims. The Maronite Church is in communion with Rome and retains in its liturgy the ancient Syriac language that was spoken by Christ. Its congregation is spread through town, village and country, through every class and profession and through every political posture. Such privileges as the Christians have enjoyed were purchased by their trade and industry, and their success has enriched their Muslim neighbours as well as themselves.

Until recently these people, many of them descended from the earliest Christians, who have kept the faith alive in biblical lands, had the support and the sympathy of every Christian nation. When they were threatened with extinction, as in 1860, their cry rang through Christendom with an imperative reverberation.

Now all that has changed. Syria, armed by the Soviet Union, governed by a single party and obedient to a harsh dictator, has imposed its will upon Lebanon. Syria has occupied, and continues to occupy, half of the country – a fact which causes no comment in the West, where only Israel's misdeeds are noticed. Through Syrian auspices the PLO was introduced into Lebanon, with the purpose of destabilising a peaceful community. The Muslim sects were divided, first from the Christians and then from each other; training camps for international terrorists were established: the area was filled with refugees and with the blood-thirsty journalists who dog their footsteps; and at last the invasion was provoked which, however justified, was to call down the wrath of the media upon Israel.

Having achieved all this, the Syrians dismissed the PLO, liquidated its garrisons and now, through evil-minded proxies, are moving towards a final solution of the problem posed by a people who depended upon their protection and who also wrought their will.

Throughout these events the Christians have endeavoured to sustain the legal order in Lebanon. Two enemies have frustrated their efforts: the Syrian state and western journalists, who have acted in character as the fifth column of dictatorial power. It is a truth obvious to all but the journalist that his ability to report on a country's troubles is a proof of its civic virtue. A real tyranny excludes the journalist from its territory, or else permits him to enter only on terms that are dictated by itself. It is precisely such tyrannies which, acting by proxy in the free states where the journalist wanders, attract his attention by a trail of blood and lay the blame for the deaths which he discovers at the door of the only power which he may safely criticise.

By such methods the Syrians have been able to persuade the western public that the Shia Muslims of Lebanon – stirred into unwonted cruelty and ignorant fanaticism – are a major force, expressing an old justly founded grievance. At the same time the public has learned to distance itself from the Christians, whose achievements and destiny ought to be its major concern. Having established a rule of law and permitted criticism, the Christians are blamed for the lawlessness of those who acknowledge no aims or interests but their own.

Thus when a Christian militia attacked the Palestinian camps, it was rightly condemned, and a political crisis was provoked from which Israel and the Lebanese Christians have failed to recover. The same camps were subsequently surrounded by Syria's Shia proxies and their populations exposed to heartless massacre. However, not a word is said. Not only is the journalist now excluded from the bloody transaction; he knows that if he is to stay at his post he needs the protection of the gangsters responsible.

An even greater cost would be paid by the journalist who reported truthfully what is happening to the 4500 Lebanese Christian soldiers held in the concentration camp at Mazze, in Syria, or to the innocent Christian villagers of the Saida and Jezzine area, now encircled by Syrian-backed forces who wish to drive them from the land which they have occupied since before the birth of the Prophet. Between March and April of this year, according to reliable reports, 60 of their villages were destroyed, 8500 of their houses burned, 12 000 of their number made homeless, 80 churches pillaged or destroyed, 17 convents razed and 200 people murdered in cold blood.

Christian nations have been offered many a *casus belli* by Lebanon's Shia Muslim fanatics, and not only by the leader who, while dedicating himself to the expulsion of justice from his homeland, rejoiced in the title of minister of justice. However, thanks to the journalists and to the diplomats whom they influence, the challenge will never be accepted. All the same, let us hope that those in the West who call themselves Christians will remember in their prayers a people who have kept alive, at such cost to themselves, the memory of Christ in lands which we should still call holy, had holiness retained its meaning for us.

14 September 1985

The Plague of Sociology

Auguste Comte, the father of sociology, was a naive and shallow thinker. But he had a concern for truth and a nose for problems. Under his tutelage sociology did not remain an academic dream, but established itself as a science. Comte was followed by four great men – Marx, Durkheim, Pareto and Weber – each of whom provided concepts and observations indispensable to a full understanding of the modern condition. Furthermore, at the fertile interface of sociology and philosophy arguments and ideas have flourished which touch on the deepest and most enduring concerns of humanity. Pope John Paul II, for example, owes many of his moral ideas to such sociologically-minded philosophers as Max Scheler.

Why then does sociology have the reputation that it has acquired? Why is it so often regarded as ideology, indoctrination and pseudo-science? Why does the mere mention of academic sociology serve to conjure images of an ignorant rabble lost in jargon, fired by doctrine and profoundly hostile to all forms of authority and power?

It seems to me that the image is not wholly unjust. Recently several academic sociologists, speaking at the British Association for the Advancement of Science, staged what amounted to a show trial of the 'New Right', denouncing their colleagues who had departed from the fold of socialism as morally corrupted and intellectually void. Not one of those colleagues was invited to reply, and the authority of the British Association was used as a badge of office with which to consign to silence all those whose opinions offended the bigots.

Academics who in this way silence discussion and who adopt a political stance as both unquestionable and the foregone conclusion of their subject are the enemies of scholarship. When the resources of a discipline are diverted to the task of fortifying a political dogma and protecting its intellectual weaknesses behind an impenetrable barrier of abstraction, and when those who question the dogma are dismissed as intellectually worthless and morally corrupt, we might justly suspect that we no longer have to do with an impartial science.

Consider the charge 'racist', so popular among members of the sociological establishment and now used to discredit the 'New Right'.The charge could be applied, on the grounds usually offered, equally to Marx, Pareto, Durkheim and Weber, and even to Comte himself. This is one small but significant instance of the way in which sociology has broken free from the intellectual discipline that created it and launched itself, a hysterical and overburdened boatload, on the sea of pure opinion – with nothing to guide it but its conviction that wherever it drifts is the right, or rather the left, direction.

Perhaps the most lamentable effect of second-rate sociology is its undermining of the natural language of moral intercourse. For bad sociology has only one intellectual device: the proliferation of spurious equivalences. Consider the favourite trick of the 'peace educators' – the representation of all power, however legitimate, however much the outcome of consent and compromise, as a form of 'structural violence'. (The trick was perfected by Mussolini's mentor, Georges Sorel, who himself took it by a devious route from Marx.)

Every social order requires a structure of authority and law whereby people are permitted to do some things and prevented from doing others. Hence every order, we are told, is founded on violence. Moreover, since those prevented and those permitted belong to different classes, every system involves 'structural violence' whereby the dominant class 'polices' the remainder. Against violence, violence is a legitimate response, and against the vast accumulation of 'structural violence' in the modern state any extreme becomes permissible – even terrorist violence.

Look at any course of 'peace studies' and you will find this nonsense purveyed as though it were a matter of dispassionate science. By the same argument, the power of the beloved over the lover, of the conductor over the orchestra, of the man who gives over the man who depends on his charity – all these legitimate relations become forms of 'structural violence'. However absurd the conclusion, we should not ignore the effect of the sociologist's language on the semi-educated. If you consider the change in modern attitudes to terrorism, in particular the changes displayed by the language of journalism, you will begin to see the extent of intellectual corruption. The terrorist gains legitimacy as soon as we are encouraged to condemn the 'system' against which he is fighting in the same terms that we condemn his deed.

'Peace education', child of sociology's most polluted slums, depends entirely on such spurious equivalences for its persuasive power. Totalitarian and democratic systems are represented as equal and opposite contenders in the game of nuclear defence, each reacting to an equivalent 'threat' presented by the other. Single-party government acting by conspiracy to suppress all rival sources of power is 'equivalent to the class oppression' of western democracy. The rule of law is 'equivalent' to a tyranny of judges. And so on.

The use of these devices by town hall fanatics and street revolutionaries is to be expected. But their repeated occurrence in the academic discipline that dominates the polytechnics and universities of Britain is the sign of an appalling intellectual coarseness. I do not suggest that the founders of sociology are entirely blameless for the present corruption. On the contrary, impatient as they were for 'deep' conclusions, they too missed the fine distinctions and painted in the same grey colours the machinations of the wicked and the actions of the good. But even in their most impetuous moments they did not mutilate the common language of morality – our best reminder that in human affairs it is the fine distinctions which matter, and upon which our happiness depends.

8 October 1985

Nelson's Monument

Why build a monument to Nelson? The simple answer is surely the correct one. Such a monument expresses gratitude: it is a testimony to the honour of the hero, from people whose freedom he protected and whose lives he inspired. The value of Nelson's monument lasts just as long as people recognise that political freedom and lawful government depend, in the end, upon personal sacrifice. Few people know the whys and wherefores of Trafalgar; few people could now describe, still fewer analyse, the threat which then was offered to our country. But almost everyone can understand the worth and the meaning of Nelson's sacrifice, and the column which carries him is no sad relic of forgotten conflicts, but a living reminder of our common interests, common allegiance and common fate.

The same could not be said of the monument which the GLC has now raised to the second Nelson. Whether or not Mandela is a hero, he is certainly not one who has spent himself on *our* behalf. On the contrary, when he trained as a guerrilla in Algeria, it was to prepare for a conflict in which we were to be the ultimate victims. When the ANC and the South African Communist Party joined together in 1961 to form Umkhonto We Sizwe – the 'armed wing of the liberation movement' – it was with the express purpose of striking a blow, not only against the white regime in South Africa, but also against the entire world of 'international capitalism', of which we are a part.

Mandela may be a hero. But it has to be said that the ANC's greatest military triumphs, such as the Pretoria bomb of 1983 which killed 19 civilians and maimed 239, were accomplished after his imprisonment and cast no glory on himself. For such victories the credit should go to Oliver Tambo, president of the ANC and long-time member of the Soviet-controlled World Peace Council, and to Moses Kotane of the South African Communist Party, who, as the ANC's external treasurer, played an indispensable role in arming the guerrillas of South Africa.

If we wish to know whose interests those 'freedom fighters' really serve, we should study more closely the affiliations of the ANC leadership. President Brezhnev gave an important clue when, speaking in Prague in 1973, he said the Soviet strategic aim was 'to gain control of the two great treasure-houses on which the West depends . . . the energy treasure-house of the Persian Gulf, and the mineral treasure-house of central and southern Africa'.

Now as then the ANC is to be the spearhead of Soviet domination. Should it accomplish its purpose, not only will the people of South Africa be deprived of their little freedom, but the West as a whole will receive a political, economic and strategic blow from which it will never recover. Londoners will surely not look kindly, then, on the statue to the second Nelson. But who knows whether they would still be permitted to pull it down?

However, perhaps the eight-foot high bust of the hero is intended to testify not to the virtues of Mandela's politics, but to the virtues of the man. For surely Mandela has virtues: courage, integrity, a desire, however abstractly conceived and however cruelly executed, for the well-being of his people. Was it not these virtues that encouraged him, in 1962, to return to South Africa, in the vain hope of marching to the citadel of power? Surely it is no ordinary character who could conceive such a design, no coward who would embark on it.

It was a favourite argument of the Greeks that virtue is one – that courage divorced from wisdom is mere foolhardiness, that wisdom without justice is selfish cunning, that justice without temperance is a corrupting prodigality. This powerful thought has never succeeded in vanquishing the evidence of history, which so often shows the thread of power in the hands of creatures no better than half-virtuous – men like Cromwell, whom Clarendon described as brave and bad.

Occasionally some artist portrays the tragedy of such a blemished hero. Like Marvell in the *Horatian Ode*, or Shakespeare in *Coriolanus*, he shows the anguish and the isolation of a life which, moved by impetuous designs and implacable ambition, has at last over-reached itself and stands threatened and despairing in fortune's failing tide.

Such a life, it seems to me, has been Mandela's. Those who told him, during his years of training, that South Africa was ripe for revolution, who promised all necessary help and who convinced him that he could now play the part of Xhosa chieftain, leading his people to freedom and power – those flatterers of his foolish pride knew well enough that they sent him home to death or life imprisonment. Only as a martyr could such a figure be useful to them; for only as a martyr would he symbolise the qualities of strength and leadership so sadly lacking in the man.

To portray in bronze or stone the life and character of so flawed a hero would be no easy task. Rodin, perhaps, might have succeeded in marking, on Mandela's noble features, the fatal imprint of an ignoble pride. A bust by such a master would be worth every penny spent on it, and set up in some public place would serve as a valuable reminder of a melancholy truth. The bust by Ian Walters, however, has all the posturing grandiloquence of the cult of personality. It is a resonant image, but it resounds not with the ring of truth but with the trashy din of propaganda. Is that all that Mandela stands for?

14 December 1985

Capitalist Equality

Socialists invariably point to America as the main offender against the egalitarian ideal. They describe a country where property, profit and advertising dominate the collective consciousness, where law is fierce, adversarial and unscrupulous, and where politics is hectoring and vulgar, devoted to the lowest of human concerns. In other words, they refer precisely to those things which assure the ordinary American that he is the equal of those who govern him.

There is no more effective equaliser than American capitalism, and if its results are offensive to the person of refined sensibilities, they are on the whole far more agreeable to those affected by them than the results of socialist planning. Moreover, thanks to the US constitution, this equality is proud, monumental and even noble – a fact recorded 150 years ago by de Tocqueville, and just as evident today.

The pursuit of equality is also an important American pastime. Reformers, pressure groups, idle professors, the media – all spend their days in search of hitherto unnoticed inequalities so that the machinery will be established that will break them down. The egalitarian causes of the modern world – civil liberties, feminism, Third Worldism, anti-racism and many more – originated not in the world of 'real socialism' but on the American campus and in the American press. It is here, in the self-intoxicated brain of the system, that the American spirit engenders its most fantastic schemes for the further emancipation of mankind. If you wish to prepare yourself for the next wave of egalitarian enthusiasm, therefore, you should attend not the fringe meetings of the Labour Party conference but the fringe courses ('feminist studies', 'Third World studies', 'ethnic studies' and a dozen more) in an American university.

In 1980 a government-funded organisation in New York, the Council on Interracial Books for Children, issued a set of guidelines for selecting 'bias-free textbooks and story books' (i.e. books with an egalitarian bias). While rehearsing the feminist objections to Grimm, Andersen, Dickens and similar corrupters of the young, the book made some interesting new suggestions as to what should be consigned to the flames.

Racism, sexism, elitism, conformism and materialism are of course unacceptable; so too, however, are ageism, youthism, even handicapism (displayed in R. L. Stevenson's positively horrid portrait of the one-legged Long John Silver). The remedy for these evils is 'affirmative action' which, with congressional help, is now being embarked upon. We are to expect a whole new kind of children's book in which one-eyed, one-legged black women of indeterminate age triumph (but with exemplary gentleness) over the evils of the capitalist system.

The anonymous authors provide us with a 'rating instrument' by which to guide our censorship. A book can be classified, for example, as 'racist by omission' (which 'means that Third World people could logically be included but are not') or 'non-racist' (where '*non* before a negative value means that the book's impact is neutral in that regard and does nothing to challenge the status quo, thereby reinforcing it'), or 'anti-racist' (the acceptable posture).

This is only one test, of course, and even if you could squeeze a few Third World people into the revised edition of *A Christmas Carol*, you are not going to get past the hurdle of handicapism without eliminating Tiny Tim. Such problems do not bother the authors. For it is obviously better that children should not read the classics than that they should acquire anti-egalitarian (or even non-egalitarian) values. (So much, however, for anti-conformism.)

Unlike British rubbish in this vein, the American is open, cheerful and friendly. However far you go, the American believes, your opponent is never your enemy. One of the merits of an egalitarian culture is that opposition is respected and compromise desired. The writers happily expose their cavernous ignorance of opposing points of view, only because they fully expect to settle for less in the way of book burning than is ideally desirable.

By contrast, in the European climate, where such matters are settled by conspiratorial elites, the egalitarian passion assumes a character of vehement hatred and will press onwards to total victory or defeat. In such circumstances political equality is not desired – and certainly not by those who campaign for it. The anti-egalitarian is therefore far safer in America, where he is treated as an equal, than in Britain, where he is not. Americans truly wish minorities to define themselves for themselves, and are generous to a fault in helping them to do so. Like every endangered species, the anti-egalitarian is assiduously protected. American academics, for instance, although just as left-leaning as their British counterparts, will permit a conservative to move freely among them and never betray the conviction that he secretly dresses in Nazi uniform, eats babies or takes bribes from the CIA.

The American liberal is a true opponent of handicapism and will therefore treat his conservative colleague graciously and warmly, providing him with special facilities suited to his disability and allowing him to compete for positions of privilege. And he will do his best to ensure that the conservative's chances of success correspond precisely to the numerical strength of his academic minority.

American equality is the result of that thing which egalitarians most vehemently deplore: open competition. A 'non-competitive' order, an order of gentle sheep, marks the end of true equality. For gentle sheep invite an ungentle shepherd. If the mass of Americans remain conscious of this truth, however, it is largely because their children's stories have so far escaped the egalitarian censor.

31 December 1985

Our Empire in America

The idea of the United States as an 'imperial' power has for a long time flourished on the left. In recent months, however, it seems to have spread from its natural breeding ground to the greatest palaces of the establishment – to the *Sunday Telegraph* and the *Spectator*, perhaps even to the government. For was there not, in Michael Heseltine's hysterical meddling in the affairs of a private company, something of the same distaste for America and its influence that finds effete expression in the writings of Peregrine Worsthorne and more solemn echoes in the isolationism of Enoch Powell?

It seems as though the ceaseless shouting of Soviet propaganda, and the self-castigation that is the greatest weakness of the American character, have at last produced their effect. There has occurred one of those strange inversions of the truth which so often pass for wisdom in the world of public opinion. Britain is now seen as a 'dependency' of the US, a 'client state', even a 'colony'. The alliance which has twice saved us from destruction, and which still protects us from the threat of it, is looked upon with a deepening suspicion, even by those who have no immediate desire to submit themselves and their neighbours to the yoke of Soviet communism.

In repudiating the Crown, the United States cast off the only link with the Old World that was truly irksome to it. Everything else that our ancestors took to America – the English language, the Common Law, Christianity, the moral and literary heritage of the Bible and the ideas of constitutional government and individual rights – every such fundamental tie was preserved, to exert precisely the same influence in the New World as it once exerted in the Old.

The British Empire lives on in America, just as the Roman Empire lived on in Byzantium, although in a form more vital, more industrious and more generous than its ancient archetype. The settlers of the New World recreated the institutions of the Old and thereby did as much to ensure the survival of European civilisation as was ever done in Europe. This year, for example, Harvard celebrates its 350th anniversary. The university remains as firm a bastion of European culture as it was in the seventeenth century, when it offered its presidency to the greatest living advocate of a liberal education: the Moravian bishop and founding father of Czech literature, Comenius.

Those who believe Britain to be a 'client' of the US, or a corner of some American 'empire', do not mean that our laws are made in Washington or our citizens conscripted into the American army. They mean that the United States has an empire of *influence* and that we, being within its boundaries, suffer a diminution in our sovereign powers. Such people forget that influence is not control, and that the American influence in Western Europe, even on the worst interpretation, is a small price to pay in order to escape control by the Soviet Union. And if you want to understand the difference between influence and control, you should compare East and West Germany, or South Yemen and Oman.

Control is one-sided, whereas influence is not. America is therefore as much within our sphere of influence as we are within that of America. Indeed, it is not so much that Britain is a 'client' of American as that America is the living body of the British Empire. Our laws, politics, language, literature and predicament vitally condition the American political process, and our security and danger are as keenly felt there as they are felt at home. Indeed, there is now far more honest loyalty to British laws and institutions in America than there is in Britain; and certainly none of the rancorous treasonableness characteristic of the new urban left.

That two countries so differently situated should govern themselves in such similar ways is indeed a sign of empire. Even today, cases in the law of one country may be persuasive authority in the law of the other. But this is because America is the continuation, in altered circumstances, of a British political tradition. The political continuity ensures that when British and American interests conflict, only gentle influence is brought to bear on us, rather than sanctions or threats. Even during the Falklands war, when the Americans saw their whole Latin American policy jeopardised by our actions, Washington did nothing to constrain our initiative and provided us, at the crucial moment, with vital reconnaissance and arms.

The British Empire was an empire of lawful government rather than military coercion. Wherever the legal heritage remains, with its associated habits of adversarial government, open discussion and public spirit, so too remains the basic loyalty upon which the Empire was founded.

Why then do the self-appointed guardians of the Old Order look down their noses at America? The *Spectator* views with appalled curiosity the demise of the British ruling class and feels, in its snobbish way, that America's egalitarian spirit is somehow to blame. In fact, however, the true executioner of the ruling class has been the political tradition which the ruling class itself established, and which launched the subjects of the Crown towards every corner of the globe, carrying with them the noble ideas of constitutional government and common law. And it is by such gifts – our most precious exports – that we retain our empire in America.

14 January 1986

In Memoriam Jaroslav Seifert

If Jaroslav Seifert, who died in Prague on 10 January, is now mourned throughout his homeland, it is not as a great poet – for he was far from that – but as a testimony to the survival of Czech culture. Seifert's personal history was an image in miniature of the history of his country. Old enough to have experienced the alienation from all things Austrian during the First World War, he joined Nezval and Teige in de-Germanising the literature of Czechoslovakia. Under the influence of Seifert and Nezval the poetry of France (and in particular the free verse of Apollinaire) became the touchstone of Czech literati and the dense metaphysical nature-worship of Otokar Březina gave way to a newer, lighter, more urban idiom, in which the techniques of surrealism were used to express the rebellious outlook of emancipated Prague.

Like other members of the 'poetist' movement, Seifert matched his internationalist aesthetic with an internationalist politics; he joined the Communist Party during the first Czechoslovak Republic and edited various party periodicals. In 1929, however, perceiving the true character of Gottwald and the fate that was being assiduously and wickedly prepared for his homeland, he left the party, thenceforth to devote himself to literature. When the Communists seized power in 1948, they lost little time in stamping out surrealism, which, with its love of recondite symbols and its Western connexions, was clearly no friend of the proletariat. Seifert continued to publish in the official press, since he was popular and had influential connexions. It was not until 1950, with the publication of *The Song of Viktorka,* that he fell properly from favour. However, he still managed to publish officially, owing to the enterprise of a brave publisher who issued his books with pre-Communist date stamps.

In 1956, after Khrushchev's secret speech, Seifert was reprieved and held various offices in the Writers' Union. In the wake of the Soviet invasion, Seifert proclaimed officially that writers have a duty to speak out for the truth, when the authorities utter nothing but lies. The authorities at once increased the volume of lies and silenced those writers who showed the slightest inclination to dispute them. Seifert was removed from his position, and there began that long official silence during which almost every writer of merit – including Seifert – could appear only in *samizdat.*

So effective was this official campaign that almost nothing is now known outside Czechoslovakia about the real cultural life of a country which has probably contributed as much to the civilisation of modern Europe as the British, the Germans or the French. The land of Čapek, Kafka, Hašek and Janáček, the birthplace of Rilke, Husserl, Mahler and Kraus is now shrouded in official silence. Its most important writers either live in exile, like Kundera and Škvorecký, or else stay fiercely at their posts, fighting a desperate battle on behalf of the culture, history and religion of their homeland.

The Communist Party has made a few feeble gestures at compromise. Some of Seifert's poems have again been officially published, and on his 80th birthday the poet was congratulated not only by *Rudé Právo* (for which he worked in its early days, when it was a genuine newspaper and a lively source of ideas) but even by President Husák. Nevertheless, this passing nod towards a dying man, representative of a dying idiom, could hardly compensate for the fact that his more interesting contemporaries – Vladimír Holan and Bohuslav Reynek, who have attempted to rescue their literature from the whimsical nothingness of surrealism, and to re-Germanise its sentiment – are no longer publishable. Moreover, writers of the younger generation are not only unpublishable, but also unmentionable, leading a shadowy existence on the borderline of persecution.

In the twilight region to which these writers have been banished, however, an extraordinary enterprise has been conceived: the enterprise of preserving and enhancing the cultural and religious heritage of Czechoslovakia. Were it not for the courageous efforts of the 'unofficial' writers who through precious *samizdat* editions introduce their countrymen to the best that is thought and said in their native language, the official war against the Czech and Slovak nations would by now have been won.

Seifert's Nobel Prize is treasured by the Czechs, not because it was a fitting recognition of literary merit, but because it was the first true sign that the 'unofficial' culture is internationally acknowledged as the true culture of Czechoslovakia, and acknowledged not through the work of fast-living exiles, but through the heroic labour of those still at home.

Seifert himself was influenced by this work of a younger generation, and in his Nobel speech he repeats the ancestral call of the Czechs and the Slovaks for a culture and an identity of their own. It is a fitting reminder of the pathos of this call that the group which published the speech – the Jazz Section of the musicians' union – is now the target of official persecution and is fighting for its life.

28 January 1986

The Dismal Pseudo-science

Thanks to Keynes, with his cocksure advice, his pseudo-scientific rigour, his political influence, social position and philosophical airs, economics became the teacher of politics and the professor of this newfangled subject became the master of those who govern us.

The mixture of sound common sense and tentative social philosophy which our ancestors knew as 'political economy' was replaced by a brazen science whose exponents tend to advance, like Keynes, from a minimum of observation and by prancing steps of *a priori* argument to conclusions which pre-empt the art of government. Thence has arisen the breed of 'economic advisers', promising final answers to questions which, because they are political, should never be answered finally.

When Keynes gave way to Friedman this appeared a victory of

common sense over speculation – and so it would have been, had not 'Friedmanism' been invented as a similar comprehensive solution, just as over-bold. Once again the problem of unemployment was treated theoretically, with little consciousness that the theories are both sketchy in themselves and more the consequences of political attitudes than the 'scientific' grounds for them. And the plain facts which have no place in the theory were again passed over as irrelevant.

But consider some of the facts. Consider, for example, the decline of discipline at home and school; the destruction of the core educational curriculum; the dwindling of literacy; the growing contempt for individual responsibility and for the ethic of work. The net result of this must surely be to make a large number of teenagers not merely unemployed but also unemployable.

Or consider the bureaucratic restrictions on the wage contract; the unjust taxation (through 'social security' payments) placed on everyone who wishes to hire another; the difficulty of dismissing an employee who turns out to be useless. The net result is that it is often crazy to employ someone, even when the work is there. Or consider the fact that many people do not want to work, or prefer to remain officially unemployed, while collecting tax-free payments for casual labour. If you mention such facts as a major cause of unemployment, socialists will condemn you as a demon, while economists will dismiss you as an amateur.

But it is difficult to have confidence in economists so long as their ardent divisions of opinion are more like *odium theologicum* than scientific debate. At least, if economics *is* a science and can aspire to an authority that all people should recognise whatever their political outlook, it is a very young science, and one whose conclusions should never be advanced dogmatically, nor adhered to unconditionally. If economists in advisory positions behave more like magicians than like scientists, it is because the power of their 'science' depends, like the power of sympathetic magic, on the disposition of people to believe in it. In which case their scientific pretensions should be taken with a pinch of salt.

No consequence of the sovereignty of economics is more dangerous than the destruction of the morality of money. Moral sense permits us to transcend self-interest and short-sightedness for the species' sake. Traditional fiscal morality has therefore proved more beneficial in the long run than the mumbo-jumbo that so often drowns its counsels. And if 'monetarism' is appealing it is not, I believe, because of its scientific credentials, but because of its moral truth. It reminds us that the state, which mediates through money in all our transactions, is under a duty not to tax us illegitimately by debasing the coin of the realm.

When theory defies the moral sense, however, it should not be listened to. During the 1960s economists persuaded themselves that the theory of Keynes applied not only to the political economy of every nation state but also to the 'international economy'. Underdevelopment, over-saving and economic stagnation could therefore be cured at once, so they thought, by 'recycling' dollars to nations which had never shown the slightest ability either to invest them wisely or to spend them well. Bankers listened to the economists, and the result will soon be catastrophic.

Common morality tells us that prudence is a virtue and that trust should neither be exploited nor betrayed. It would have reminded the banker that the dollars which he loaned to governments that had not given the slightest evidence of their probity were not his to lend, that he held them in trust, to invest wisely on behalf of clients to whom he was answerable, and that the only security for an investment is proof of a return.

It is precisely such self-evident moral truth that the pseudo-scientific language of international Keynesianism ('recycling', 'pump-priming', the 'world economic order') is designed to obscure. Once the economic advisers entered the scene and 'demoralised' the problem, the meagre store of common sense was dissipated and madness triumphed in 'scientific' form.

We may not be able to solve the problem of unemployment, but perhaps we could at least understand it, were we to refuse the terms which economists recommend to us and to trust instead the language of morality.

11 February 1986

Freud and Fraud

If we really wish to explain the increase in crime, we should consider the following hypothesis: that crime is explained by our desire to explain it. As we look for the causes of our behaviour, so we take attention away from the act itself, fencing it round with excuses, isolating it from judgement and making inaccessible the only ground in which the seeds of morality can be sown: the ground of individual responsibility. Surely it is this habit of explanation – this obsession with the 'genealogy' of our acts and intentions – which has most effectively 'transvalued' our values. That which Nietzsche so joyfully recommended is precisely what, in retrospect, we have greatest reason to deplore: the destruction of morality by the habit of explaining it.

It would be wrong to assume, however, that the new 'sciences' of man really *do* explain our behaviour. Their scientific guise is often no more than a mask, behind which a more serious moral purpose advances: the purpose of lowering the price of absolution. Left to his own in a godless universe, modern man sees no reason to deny himself and desires only the excuses that will justify him in the eyes of creatures like himself. And since he recognises no authority higher than science, it is to science that he turns for his exculpation. The sciences which are chosen as his idols are those which are most prodigal of excuses, which rain down upon him a stream of whitewashing explanations and which tell him in one and the same breath that he deserves our sympathy and that he cannot be blamed.

Perhaps no science has been a more powerful source of absolution than the psycho-analysis of Freud. Here, in a single theory, the wandering conscience finds a complete kit for survival in a demoralised world. The sinner becomes a patient, and if he seems to do wrong, it is not really he who does it but an Unconscious whose machinations are unknown to him. If he is tormented by conscience, then this too is the work of the Unconscious, which erects before his inner eye the spectre of a Super Ego whose authority can be instantly discounted as the survival of a primitive fear.

As the stage of personality is vacated by responsibility, however, it becomes the scene of a new and more spectacular drama – a noble tragedy in which the self is justified in the very act of being overwhelmed. Psycho-analysis simultaneously removes the individual from the sphere of praise and blame and returns him to it vindicated, a hero who has been finally justified by the fate to which he must succumb. And psycho-analysis does all this without the slightest moral penalty: the only cost is financial, and who would not part with money for the sake of a clean conscience and an inexhaustible store of new excuses?

Of course, there has been no shortage of critics anxious to point to the scientific deficiencies of psycho-analytic theory: its dependence on metaphor, myth and imagery; its blithe indifference to evidence and refutation; its lack of experimental method; its self-serving definition of 'illness', 'therapy' and 'cure'. However, devotees of this 'science' are impatient with such feeble, external criticism. Their attitude is typified by Freud who, presented with a dream which seemed to refute his wish-fulfilment theory, replied: 'No, your dream is an expression of the unconscious wish to refute my theory'. For the whole purpose of these pseudo-sciences of the soul is to make their exponents and their adepts *immune from criticism*, even from the criticism which their scientific pretension invites.

To break into this charmed circle and rescue the trapped moral sense is no easy task. One method, however, promises success: this is to treat the science of the soul as it treats morality, to search for its genealogy and so to 'transvalue' it. As Ernest Gellner shows in a brilliant book *(The Psychoanalytic Movement)* the result is the downfall of every claim to authority that the Freudians have made. Professor Gellner describes the genesis of Freudian psychology in modern man's most dominating fear: the fear of other people. The Freudian doctrines, he argues, are superstitious reponses to that fear, which enclose it, nurture it and promise a final redemption.

The idea of an Unconscious is introduced in order to devalue all certainties and to place the patient's psyche outside of his own reach. The analyst thereby becomes priest in a solemn *rite de passage*, conducting the patient from unbelief to holy enlightenment. Gellner describes powerfully, and in the most brightly coloured prose, the causality of Freudian dogma in this concealed religious urge. In doing so he destroys its scientific claims and devalues its morality. But he also praises, in a manner that is at once serious and ironical, these novel certainties so neatly tailored to the modern conscience and so carefully separated from every suggestion of blame.

Gellner stops short, however, of drawing the most important conclusion. While this modern superstition erodes the moral sense, the religion upon which our civilisation was built did just the opposite, upholding and supporting the idea of moral responsibility and giving divine authority to its absolute commands. The secular superstitions offer excuses where religion offered fear, anger and blame; and while it compelled man against his will to be good, they entice him along the path of immorality.

When laws are made, institutions governed and even churches led by those in the grip of these exculpating idolatries, should we really be surprised that the people turn more cheerfully to crime?

25 February 1986

Rights and Wrongs

Alterations in the language of public debate, and in the categories through which the social world is understood and acted on, are of decisive importance. The totalitarian movements of our century have shown that the seizure of language is an effective step towards the seizure of power. They have also shown that a wholly unnatural form of government may be maintained indefinitely by the unceasing broadcast of potent lies, and by the destruction of the language in which the truth may find expression.

In a less extreme and less violent way, the language of public debate has been important in shaping western democratic politics. In particular, the shift on the left away from traditional socialism has followed an increasing lack of confidence in the language through which socialism had been justified. 'Equality', 'social justice', 'public ownership' – these notions have lost their superficial clarity and their rhetorical appeal. There has therefore been an interesting return to the original idea of left-wing politics: the idea of the Rights of Man. It is through the conception of a human right that egalitarian values now find their most influential expression.

Ironically, therefore, the idea which once defended individual liberty, private property and the restriction of sovereign power is now a weapon against private property, against 'bourgeois' liberties and against those who seek to 'roll back the frontiers of the state'. The idea of 'rights' is indeed a potent weapon in the hands of the radical, not least because the old guard lacks the strength to attack with it and has forgotten how to use it as a shield.

During the miners' strike, the National Council for Civil Liberties – a body with impeccable left-wing credentials – was much exercised by the need to defend Arthur Scargill and his militants. The right of the working miners to proceed peacefully about their business had to be set aside in favour of a 'right to picket'. And as Professor Dworkin has told us, the rights of militant radicals include the right to 'match rhetoric to outrage', and hence to make as much abusive noise as may further the egalitarian purpose.

By a few deft sleights of hand, the NCCL was able to take the lesson offered by the new school of jurisprudence and to invent as many rights as the left-wing conscience deemed necessary for the defence of illegality. This was just one instance of the tricks which the language of 'rights' has now been taught to play.

Consider also the 'right to work'. For the traditional liberal, this denotes the freedom to go about one's business undisturbed. Such a right is of course threatened by violent picketing. For the leftist a freedom that can be exercised only by the fortunate is a freedom which violates equality. Such a freedom must therefore not be given the status of a right. Instead a new 'right to work' has been invented: not a liberty, this time, but a claim. This right is honoured not by leaving its holder undisturbed, but by actively looking after him. The new 'right to work' requires a vast effort of social mobilisation if it is to be upheld. Jobs and opportunities must be created and the economy fashioned accordingly. If this involves the restriction of those 'bourgeois' liberties that flourish in the market-place, then so much the worse for bourgeois liberties. Some must be forced, so that others may be free.

The notion of a 'claim right' is not new to jurisprudence. For instance, if I contract with you and perform my part of the bargain, then I have a claim against you. If you refuse to honour your promise, then you violate my rights. But claims arise only when duties are fulfilled, and it is a singular feature of the new ideology of rights that duties are seldom mentioned (least of all by those who enjoin us to 'take rights seriously' – see R. Dworkin, *Taking Rights Seriously*).

Furthermore, in traditional liberal thinking the rights of the citizen were not claims, but liberties: they were granted to the citizen in return for his obedience, and were to guarantee that he retained an effective veto in all matters that most intimately concerned him. The new 'right to work', however, is not a veto but a command. It obliges the state not to stand outside my threshold, but to cross the threshold of others so as to compel them to my aid. But if the state really does have the duty to uphold these novel claims, by what duty do I gain my title to them? What do I owe to the state in return for the enormous claims that I am encouraged to make against it?

The duty to obey the law has been taken fairly lightly by the left. The last Labour Party conference showed that it is not obedience but disobedience which defines the egalitarian idea of citizenship. Labour is encouraged by the new jurisprudence, which seeks constantly to augment the store of rights (including the 'right to civil disobedience') while diminishing the fund of duties. In jurisprudence as elsewhere, egalitarianism inflates the moral currency and erodes the capital of civil virtue.

In this way the language of rights has taken on a new meaning. Instead of guaranteeing those freedoms whereby the competent could govern, it now tips the balance permanently against all forms of human excellence and against every species of elite. At the same time it becomes the source of a new corruption. No duties are imposed on the man whose 'right to work' is to be inflicted on the public purse. Even the duty of obedience is set aside by the champions of the underdog. And this steady erosion of legality, responsibility and public spirit is effected in the name of that old chimera – the Rights of Man.

11 March 1986

Sense and Censorship

'The peculiar evil of silencing the expression of an opinion is that it is robbing the human race; posterity as well as the existing generation; those who dissent from the opinion, still more than those who hold it. If the opinion is right, they are deprived of the opportunity of exchanging error for truth: if wrong, they lose, what is almost as great a benefit, the clearer perception and livelier impression of truth, produced by its collision with error.'

John Stuart Mill's words encapsulate what was, until recently, a common premise of British politics and a cornerstone of our education system. It was assumed that, within the limits of decency and public order, a British citizen is free to speak his mind, and that political decisions should not be taken before a period of free public discussion. It was also assumed that no educational institution at the higher level, whether college, university or polytechnic, could engage in censorship and still retain its academic standing.

Of course, public pressures make the expression of certain opinions difficult. Those who speak on the 'right' know that they must contend with a fearful barrage of *bien pensant* hostility. Nevertheless, they learn in due course to despise fashionable opinion and to ignore those who live by it. Even in the strongholds of the left establishment, therefore – in universities and polytechnics – it has been possible for a right-winger to speak his mind. If his prospects have suffered, it has been merely because, in the opinion of his respectable colleagues, right-wing convictions are so conclusive a sign of a defective intelligence as to outweight the evidence of a lifetime's teaching or research.

In recent months, however, the position of the right-winger has appreciably worsened. His opinions are now widely censored, not only in public debate but also in places of learning. This is especially so when those opinions touch on the question of ethnic minorities, where to diverge from the left-wing orthodoxy in the smallest particular is to risk the charge of 'racism'.

In fact most people do diverge from this orthodoxy and are deeply insulted by the accusation that despite their record of hospitality to immigrants they are really 'racist'. The suppression of their viewpoint could lead in the end to a dangerous reaction. Nevertheless, to speak out for the majority over this issue, on which the majority are judged to be 'right wing', is to risk harassment and slander.

Such has been the fate of the *Salisbury Review*. Some time ago one of its contributors, Ray Honeyford, questioned the orthodox view of multi-cultural education. Through a long campaign of organised intimidation he was forced to withhold his opinions from the press and finally to resign from his job as a headmaster. Another contributor, Jonathan Savery, expressed his support for Honeyford's arguments, drawing on his own considerable experience as a teacher of ethnic minorities. He too is being victimised. Avon Education Authority has summoned him to a 'disciplinary hearing', while the local NUT has launched a campaign of denigration, circulating documents calculated to inflame opinion against him and to prejudice the outcome of his 'trial'.

Nobody who writes for the *Salisbury Review* is really safe from harassment and slander. Whether they write about 'weasel words' (F.A. Hayek), 'the politics of language' (Sally Shreir) or the difference between the sexes (myself) the left-wing press will find ways to discover therein a secret element of 'racism' and so to justify its damaging accusations. The editor was invited recently by Leeds city council to speak publicly on the subject of 'peace education' and then hastily 'disinvited' when it was discovered that, on this subject too, his opinions would prove disagreeable to the fascist left.

For Honeyford, 'disinvitation' is a common experience. When the students of Oxford Polytechnic invited him to a conference, he was not surprised to receive a letter from the dean of the faculty of educational studies suggesting that 'there may be a number of reasons why you might consider it appropriate to decline the invitation'; nor was he surprised when, after he had expressed his inability to discover such reasons, the conference was cancelled.

Likewise, when Honeyford was invited by a student body to speak at Bristol Polytechnic, he was again promptly disinvited. Bristol Polytechnic is in fact curiously open about its left-wing bias. Last year it organised, through its department of humanities, a conference on 'literature-teaching-politics', so as to 'provide an opportunity for those on the left concerned with the teaching and studying of literature, modern languages and cultural studies to discuss common concerns and problems'.
expressly for those 'on the right' – still less an institution that is publicly funded. But so habituated have we become to bias and intimidation that no one dares to object to Bristol Polytechnic, either for excluding right-wingers from its conferences or for forbidding them to speak to its students. Gestures that should cause an immediate cessation of public funds are made with impunity, by people for whom education is less a means to truth than an excuse for politics.

25 March 1986

Charity and Politics

The preamble to the Charitable Uses Act of 1601 gives no definition of charity. Nevertheless, in the cases that it mentions and in the subsequent history of the common law, four broad areas have been defined as charitable: religion, education, the relief of poverty and other purposes beneficial to the community. Those categories must be understood not abstractly, but in the light of a long history of cases through which the courts have tried to offer a consensual idea of public benefit.

Two firm principles have emerged from the judicial reasoning. The first is that charities should not merely serve the private interests of the donor. They should not, for example, be designed as a reward to employees or as a family endowment. Second, charities should not be political in intention, even if they are sometimes political in effect.

The consequences of this second principle have been profound: charities are exempt from taxation, and to exclude political organisations from this privilege is drastically to curtail their power. There seems to be little agreement, however, as to the reason for the exclusion. Lawyers and jurisprudents have written as though it were an historical accident, a quirk of the common law, subsequently enshrined in fiscal thinking and now lending a permanent colour to our politics.

In fact there are good reasons for the exclusion of political activity from the field of charity. Politics is never better than a means to an end, while education, worship and the relief of suffering are ends in themselves. In these latter activities man is at rest, doing what he knows to be intrinsically worthwhile. In the experiences of worship, learning and kindness are enshrined our first ideas of peace. Politics, by contrast, is directed always to a further goal. It has no intrinsic value, but must look for its justification in barely foreseeable consequences. Politics is a paradigm of restlessness – an experience in which man is always seeking, never finding, and always in conflict with his kind.

The exclusion of politics from the privileges granted to charity can be seen, therefore, as part of the de-politicisation of society. It expresses an important motive of the English law, which is the generation and protection of civil society as an entity independent of the state. The law of charity encourages those activities in which we are at peace and the value of which is unquestioned by those engaged in them. At the same time it refuses to encourage politics, in which our conflicts are heightened and where value is never more than instrumental.

Moreover, through charitable endowment churches, schools, colleges and relief organisations are maintained outside the control of the state. The existence of these institutions constitutes a severe limitation on the scope and the authority of political power. Through their fiscal privileges such institutions are able to defy attempts to control our lives and to mobilise our actions. Totalitarian states, therefore, usually forbid gifts to charity. For such states are the enemies of civil society and seek rather to control the thought and activity of the citizen than to permit his nature to flourish according to its own intrinsic purposes.

Our de-politicised law of charity is an important component of a free social order. Everyone should therefore view with alarm the increasing defiance of the law by established charities. Many of these are turning themselves into left-wing campaigning organisations, while the Charity Commissioners – whose role is to uphold and to advertise the law – neither take action against them nor notice the fault.

Consider, for example, the intensive campaign mounted by Oxfam, Christian Aid and associated bodies in support of the Marxist government of Nicaragua. This campaign has produced a flood of literature, and even advertisements on the Underground, inviting us to 'pray that Nicaragua be left to grow in peace' (the last four words being no more than an afterthought). It may be the case, as these charities claim, that the Sandinistas are leading the people of Nicaragua towards peace, justice and a Christian polity; it may also be the case, as Nicaraguans like Humberto Belli have forcefully argued, that they are leading the people towards Marxist enslavement beneath a mantle of deliberate deception. (See Belli's *Breaking Faith*, published by the Pueblo Institute.)

But is it the role of charities to enter this debate, or to spend considerable sums, as Oxfam does, on propaganda indistinguishable in language and content from that issued by the Sandinistas and their left-wing allies? A particularly disturbing example is Oxfam's campaigning booklet *Nicaragua – The Threat of a Good Example?* by Dianna Melrose. This carefully arranged pastiche of opinions, facts and images, backed by a reading list of exclusively left-wing material, invites us to campaign in support of the new socialist order in Nicaragua, to put appropriate pressure on the British government and the European Economic Community, to follow various paths towards sabotaging US foreign policy. To use Oxfam's good name to win credibility for a cause that is immensely controversial and in all probability counter to Britain's long-term interests is a species of deception comparable to that practised daily by the Sandinistas. Are we to believe that Oxfam, too, is another *manto*, another mask for dictatorial power?

The Charity Commissioners have been many times alerted to Oxfam's propaganda on behalf of 'Third World socialism' by those on whom it is bestowed. Yet they have persistently refused to take action. Perhaps the time has come for those who give money to such charities to reflect again as to whether it is either honestly raised or wisely used.

8 April 1986

L'invitation au voyage

People are becoming less and less able to understand foreigners. The reason, I believe, is the lamentable tendency to rely on first-hand experience. Rather than read Herodotus or Plutarch at home, we drag our uninstructed senses through foreign cities and acquire not the first understanding of the people who live in them. Few modern Englishmen know the language, fewer still the history and culture of the places to which they travel. Their experience of foreigners is therefore without concepts, a bundle of pure impressions, in which the characters are schematic, hazy and unreal. Only considerable culture and a haughty independence of mind can render travel intelligible. For most people, the disjointed experience of foreign parts sinks rapidly into the waste of consciousness, to lie there in disordered and unmeaning fragments, like shells collected on an empty holiday.

Travel narrows the mind, providing a surfeit of impressions and a dearth of interpretations. Sometimes, however, a meaning emerges, and sometimes this meaning is the aim. For instance, you might make a pilgrimage to some holy place – or a journey to those with whom your destiny is somehow mingled. Nevertheless, failing those laudable purposes it is better by far to remain at home, studying the language, the thought and the customs of strangers and dreaming of their habitats with the aid of a large cigar.

If it is not easy to act so wisely, it is partly because cigars are so expensive. When the experience of concentrated wanderlust is priced at £3 a time, we are tempted to travel in search of cheaper satisfactions, just as we used to travel in search of wine. As a matter of fact, travel may very well be justified by this consideration. For British citizens are able to bring home 50 cigars free of tax. Since you may save up to £3 on the price of each smoke, you can often end up paying for the journey. The important thing, therefore, is to ensure that your friends and your places of pilgrimage are located in areas where decent cigars are still obtainable.

Roughly speaking, there are two such areas. The first consists of all those places where Cuban cigar makers, driven from their homes by communism, have settled down to their old employment; the second consists of those places which import the shoddier but still acceptable cigars that continue to be made in Cuba. While Cuba remains communist, a first-rate cigar will be unobtainable: the choice, therefore, lies between a craftsman-like cigar produced from second-class materials, and first-class materials hammered into rough but smokable cylinders of proletarian poison.

If it is the communist product that appeals to you, then there is no need to travel so far as Cuba. At Warsaw airport, for example, you can buy Cuban cigars so cheaply as to save up to £100 on a single purchase. Since this amounts to 70 per cent of the air fare, and since you can make up the remaining 30 per cent by exchanging Leith's or Wilton's for the charming old Basilisk on the Stary Rynek, you could spend your next festive weekend in Warsaw at no cost, and with great benefit to your subsequent mental composure.

It has to be said, however, that the Cuban cigars available in communist countries are not so good as the best of those that are made from Caribbean leaf elsewhere. Now of all the places where the Cuban diaspora has settled, by far the most interesting is New York. In lower Manhattan you can find on almost every block a den, often no wider than a newspaper kiosk but usually stretching back into a long and fragrant inner recess, where the members of a family work at the long leaves stacked and graded on the benches beside them. These leaves come from Dominica, Guatemala and El Salvador and lack the flavour of their Cuban rivals. The good patriots who roll them into smart coronas will not hesitate to remind you of their defects. Nevertheless, the product is smooth, delicate and lively and, at a dollar a time, also cheap enough to pay for the journey back to London.

For half that price, however, you can obtain a presentable cigar from the bulk distributors. By far the best of these is the New York firm of JR Cigars, on East 45th Street. Here, in addition to seconds, every quality and variety of non-Cuban cigar is available at prices that can be matched by no West European airport. Simply to open the door of this shop, and to be swamped by the heady aroma of fermentation is to discover a justification for the market economy far stronger than any mentioned in the works of Friedman or Hayek. JR Cigars is the very heart, the nub, the spirit of New York – the place where an industry, driven by madness and cruelty from its natural home, finds profit for itself and pleasure for mankind in the pure thrill of buying and selling. To look around this shop, piled to the ceiling with boxes from Jamaica, Dominica, Honduras, Mexico, Guatemala, the Philippines and from every point of North America, is to be confronted with an extraordinary proof of the power of the free economy – the power that comes from pure permission.

An industry that by rights should have died entirely thrives in abundance, finding new raw materials, new distributors, new producers and new purchasers, and finding also that life-enhancing rush to the centre which has made New York the place where all that is exchangeable may be obtained for its market price.

In JR Cigars the customer may also buy the very best of Jamaican smokes, matured in humid chambers for a year or more. For just two dollars he can acquire a forest of symbols, a paradise garden, a lake of dreams. Furnished with these self-contained adventures of the imagination, he could survive at home for 50 days without the faintest desire for travel. For such a result, the journey is almost excusable.

20 May 1986

Bentham and Birkbeck

The University of London began life in 1826. Three years earlier, at the Crown and Anchor Tavern in the Strand, the London Mechanics Institution was founded to provide evening education to the new working class. The institution began to flourish, and by 1835 its founder, Dr George Birkbeck, had the pleasure of observing more than a thousand students in attendance – 800 of them being 'mechanics'.

In 1866 the institution began to teach for the London University degree and decided to name itself after the man who created it. By 1890 Birkbeck College had 4000 students and counted among its graduates Sir Arthur Pinero, Annie Besant, Sidney Webb and Ramsay MacDonald, who was to become prime minister and also first president of the Friends of Birkbeck. By 1920 the college was a fully integrated part of the University of London, providing for people occupied in day-time employment a unique opportunity to study for degrees at every level.

Victorian philanthrophy aimed to destroy the proletariat. By the ways of self-help and self-improvement, people were to rise from the dregs of society and join the new order of mobile artisans. Charities were founded in order to offer the first helping hand and to open new and accessible channels to advancement. Birkbeck's final incorporation into the University of London was the vindication of its charitable purpose: it was now clear to all who came to it that the education which Birkbeck offered was not some cheap substitute, but the real thing, and that the student could advance by this peculiar route to the very advantages from which he had supposed himself excluded.

By and large Victorian philanthropy was successful, and the urban proletariat dwindled. This fact is reflected in Birkbeck's present membership: civil servants, carpenters, translators, teachers, roadsweepers, milkmen, musicians, nurses and bank clerks all gather after hours in Malet Street to study subjects both useful and sublime.

A hundred years ago a visitor to the college commented favourably on its atmosphere, remarking that there was 'no dawdling or larking visible'. If you chanced to visit this place today, coming perhaps from one of those soulless factories of the mind engendered by Lord Robbins, you would be equally struck by the absence of dawdling or larking, and by the prevailing dedication to an ideal of learning that is elsewhere in decline.

For students come to Birkbeck at their own insistence and their own expense. They have what in sociologese is called 'motivation' – which is to say that they are not carried like flotsam on the tide of public charity but strike out on a path of their own, towards destinations which, however distant, however irrelevant, are chosen as their personal responsibility.

A tradition of learning depends upon people giving themselves, in this way, to the pursuit of useless knowledge, just as an economy depends on the disposition of people to take hold of their own destinies and to help themselves to what they want. Birkbeck is not merely a product of Victorian values: it is also a continuing expression of them, and a proof of their lasting authority.

Not every product of the 19th century has been equally beneficial. From a glass cupboard in the nearby University College radiates the spirit of Jeremy Bentham – the cheerful, improving rationalist whose maxims stroll through the minds of bureaucrats, prompting them to destroy whatever they can find no reason to preserve. For a century and a half the Benthamite mentality has dominated the affairs of state, weighing laws, customs and institutions in the balance of profit and presumptuously assuming the title to a wisdom which no mortal mind can really claim. Of course, we may now regret the fact that educational establishments were surrendered to the care of a state which seemed to offer such generous protection. But until the wholesale denationalisation of learning, universities will depend upon the Benthamite jurisdiction of well-meaning bureaucrats.

One such bureaucrat is Sir Peter Swinnerton-Dyer, chairman of the University Grants Committee. Having surveyed the affairs of London University, Sir Peter finds no special reason for the fiscal privileges enjoyed by Birkbeck. Why, he asks, should part-time students in London be 'better-resourced' than those elsewhere? (Other universities after all, have found it 'cost-effective' to share resources between part-time and full-time students.) However hard he looks, Sir Peter cannot discern that special reason which would entitle Birkbeck to survive and flourish in its customary manner, and if no reason can be given for its survival, why should it survive?

Benthamite rationality has survived the onslaught of Coleridge, Carlyle, Arnold, Ruskin and Leavis. For there seems to be no way whereby the chasm can be bridged between those who see the world as replete with intrinsic values and those who find nothing significant save the long-term profit and loss. That bureaucracies are inhabited by people of the second kind lies in the nature of things. Nevertheless, one thought should be considered by those who would resist the tyranny of instrumental reasoning.

Institutions are not things but persons: they have a life, a will and a responsibility of their own. Their death is always a matter of concern both to themselves and to those who have joined with them in friendship. And our attitude to a person should respect not just his present and his future, but also his past. For it is by the past that his merits can be understood and measured. So it is with Birkbeck College, an institution whose place in the history of England entitles it not just to the affection of those with whom it has entered into friendship, but also to the respect of those on whom the future of British education depends.

2 August 1986

Index of Names

Subject Index